THE DOCTRINE OF
AWAKENING

THE DOCTRINE OF
AWAKENING

THE ATTAINMENT OF SELF-MASTERY

ACCORDING TO

THE EARLIEST BUDDHIST TEXTS

JULIUS EVOLA

TRANSLATED FROM THE ITALIAN BY

H. E. MUSSON

Inner Traditions
Rochester, Vermont

Inner Traditions International
One Park Street
Rochester, Vermont 05767

Originally published in Italian as *La dottrina del risveglio*
Copyright © 1995 by Edizioni Mediterranee
English-language edition copyright © 1996 by Inner Traditions International

LIBRARY OF CONGRESS CATALOGING-IN-PUBLICATION DATA

Evola, Julius, 1898–1974.
    [La dottrina del risveglio. English]
    The doctrine of awakening : the attainment of self-mastery according to the earliest Buddhist texts / Julius Evola ; translated by H. E. Musson.
      p.   cm.
    Includes index.
    ISBN 0-89281-553-1
    1. Spiritual life—Buddhism. 2. Buddhism—Doctrines. I. Musson, H. E.
BQ4302.E9613 1995
294.3'422—dc20
                                      95-21532
                                        CIP

Printed and bound in the United States

10 9 8 7 6 5 4 3 2 1

Text design and layout by Charlotte Tyler
This book was typeset in Times with Bodega Sans Old Style as a display typeface

Distributed to the book trade in Canada by Publishers Group West (PGW), Toronto, Ontario
Distributed to the book trade in the United Kingdom by Deep Books, London
Distributed to the book trade in Australia by Millennium Books, Newtown, N.S.W.
Distributed to the book trade in New Zealand by Tandem Press, Auckland
Distributed to the book trade in South Africa by Alternative Books, Randburg

꒰ᤳ꒱

A Note on Sources

In this work we have, apart from the two last chapters, based ourselves exclusively upon the *Sutta-piṭaka*, which contains the most important and most ancient portion of Pāli Buddhism.

Many of the Buddhist teachings are set forth in the form of *leitmotif*, that is to say, of passages that recur in various texts, almost in identical form. Wherever possible we have referred to these motifs in their contexts in the *Majjhima-nikāya*. There was moreover a specific reason for this, namely, that there is accessible to the Italian public a really first-class translation of this text, and which is also a noteworthy work of art, made by K. E. Neumann and G. de Lorenzo (*I discorsi di Buddho* [Bari, 1916–27] 3 vols.). We have done our best to make the maximum use of this translation. For the other texts we give the reader the following references should he or she wish to refer to them.

Dīgha-nikāya in *Sacred Books of the Buddhists*, trans. T. W. Rhys Davids (London, 1899–1910). For the sutta no. 16, which is the *Mahāparinibbāna-sutta*, we have also made use of the Chinese version, translated into Italian by C. Puini (Lanciano, 1919).

Saṁyutta-nikāya, trans. C. A. F. Rhys Davids and F. L. Woodward. Pāli text edition (London, 1922–24), 4 vols.

Anguttara-nikāya, ed. Nyānatiloka (*Die Reden des Buddhas*) [Munich and Neubiberg, 1922–23].

Of the *Dhammapada* there exists the Italian translation by P. E. Pavolini, Lanciano, ed. *Cultura dell'anima*.

The quotations from these, as from other texts, follow the paragraphing of the originals. Concerning those that have been made available by H. C. Warren, *Buddhism in Translations* (Cambridge, Mass., 1909, first published 1896), we have given in brackets the letter W.

For the *Vinaya-piṭaka*, see *Sacred Books of the East*, vol. 13, *Dhamma-saṅgani*, trans. C. A. F. Rhys Davids (London, 1900).

Contents

Translator's Foreword

Of the many books published in Italy and Germany by Julius Evola, this is the first to be translated into English. The book needs no apology; the subject—Buddhism—is sufficient guarantee of that. But the author has, it seems to me, recaptured the spirit of Buddhism in its original form, and his schematic and uncompromising approach will have rendered an inestimable service even if it does no more than clear away some of the woolly ideas that have gathered round the central figure, Prince Siddhattha, and round the doctrine that he disclosed.

The real significance of the book, however, lies not in its value as a weapon in a dusty battle between scholars, but in its encouragement of a practical application of the doctrine it discusses. The author has not only examined the principles on which Buddhism was originally based, but he has also described in some detail the actual process of "ascesis" or self-training that was practiced by the early Buddhists. This study, moreover, does not stop here; it maintains throughout that the doctrine of the Buddha is capable of application even today by any Western person who really has the vocation. But the undertaking was never easy, and the number who, in this modern world, will succeed in pursuing it to its conclusion is not likely to be large.

H. E. M.
[1948]

Preface

In his autobiography *Il cammino del cinabro* (The Cinnabar Path), Julius Evola recalled:

> "During the last years of the 1930s I devoted myself to working on two of my most important books on Eastern wisdom: I completely revised *L'uomo come potenza* [Man As Power], which was given a new title, *Lo yoga della potenza* [The Yoga of Power], and wrote a systematic work concerning primitive Buddhism entitled *La dottrina del risveglio* [The Doctrine of Awakening]."

The recent discovery of the correspondence between Evola and his publisher allows us to specify the sequence of events and modify it, at least in part. In a letter dated October 20, 1942, Evola wrote to Laterza with a proposal:

> "It is a new book entitled *La dottrina del risveglio,* carrying the subtitle *Saggio sull'ascesi buddista* [Essay on Buddhist Asceticism]. This is a work that I have almost completed concerning the practical and virile aspect of Buddhist teachings, with particular emphasis on the striving after the Unconditioned. I believe that my book's exposition of Buddhist teachings on this basis, explained in a way that everybody will understand, constitutes something original and will be of interest to more than a handful of specialized scholars.

After Laterza accepted this project, the final manuscript was mailed on November 30, 1942. It was sent to press in February 1943, and the last revisions were made during the first ten days of August. The book was finally printed in September 1943 during a period of radical political and military upheaval. The author was able to see a copy of *La dottrina* only after the war was over.

About his book, Evola wrote, "I have paid a debt that I had toward Buddha's doctrine," which had "a definite influence in helping me overcome the inner crisis I experienced right after World War I." He also added:

> Later on, I made a practical and rewarding use of Buddhist texts, in order to strengthen a detached awareness of the principle of "being." He who was a prince of the Śākya pointed out a series of inner disciplines that I felt were very congenial to my spirit, just as I felt religious, and especially Christian, asceticism totally alien to me.

Evola was neither a Buddhist nor a Buddhist scholar, and always considered it a misunderstanding that some would classify him as such. Buddhism was a "way," one among other "ways" available to people who live in the last age, the Kali Yuga. In his autobiography Evola explained his need to explore and to point out to others the various spiritual paths that could be found in Eastern and Western traditions; these paths, he believed, helped one to remain steady in this "age of dissolution." After expounding the "wet path," the path "of affirmation, of the assumption, use, and transformation of immanent forces that are freed until Śakti's awakening, which is the power root of every vital energy and especially of sex" in the *Yoga of Power*, in *The Doctrine of Awakening* he indicated a "dry path," an intellectual approach of pure detachment. Some people have thought of these paths as opposites, but Evola explicitly declared them to be "equivalent, as far as the final goal is concerned, provided they are followed to the end, though one may be preferred to the other depending on the circumstances, one's own nature, and inner, existential dispositions." These words need to be emphasized. They were written in 1963 and express the same point of view as twenty years earlier. Evola noted then that his book was

> the counterpart to some of my previous works in which I have popularized doctrines that have indicated different ways to achieve the same goal, namely, the deconditioning of the human being, enlightened awakening, and the initiatory opening of one's consciousness.

This is the underlying theme of Evola's multiform and apparently contradictory (to a superficial reader) literary production: to indicate paths of inner salvation available to those who live in the fourth age. Evola wrote:

> If, on the one hand, this civilization is harvesting more victims than any other known pagan idol, on the other hand, its nature is such that in it, even heroism, sacrifice, and struggle display, almost without exception, a lightless, "elementary," and merely earthly character, due precisely to the lack of any transcendent reference point.

In these desperate times, Evola has indicated a number of "transcendent reference points" for us through his works, each one different from the others and adaptable to different personalities. The techniques of spiritual realization that are part of Western Hermeticism are discussed in *The Hermetic Tradition* (1931; English translation, 1995); the "initiatory content" of the symbolism of medieval knightly literature is covered in *The Mystery of the Grail* (1937; translation forthcoming); the "esotericism" present in Taoism is discussed in his introductions to the *Tao-te-ching* (1923 and 1959), which essays have been published in English under the title *Taoism: The Magic, the Mysticism* (1995); the "path of magic" is the subject of his contributions to *Introduzione alla magia* (1955); and finally, the "path of sex" is discussed in *Eros and the Mysteries of Love: The Metaphysics of Sex* (1958; translation 1983). To these one could add "political" versions of the "wet path" in his *Gli uomini e le rovine* (1953; [Men amid Ruins]) and the "dry path" in *Cavalcare la tigre* (1961; [Riding the Tiger]). These can be seen as Evola's attempts, at times on the external plane, at other times on the inner plane, to promote a change in the mentality of the Italian man, whom he stereotypes as a mandolin-playing, macaroni-eating fellow who is all pizza, mafia, and church. Evola proposed both the path of action and the path of meditation as the means to effect this change. During both the fascist and democratic regimes this intent always informed his work, though he also knew he was addressing a country of Catholics. This helps to explain why he introduced the Buddhist "Doctrine of Awakening," since as a system or technique it could be grafted onto any religion without coming into conflict with any specific doctrines.

In *The Doctrine of Awakening* Evola wove together several traditions. For example, in the Fulfilled or Awakened One whom he describes we find an echo of the inner and outer characteristics of his understanding of the "Roman style"; moreover, in primitive Buddhism he finds again the traits of a nontheistic spirituality (that has nothing to do with morality); of self-mastery; and of the achievement of a degree of spirituality that is closer to the divine. According to Evola, Tantrism and primitive Buddhism are like two faces of the same coin and indicate a "detached path of asceticism that is almost 'Olympian.'"

Moreover, the identification of primitive Buddhism and Tantrism as methods, systems, or paths available to modern Westerners is owing to the fact that, according to Evola, they belong to the "cycle in which modern humanity happens to live." More exactly, "primitive Buddhism has been formulated in view of an existential condition of man that, though distant from that of Western materialism and the correlative eclipse of every living traditional wisdom, nevertheless already possessed its warning signs and seeds." Thus, primitive Buddhism presents itself as a "complete and virile system of asceticism formulated during the cycle to which modern man belongs." In modern man, whose life is "almost external to himself, semisomnambulistic, moving between psychological reflexes and images that hide from him the deepest and purest substance of life," we can see a shift from a purely individual consciousness to a saṁsāric consciousness that assumes indefinite possibilities of existence or rebirths *(gati).*

In regard to the practical actualization of an "ascetic" doctrine that seems to have been conceived for a concrete lifestyle very different from that of the modern Westerner, the problems can be overcome precisely through the apparently most difficult one, namely, "detachment from the world." Evola explains that the Pāli texts indicate three types of detachment: physical, mental, and physical-mental. Today the second type is the most viable one:

> Once detachment, *viveka,* is interpreted mainly in this internal sense, it appears perhaps easier to achieve it today than in a more normal and traditional civilization. One who is still an "Aryan" spirit in a large European or American city, with its skyscrapers and asphalt, with its politics and sport, with its crowds who dance and shout, with its exponents of secular culture and of soulless science and so on—among all this he may feel himself more alone and detached and nomad than he would have done in the time of the Buddha, in conditions of physical isolation and of actual wandering. The greatest difficulty, in this respect, lies in giving this sense of internal isolation, which today may occur to many almost spontaneously, a positive, full, simple, and transparent character, with elimination of all traces of aridity, melancholy, discord, or anxiety. Solitude should not be a burden, something that is suffered, that is borne involuntarily, or in which refuge is taken by force of circumstances, but rather, a natural, simple, and free disposition. In a text we read: "Solitude is called wisdom *[ekattaṁ monam akkhātaṁ],* he who is alone will find that he is happy"; it is an accentuated version of *"beata solitudo, sola beatitudo."* (see p. 103)

This is a theme that Evola will develop in his *Cavalcare la tigre,* a book conceived and partially written in the early 1950s and published in the 1960s. *Cavalcare la tigre* points out an "existential path" that, like the "Doctrine of Awakening," is meant for "a very restricted circle of people who are endowed with a not too common inner strength." At the center of that work, as in *Doctrine,* there is the problem of the "inviolability of being" vis à vis the devouring Becoming that surrounds us. The themes of "he who stays by going and goes by staying"; of *katam karaniyam,* "done is what needed to be done," or "the work has been completed because it had to be, without reasons why or benefits"; of surviving death, which "can logically be conceived only for those few who, as human beings, were able to realize themselves as more than mere human beings"; of "everybody is lord unto himself, there is no other lord, and by dominating yourself you will have a master the like of whom it is hard to find" (as is written in the *Dhammapada*) are all taken up, developed, and adapted to the theses of *Cavalcare la tigre*.

The Prince Siddhartha whom Evola describes is certainly not the one depicted by Hermann Hesse in his novel, which has become a sort of *livre de chevet* to many contemporary readers, especially the young ones. The historical Siddhartha was a prince of the Śākya, a *kṣatriya* (belonging to the warrior caste), an "ascetic fighter" who opened a path by himself with his own strength. Thus Evola emphasizes the "aristocratic" character of primitive Buddhism, which he defines as having the "presence in it of a virile and warrior strength (the lion's roar is a designation of Buddha's proclamation) that is applied to a nonmaterial and atemporal plane . . . since it transcends such a plane, leaving it behind." The "essential nucleus of Buddhism is therefore metaphysical and initiatory," he wrote, while its interpretation "as a mere moral code based on compassion, humanitarianism, and escape from life because life is 'suffering,' is absolutely extrinsic, profane, and superficial."

Thus, we can understand the number of polemics this "essay on Buddhist asceticism" generated among the representatives of different interpretations of Buddhism, who accused Evola of "arbitrariness." Despite their disapproval, a number of British and French Buddhist centers and international scholars of Buddhism have expressed their esteem for Evola's work.

GIANFRANCO DE TURRIS
translated by Guido Stucco

Introduction

Julius Evola and Buddhism

Evola published his *Doctrine of Awakening (La dottrina del risveglio)* in 1943, a time when history took a tragic turn, particularly in Italy where the outbreak of a most cruel civil war occurred in the context of a world conflict that seemed to sentence European civilization to death. Entire cities, turned into ashes, had ceased to exist, and this was just the prelude to the imminent apocalypse. In this tragic atmosphere, in which intellectuals were expected to assume a fighting attitude based on the values of action, courage, and heroism, Evola wrote a book on Buddhism for his readers! Keeping in mind the image that the West had formed of Eastern traditions, and more specifically, of the teachings of Śākyamuni, one can see how in Italy, among the numerous potential readers of such an unexpected work, there were some who saw in this "essay on Buddhist asceticism" a sort of provocation. This was especially so considering that Evola's aristocratic origins did not seem particularly to predispose him to be interested in a religion in which monks, alienated from the world, played a predominant role.

This reaction to the work was obviously a misunderstanding. It ignores the fact that the future Buddha was also of noble origins, that he was the son of a king and heir to the throne and had been raised with the expectation that one day he would inherit the crown. He had been taught martial arts and the art of government, and having reached the right age, he had married and had a son. All of these things would be more typical of the physical and mental formation of a future samurai than of a seminarian ready to take holy orders. A man like Julius Evola was particularly suitable to dispel such a misconception.

He did so on two fronts in his *Doctrine*: on the one hand, he did not cease to recall the origins of the Buddha, Prince Siddhartha, who was destined to the throne of Kapilavastu; on the other hand, he attempted to demonstrate that Buddhist asceticism is not a cowardly resignation before life's vicissitudes, but rather a struggle of a spiritual kind, which is not any less heroic than the struggle of a knight on the battlefield. As Buddha himself said (*Mahāvagga*, 2.15): "It is better to die fighting than to live as one vanquished." This resolution is in accord with Evola's ideal of overcoming natural resistances in order to achieve the Awakening through meditation; it should be noted, however, that the warrior terminology is contained in the oldest writings of Buddhism, which are those that best reflect the living teaching of the master. Evola works tirelessly in his book to erase the Western view of a languid and dull doctrine that in fact was originally regarded as aristocratic and reserved for real "champions."

After Schopenhauer, the unfounded idea arose in Western culture that Buddhism involved a renunciation of the world and the adoption of a passive attitude: "Let things go their way; who cares anyway." Since in this inferior world "everything is evil," the wise person is the one who, like Simeon the Stylite, withdraws, if not to the top of a pillar; at least to an isolated place of meditation. Moreover, the most widespread view of Buddhists is that of monks dressed in orange robes, begging for their food; people suppose that the only activity these monks are devoted to is reciting memorized texts, since they shun prayers; thus, their religion appears to an outsider as a form of atheism.

Evola successfully demonstrates that this view is profoundly distorted by a series of prejudices. Passivity? Inaction? On the contrary, Buddha never tired of exhorting his disciples to "work toward victory"; he himself, at the end of his life, said with pride: *katam karaniyam*, "done is what needed to be done!" Pessimism? It is true that Buddha, picking up a formula of Brahmanism, the religion in which he had been raised prior to his departure from Kapilavastu, affirmed that everything on earth is "suffering." But he also clarified for us that this is the case because we are always yearning to reap concrete benefits from our actions. For example, warriors risk their lives because they long for the pleasure of victory and for the spoils, and yet, in the end they are always disappointed: the pillaging is never enough and what has been gained is quickly squandered. Also, the taste of victory soon fades away. But if one becomes aware of this state of affairs (this is one aspect of the Awakening), the pessimism is dispelled since reality is what it is, neither good nor bad in itself; reality is inscribed in Becoming, which cannot be interrupted. Thus, one must live and act with the awareness that the only thing that matters is each and every moment. Thus, duty *(dhamma)* is claimed to be the only valid reference point: "Do your duty," that is, "let your every action be totally disinterested."

Evola demonstrated that this ideal was also shared by the itinerant knights of the Western Middle Ages, who put their swords at the service of every noble cause without looking for any compensation. They fought because they prepared all their lives to offer their services and not because they wanted to become rich by looting their enemies. Were they pessimists? Certainly not. At the end of their lives they too could say, like Buddha, "done is what needed to be done." Nor were they optimists, since the principle "everything is working for the better, and in the best possible way" is not any less illusory than its opposite.

Finally, the term "asceticism" is also susceptible to being misunderstood by those who view Buddhism from the outside. Evola reminds his readers that the original meaning of the term *asceticism* is "practical exercise," or "discipline"—one could even say "learning." It certainly does not mean, as some are inclined to think, a willingness to mortify the body that derives from the idea of penance, and even leads to the practice of self-flagellation, since it is believed that one must suffer in order to expiate one's sins. Asceticism is rather a school of the will, a pure heroism (that is, it is disinterested) that Evola, a real expert in this subject, compares to the efforts of a mountain climber. To the layman, mountain climbing may be a pointless effort, but to the climber it is a challenge in which the test of courage, perseverance, and heroism is its only purpose. In this we recognize an attitude that Brahmanism knew under certain forms of yoga and Tantrism. A few years earlier Evola had devoted his book *L'uomo come potenza* ([Man As Power] 1926) to celebrating such an attitude.

In the spiritual domain, the procedure is the same. Buddha, as we know, was tempted early in his life by a form of asceticism that was similar to that of a hermit living in the desert. This approach involved prolonged fasts and techniques aimed at breaking the body's resistance. Siddhartha, however, realized himself and achieved the Awakening only when he understood this type of asceticism to be a dead end. Turning away from the indignant protests of his early companions, he stopped mortifying his body, ate to placate his hunger, and returned to the world of human beings. But it was then that his detachment started to develop: the world no longer had a grasp on him, since he had become a "hero," or like the ancient Greeks would have said, a "god."

This is the profound meaning of Prince Siddhartha's teachings, of he who became the "Enlightened One" (Buddha) or the "ascetic of the regal dynasty of the Śākya" (Śākyamuni). The value of Evola's book lies in his clarification of this authentic Buddhism. Evola utilized a great number of original sources, especially those that were gathered in the Pāli canon (Pāli being the language employed by Buddha in his teaching career). And yet, Evola's erudition is not running with his pen; his learning is not an end in itself, but rather fulfills its essential but subordinate role as a demonstrative means. Evola's work, as he himself indicated in his original subtitle, is an "essay," a summary, and not a summa. It is not a history of primitive Buddhism, but a reflection on the real nature of Buddhist asceticism and on its possible integration in the modern world.

Who knows what Evola was thinking when he wrote this book? For my part, I am inclined to believe that, having a foreboding of the imminent tragedy ahead of him, he wished to illustrate the virtue of perseverance and faithfulness, even if it meant fighting in a no-win situation. And when in 1945 in Vienna he received the terrible wound that paralyzed him for the remaining thirty years of his life, we can believe that, overcoming his pain and the disappointment of no longer being able to climb the peaks that had always attracted him, he must have said to himself that having been born in that time and place, he had done what he needed to do, that is, give witness to Truth. And if in this dark age, in which the universe is approaching the end of one of its cycles (a necessary thing if a new world is to appear, according to the cyclical view of time), people are not able to receive such a testimony, so what? As Buddha himself said: "He who has awakened is like the lion who roars to the four directions." Who knows where and how this roar will echo? In any event, it is the roar of a victor, and this is the only thing that matters.

JEAN VARENNE
translated by Guido Stucco

PART I

Principles

1

Varieties of Ascesis

The original meaning of the term *ascesis*—from *ἀσκέω,* "to train"—was simply "training" and, in a Roman sense, discipline. The corresponding Indo-Aryan term is *tapas* (*tapa* or *tapo* in Pāli) and it has a like significance; except that, from the root *tap,* which means "to be hot" or "to glow," it also contains the idea of an intensive concentration, of glowing, almost of fire.

With the development of Western civilization, however, the term *ascesis* (or its derivatives) has, as we know, taken on a particular meaning that differs from the original. Not only has it assumed an exclusively religious sense, but from the general tone of the faith that has come to predominate among Western peoples, asceticism is bound up with ideas of mortification of the flesh and of painful renunciation of the world: it has thus come to represent the method that this faith usually advocates as the most suitable for gaining "salvation" and the reconciliation of man, weighed down by original sin, with his Creator. As early as the beginnings of Christianity the name "ascetic" was applied to those who practiced mortification by flagellation of the body.

Thus, with the growth of modern civilization, all that asceticism stood for gradually and inevitably became the object of strong dislike. If even Luther, with the resentment of one unable to understand or tolerate monastic disciplines, could refuse to recognize the necessity, value, and usefulness of any ascesis, and could substitute it by exaltation of pure faith, then humanism, immanency, and the new life cult were brought from their standpoint to heap discredit and scorn upon asceticism, broadly associating such tendencies with "medieval obscurantism" and with the aberrations of "historically outdated ages." And even when asceticism was not dismissed out of hand as pathological or as a kind of sublimated masochism, all sorts of incompatibilities to our ways of life were affirmed. The best known and most overworked of these is the antithesis supposed to exist between the ascetic, static, and emasculated

Orient, renouncer and enemy of the world, and the dynamic, positive, heroic, and progressive Western civilization.

Unfortunate prejudices such as these have succeeded in gaining a foothold in people's minds; even Friedrich Nietzsche sometimes seriously believed that asceticism only attracted the "pallid enemies of life," the weak and disinherited, and those who, in their hatred of themselves and the world, undermine with their ideas the civilizations created by a superior humanity. Furthermore, recent attempts have been made to provide "climatic" explanations of asceticism. Thus, according to Günther, the Indo-Germans, under the influence of an enervating and unaccustomed climate in the Asiatic lands they had conquered, came slowly to regard the world as suffering, turning their energies away from affirmation of life and toward a seeking for "liberation" by means of various ascetic disciplines. We need hardly discuss the low level to which asceticism has been brought by recent "psychoanalytical" interpretations.

In the West, then, a tight net of misunderstanding and prejudice has been drawn round asceticism. The one-sided meaning given to asceticism by Christianity, through its frequent association therein with entirely misguided forms of spiritual life, has produced inevitable reactions: these have usually—and not without a certain antitraditional and antireligious bias—stressed only the negative side of what *one* kind of ascesis has to offer the "modern" spirit.

Our own contemporaries, however, as though the position were inverted, are now again using expressions of this nature in the original sense, though adapting them to their own entirely materialistic plane. Thus we hear of a "mystique of progress," a "mystique of science," a "mystique of labor" and so on, and likewise of an ascesis of sport, an ascesis of social service and even of an ascesis of capitalism. In spite of the confusion of ideas, there is definitely to be found here a certain element of the original meaning of the word *ascesis:* this modern use of the word or its derivatives does, in fact, imply the simple idea of training, of intensive application of energy, not without a certain impersonality and neutralization of the purely individual and hedonistic element.

Be that as it may, it is important at the present time that intelligent people should once again understand the value of asceticism in a comprehensive view of the universe and thus what it may signify at successive spiritual levels, independently of the mere religious concepts of a Christian type as well as of the modern distinctions; for which they should refer to the fundamental traditions and the highest metaphysical concepts of the Aryan races. As we wished to discuss asceticism in this sense, we asked ourselves: what example can history furnish as the best suited for examination as a comprehensive and universal ascetic system that is clear and undiluted, well tried and well set out, in tune with the spirit of Aryan man and yet prevailing in the modern age?

We eventually decided that the answer to our question could only be found in the "Doctrine of Awakening," which, in its original form, satisfies all these conditions. The "Doctrine of Awakening" is the real signification of what is commonly known as Buddhism. The term *Buddhism* is derived from the Pāli designation *Buddha* (Sanskrit: *Buddha*) given to its founder; it is, however, not so much a name as a title. *Buddha,* from the root *budh*, "to awaken," means the "Awakened One"; it is thus a designation applied to one who attains the spiritual realization, likened to an "arousing" or to an "awakening," which Prince Siddhattha announced to the Indo-Aryan world. Buddhism, in its original form—the so-called Pāli Buddhism—shows us, as do very few other doctrines, the characteristics we want: (1) it contains a complete ascetic system; (2) it is universally valid and it is realistic; (3) it is purely Aryan in spirit; (4) it is accessible in the general conditions of the historical cycle to which present-day humankind also belongs.

We have implied that asceticism, when considered as a whole, can assume various meanings at successive spiritual levels. Simply defined, that is to say as "training" or discipline, an ascesis aims at placing all the energies of the human being under the control of a central principle. In this respect we can, properly speaking, talk of a technique that has, in common with that of modern scientific achievements, the characteristics of objectivity and impersonality. Thus an eye, trained to distinguish the accessory from the essential, can easily recognize a "constant" beyond the multiple variety of ascetic forms adopted by this or that tradition.

In the first place, we can consider as accessory all the particular religious conceptions or the particular ethical interpretations with which, in very many cases, asceticism is associated. Beyond all this, however, it is possible to conceive of and to work out what we may call a pure ascesis, that is to say, one made up of techniques for developing an interior force, the use of which, to begin with, remains undetermined, like the use of the arms and machines produced by modern industrial techniques. Thus, while "ascetic" reinforcement of the personality is the foundation of every transcendental realization, whether in the form of one historical tradition or another, it can likewise be of great value on the level of the temporal aspirations and struggles that absorb practically all the energies of modern Western people. Furthermore, we could even conceive of an "ascesis of evil," for the technical conditions, as we may call them, needed to achieve any positive success in the direction of the "evil" are not different in kind from those needed, for example, to attain sainthood. Nietzsche himself, as we have already pointed out, partly shared the modern widespread prejudice against asceticism: when dealing with his "Superman" and when formulating the *Wille zur Macht,* did he not take into account various disciplines and forms of self-control that are clearly of an ascetic nature? Thus, at least within certain limits, we can quote the words of an old medieval tradition: "One the Art, One the Material, One the Crucible."

Now, few other great historical traditions allow us to isolate so easily the elements of a pure ascesis as does the "Doctrine of Awakening," that is to say, Buddhism. It has been justly said of Buddhism that in it the ascetic problems "have been stated and resolved so clearly and, one could almost say, so logically that, in comparison, other forms of mysticism seem incomplete, fragmentary and inconclusive"; and that, far from being weighed down by every kind of emotional and sentimental element, an austere and objective style of intellectual clarity so much predominates that one is almost forced to compare it with the modern scientific mentality.[1] In this respect two points must be emphasized.

First, the Buddhist ascesis is *conscious,* in the sense that in many forms of asceticism—and in the case of Christian asceticism almost without exception—the accessory is inextricably tied up with the essential, and ascetic realizations are, one might say, indirect because they result from impulses and workings of the mind determined by religious suggestions or raptures; while in Buddhism there is direct action, based on knowledge, conscious of its aim and developing throughout in controlled stages. "Just as a practiced turner or turner's apprentice, when turning quickly, knows 'I am turning quickly,' and when turning slowly, knows 'I am turning slowly'"; and "as a practiced butcher or butcher's apprentice who butchers a cow, takes it to the marketplace and dissects it piece by piece; he knows these parts, he looks at them and examines them well and then sits down"—here are two trenchant similes, chosen from many, and typical of the style of consciousness of every ascetic or contemplative procedure in the Doctrine of Awakening.[2] Another image is furnished by clear and transparent water through which can be seen everything lying on the bottom: symbolical of a mind that has left behind all unrest and disturbance.[3] And it will be seen that this style persists throughout, on every level of Buddhist discipline. It has been well said that "this path through consciousness and awakening is as clearly described as a road on an accurate map, along which every tree, every bridge and every house is marked."[4]

Second, Buddhism is almost the only system that avoids confusion between asceticism and morality, and in which the purely instrumental value of the latter in the interests of the former is consciously realized. Every ethical precept is measured against an independent scale, that is, according to the positive "ascetic" effects that result from following these precepts or failing to follow them. From this it can be seen that not only have all religious mythologies been surpassed, but also all ethical

1. B. Jansink, *La mistica del buddismo* (Turin, 1925), p. 304.
2. *Majjhima-nikāya*, 10.
3. Cf., e.g., *Jātaka,* 185.
4. E. Reinhold, in the introduction to the works of K. E. Neumann quoted by G. de Lorenzo, *I discorsi di Buddho* (Bari, 1925), vol. 2, p. 15.

mythologies. In Buddhism, the elements of *sīla*, that is, of "right conduct," are considered purely as "instruments of the mind":[5] it is not a question of "values" but of "instruments," instruments of a *virtus*, not in the moralistic sense but in the ancient sense of virile energy. Here we have the well-known parable of the raft: a man, wishing to cross a dangerous river and having built a raft for this purpose, would indeed be a fool if, when he had crossed, he were to put the raft on his shoulders and take it with him on his journey. This must be the attitude—Buddhism teaches—to all that is labeled by ethical views as good or evil, just or unjust.[6]

Thus we can fairly claim that in Buddhism—as also in yoga—asceticism is raised to the dignity and impersonality of a science: what is elsewhere fragmentary here becomes systematic; what is instinct becomes conscious technique; the spiritual labyrinth of those minds that achieve a real elevation through the workings of some "grace" (since it is only accidentally and by means of suggestions, fears, hopes, and raptures that they discover the right way) is replaced by a calm and uniform light, present even in abysmal depths, and by a method that has no need of external means.

All this, however, refers only to the first aspect of asceticism, the most elementary in the ascetic hierarchy. When an ascesis is understood as a technique for the conscious creation of a force that can be applied, in the first place, at any level, then the disciplines taught by the Doctrine of Awakening can be recognized as those that incorporate the highest degree of crystallinity and independence. However, we encounter inside the system a distinction between the disciplines that "suffice for this life" and those that are necessary to take one beyond.[7] Ascetic achievement in Buddhism is exploited essentially in an upward direction. This is how the sense of such achievements is expressed in the canon: "And he reaches the admirable path discovered by the intensity, the constancy and the concentration of the will, the admirable path discovered by the intensity, the constancy and the concentration of the energy, the admirable path discovered by the intensity, the constancy and the concentration of the spirit, the admirable path discovered by the intensity, the constancy and the concentration of investigation—with a heroic spirit as the fifth." And this continues: "And thus attaining these fifteen heroic qualities, he is able, O disciples, to achieve liberation, to achieve awakening, to attain the incomparable sureness."[8] In this connection another text considers a double possibility: "Either certainty in life, or no return after death."[9] If, on the highest level, "sureness" is linked with the state of "awakening," the alternatives can be similarly interpreted on a lower level, and we

---

5. *Majjh.*, 53.
6. Ibid., 22.
7. Cf., e.g., *Majjh.*, 53.
8. *Majjh.*, 16.
9. Ibid., 10.

may think of a more relative sureness in life, created by a preliminary group of ascetic disciplines and able to prove its value in all fields of life, and yet that is essentially a foundation for an ascesis of a higher nature. It is in this sense that we can talk of an "intensive application," which is considered to be the keystone of the whole system and which, when "developed and constantly practised, leads to two-fold health, health in the present and health in the future."[10] "Sureness," in ascetic development—*bhāvanā*—is associated with unshakable calm—*samatha*—which may be considered as the highest aim of a "neutral" discipline, and which can be pursued by one who yet remains essentially a "son of the world"—*putthujjana.* Beyond this there is an unshakable calm—*samatha*—which is associated with knowledge—*vipassanā*—and which then leads to "liberation."[11]

Here we have, then, a new conception of the ascesis, on a higher plane than the last, and taking us to a level above normal perception and individual experience; and at the same time it becomes clear why Buddhism, on this higher level also, gives us positive points of reference such as we find in few other traditions. The fact is that Buddhism in its original form carefully avoids anything that savors of simple "religion," of mysticism in its most generally accepted sense, of systems of "faith" or devotion, or of dogmatic rigidity. And even when we consider that which is no longer of that life, that which is "more than life," Buddhism, as the Doctrine of Awakening, offers us those very traits of severity and nudity that characterize the monumental, and features of clarity and strength that may be called, in a general sense, "classical"; a virile and courageous attitude that would seem Promethean were it not indeed essentially Olympian. But before this can be appreciated, once again various prejudices must be removed. And here it is well to discuss two points.

It has been claimed that Buddhism, in its essentials, and leaving out of account its later popular forms, entirely centered as they were on a deified concept of its founder, is not a religion. This is true. We must, however, be quite clear as to what we mean when we say this. The peoples of the West are so inured to the religion that has come to predominate in their countries that they consider it as a kind of unit of measure and as a model for every other religion: they are near denying the dignity of true religion to any concept of the supersensory and to man's relationship to it, when the concept in any way differs from the Judeo-Christian type. The result of this has been that the most ancient traditions of the West itself—beginning with the Aryo-Hellenic and the Aryo-Roman—are no longer understood in their real significance

---

10. *Anguttara-nikāya*, 3.65; 10.15. Cf. *Saṁyutt.*, 35.198, where the disciplines are stated to be valid for this life since, in it, they create self-possession, and yet build the firm foundations for the destruction of the *āsava*, that is, for the task of following the upward path.

11. In *Angutt.*, 4.170 it is said that the bonds give way and the path opens when *samatha* is combined with *vipassanā*.

or effective value;[12] so it is easy to imagine what happened to older and often more remote traditions, particularly to those created by the Aryan races in Asia. But, indeed, this attitude should be reversed: and just as "modern" civilization is an anomaly when compared with what has always been true civilization,[13] so the significance and the value of the Christian religion should be measured according to that part of its content that is consonant with a vaster, more Aryan, and more primordial concept of the supersensory.

We need not dwell on this point since we have already dealt with it elsewhere; Dahlke sums up the matter, saying that one characteristic of Western superficiality is the tendency always to identify religion as a whole with religion based on faith.[14] Beyond those who "believe" are those who "know," and to these the purely "mythological" character of many simply religious, devotional, and even scholastically theological concepts is quite clear. It is largely a question of different degrees of knowledge. Religion, from *religo,* is, as the word itself indicates, a reconnecting and, more specifically, a reconnecting of a creature to a Creator with the eventual introduction of a mediator or of an expiator. On the basis of this central idea can be built up a whole system of faith, devotion, and even mysticism that, admittedly, is capable of carrying an individual to a certain level of spiritual realization. However, it does so to a large extent *passively* since it is based essentially on sentiment, emotion, and suggestion. In such a system no amount of scholastic explaining will ever completely resolve the irrational and subintellectual element.

We can easily understand that in some cases such "religious" forms are necessary; and even the East, in later periods, has known something of the kind, for instance, the way of devotion—*bhakti-marga* (from *bhaj,* "to adore")—of Rāmānuja and certain forms of the Śakti cult: but we must also realize that there may be some who have no need of them and who, by race and by calling, desire a way free from "religious" mythologies, a way based on clear knowledge, realization, and awakening. An ascetic, whose energies are employed in this direction, achieves the highest form of ascesis; and Buddhism gives us an example of an ascesis that is outstanding of its kind—in saying "of its kind" we wish to point out that Buddhism represents a great historical tradition with texts and teachings available to all; it is not an esoteric school with its knowledge reserved for a restricted number of initiates.

In this sense we can, and indeed we must, state that Buddhism—referring always to original Buddhism—is *not* a religion. This does not mean that it denies supernatural and metaphysical reality, but only that it has nothing to do with the way of

---

12. Cf. W. F. Otto, *Die Götter Griechenlands* (1935), 1, 2, and *passim.*
13. Cf. R. Guénon, *Orient et Occident* (Paris, 1924); *La Crise du monde moderne* (Paris, 1925). [English translations: *East and West* (London, 1941), and *The Crisis of the Modern World* (London, 1943)].
14. P. Dahlke, *Buddhismus als Religion und Moral* (Munich and Neubiberg, 1923), p. 11.

regarding one's relationship with this reality that we know more or less as "religion." The validity of these statements would in no way be altered were one to set out in greater detail to defend the excellence of the theistic point of view against Buddhism, by charging the Doctrine of Awakening with more or less declared atheism. This brings us to the second point for discussion, but which we need only touch upon here as it is dealt with at length later in this work.

We have admitted that a "religiously" conceived system can carry an individual to a certain level of spiritual realization. The fact that this system is based on a theistic concept determines this level. The theistic concept, however, is by no means either unique or even the highest "religious" relationship such as the Hindu *bhakti* or the predominant faiths in the Western or Arab world. Whatever one may think of it, the theistic concept represents an incomplete view of the world, since it lacks the extreme hierarchic apex. From a metaphysical and (in the higher sense) traditional point of view, the notion on which theism is based of representing "being" in a personal form even when theologically sublimated, can never claim to be the ultimate ideal. The concept and the realization of the extreme apex or, in other words, of that which is beyond both such a "being" and its opposite, "nonbeing," was and is natural to the Aryan spirit. It does not deny the theistic point of view but recognizes it in its rightful hierarchic place and subordinates it to a truly transcendental concept.

It is freely admitted that things are less simple than they seem in Western theology, especially in the realm of mysticism, and more particularly where it is concerned with so-called "negative theology." Also in the West the notion of a personal God occasionally merges into the idea of an ineffable essence, of an abysmal divinity, as the ἕν conceived by the Neoplatonists beyond the ὄν, as the *Gottheit* in the neuter beyond the *Gott,* which, after Dionysius the Areopagite, appeared frequently in German mysticism and which exactly corresponds with the neuter *Brahman* above the theistic *Brahmā* of Hindu speculation. But in the West it is more a notion wrapped in a confused mystical cloud than a precise doctrinal and dogmatic definition conforming to a comprehensive cosmic system. And this notion, in point of fact, has had little or no effect on the "religious" bias prevalent in the Western mind: its only result has been to carry a few men, confused in their occasional intuitions and visions, beyond the frontiers of "orthodoxy."

That very apex that Christian theology loses in a confused background is, instead, very often placed consciously in the foreground by the Aryo-Oriental traditions. To talk in this respect of atheism or even of pantheism betrays ignorance, an ignorance shared by those who spend their time unearthing oppositions and antitheses. The truth is that the traditions of the Aryans who settled in the East retain and conserve much of what the later traditions of races of the same root who settled in the West have lost or no longer understand or retain only fragmentarily. A contributing factor here is the undoubted influence on European faiths of concepts of Semitic and Asiatic-Mediterranean origin. Thus to accuse of atheism the older traditions, particularly the Doctrine of Awakening, and also other Western traditions that reflect the same spirit, only betrays an attempt to expose and discredit a higher point of view on the part of a lower one: an attempt that, had circumstances been reversed, would have been qualified out of hand by the religious West as Satanic. And, in fact, we shall see that it was exactly thus that it appeared to the doctrine of the Buddha (cf. p. 85–86).

The recognition of that which is "beyond both 'being' and 'nonbeing'" opens to ascetic realization possibilities unknown to the world of theism. The fact of reaching the apex, in which the distinction between "Creator" and "creature" becomes metaphysically meaningless, allows of a whole system of spiritual realizations that, since it leaves behind the categories of "religious" thought, is not easily understood: and, above all, it permits a direct ascent, that is, an ascent up the bare mountainside, without support and without useless excursions to one side or another. This is the exact meaning of the Buddhist ascesis; it is no longer a system of disciplines designed to generate strength, sureness, and unshakable calm, but a system of spiritual realization. Buddhism—and again later we shall see this distinctly—carries the will for the unconditioned to a limit that is almost beyond the imagination of the modern Westerner. And in this ascent beside the abyss the climber rejects all "mythologies," he proceeds by means of pure strength, he ignores all mirages, he rids himself of any residual human weakness, he acts only according to pure knowledge. Thus the Awakened One (Buddha), the Victor (Jina) could be called he whose way was unknown to men, angels, and to Brahmā himself (the Sanskrit name for the theistic god). Admittedly, this path is not without dangers, yet it is the path open to the virile mind—*viriya-magga*. The texts clearly state that the doctrine is "for the wise man, the expert, not for the ignorant, the inexpert."[15] The simile of the cutting grass is used: "As *kusa* grass when wrongly grasped cuts the hand, so the ascetic life wrongly practised leads to infernal torments."[16] The simile of the serpent is used: "As a man who wants serpents goes out for serpents, looks for serpents, and finding a powerful serpent grasps it by the body or by the tail; and the serpent striking at him bites his hand or arm or other part so that he suffers death or mortal anguish—and why is this? Because he wrongly grasped the serpent—so there are men who are harmed by the doctrines. And why is this? Because they wrongly grasped the doctrines."[17]

It must be thus quite clear that the Doctrine of Awakening is not itself one par-

15. *Majjh.*, 2.
16. *Dhammapada*, 311.
17. *Majjh.*, 22.

ticular religion that is opposed to other religions. Even in the world in which it grew, it respected the various divinities and the popular cults of religious type that were attached to them. It understood the value of "works." Virtuous and devout men go to "heaven"—but a different path is taken by the Awakened Ones.[18] They go beyond as "a fire which, little by little, consumes every bond,"[19] both human and divine. And it is fundamentally an innate attribute of the Aryan soul that causes us never to meet in the Buddhist texts any sign of departure from consciousness, of sentimentalism or devout effusion, or of semi-intimate conversation with a God, although throughout there is a sense of strength inexorably directed toward the unconditioned.

We have now elaborated the first three reasons why Buddhism in particular is so suitable as a base for an exposition of a complete ascesis. Summing up: the first is the possibility of extracting easily from Buddhism the elements of an ascesis considered as an objective technique for the achievement of calm, strength, and detached superiority, capable in themselves of being used in all directions. The second is that in Buddhism the ascesis has also the superior signification of a path of spiritual realization quite free from any mythology, whether religious, theological, or ethical. The third reason, finally, is that the last stretch of such a path corresponds to the Supreme in a truly metaphysical concept of the universe, to a real transcendency well beyond the purely theistic concept. Thus while the Buddha considers the tendency to dogmatize as a bond, and opposes the empty sufficiency of those who proclaim: "Only this is truth, foolishness is the rest,"[20] yet he maintains firmly the knowledge of his own dignity: "Perhaps you may wish, disciples, thus knowing, thus understanding, to return for your salvation to the rites and the fantasies of the ordinary penitent or priest?" "No, indeed," is the answer. "Is it thus then, disciples: that you speak only of that on which you yourselves have meditated, which you yourselves have known, which you yourselves have understood?" "Even so, Master." "This is well, disciples. Remain, then, endowed with this doctrine, which is visible in this life, timeless, inviting, leading onward, intelligible to all intelligent men. If this has been said, for this reason has it been said."[21] And again: "There are penitents and priests who exalt liberation. They speak in various manners glorifying liberation. But as for that which concerns the most noble, the highest liberation, I know that none equals me, let alone that I may be surpassed."[22] This has been called, in the tradition, "the lion's roar."

18. *Dhammapada*, 126.
19. Ibid., 31.
20. Cf., e.g., *Suttanipāta*, 4.12; 13.17–19.
21. *Majjh.*, 38.
22. *Dīgha-nikāya*, 8.21.

2

⚜

The Aryan-ness of
the Doctrine of Awakening

We have yet to say something of the "Aryan-ness" of the Buddhist doctrine.

Our use of the term *Aryan* in connection with this doctrine is primarily justified by direct reference to the texts. The term *ariya* (Skt.: *ārya*), which in fact means "Aryan," recurs throughout the canon. The path of awakening is called Aryan—*ariya magga;* the four fundamental truths are Aryan—*ariya-saccāni;* the mode of knowledge is Aryan—*ariya-naya;* the teaching is called Aryan (particularly that which considers the contingency of the world[1]) and is, in turn, addressed to the *ariya;* the doctrine is spoken of as accessible and intelligible, not to the common crowd, but only to the *ariya.* The term *ariya* has sometimes been translated as "saint." This, however, is an incomplete translation; it is even discordant when we consider the notable divergence between what is concerned and all that "saintliness" means to a Western man. Nor is the translation of *ariya* as "noble" or "sublime" any more satisfactory. They are all later meanings of the word, and they do not convey the fullness of the original nor the spiritual, aristocratic, and racial significance that, nevertheless, is largely preserved in Buddhism. This is why Orientalists, such as Rhys Davids and Woodward, have maintained that it is better not to translate the term at all, and they have left *ariya* wherever it occurs in the texts, either as an adjective or as a noun meaning a certain class of individuals. In the texts of the canon the *ariya* are the Awakened Ones, those who have achieved liberation and those who are united to them since they understand, accept, and follow the *ariya* Doctrine of Awakening.[2]

It is necessary, however, that we should emphasize the Aryan-ness of the Buddhist doctrine for various reasons. In the first place, we must anticipate those who

---

1. Cf. *Saṁyutta-nikāya*, 35.84; 42.12.
2. The racial significance of the term *ariya* is clear in certain texts, e.g., where it is considered as a difficult birth to achieve and where it is a privilege to be born in the land of the Aryans (*Aṅguttara*, 6.96).

will put forward the argument of Asiatic exclusiveness, saying that Buddhism is remote from "our" traditions and "our" races. We have to remember that behind the various caprices of modern historical theories, and as a more profound and primordial reality, there stands the unity of blood and spirit of the white races who created the greatest civilizations both of the East and West, the Iranian and Hindu as well as the ancient Greek and Roman and the Germanic. Buddhism has the right to call itself Aryan both because it reflects in great measure the spirit of common origins and since it has preserved important parts of a heritage that, as we have already said, Western man has little by little forgotten, not only by reason of involved processes of intermarriage, but also since he himself—to a far greater extent than the Eastern Aryans—has come under foreign influences, particularly in the religious field. As we have pointed out, Buddhist asceticism, when certain supplementary elements have been removed, is truly "classical" in its clarity, realism, precision, and firm and articulate structure; we may say it reflects the noblest style of the ancient Aryo-Mediterranean world.

Furthermore, it is not only a question of form. The ascesis proclaimed by Prince Siddhattha is suffused throughout with an intimate congeniality and with an accentuation of the intellectual and Olympian element that is the mark of Platonism, Neoplatonism, and Roman Stoicism. Other points of contact are to be found where Christianity has been rectified by a transfusion of Aryan blood that had remained comparatively pure—that is to say, in what we know as German mysticism: there is Meister Eckhart's sermon on detachment, on *Abgeschiedenheit,* and his theory of the "noble mind," and we must not forget Tauler and Silesius. To insist here, as in every other field of thought, on the antithesis between East and West is pure dilettantism. The real contrast exists in the first place between concepts of a modern kind and those of a traditional kind, whether the latter are Eastern or Western; and secondly, between the real creations of the Aryan spirit and blood and those which, in East and West alike, have resulted from the admixture of non-Aryan influences. As Dahlke has justly said, "Among the principal ways of thought in ancient times, Buddhism can best claim to be of pure Aryan origin."[3]

This is true also more specifically. Although we can apply the term Aryan as a generalization to the mass of Indo-European races as regards their common origin (the original homeland of such races, the *ariyanem-vaējō,* according to the memory consciously preserved in the ancient Iranian tradition, was a hyperborean region or, more generally, northwestern),[4] yet, later, it became a designation of caste. *Ārya*

---

3. P. Dahlke, *Buddhismus als Weltanschauung* (Munich and Neubiberg, undated), p. 35. [English translation, *Buddhism and Science* (London, 1913), p. 29.]

4. In this connection cf. our works: *Rivolta contro il mondo moderno* (Milan, 1934) [English translation, *Revolt Against the Modern World* (Rochester, Vt., 1995)]; *Sintesi di dottrina della razza* (Milan, 1941).

stood essentially for an aristocracy opposed, both in mind and body, not only to obscure, bastard, "demoniacal" races among which must be included the Kosalian and
Dravidian strains found by the Hyperboreans in the Asiatic lands they conquered,
but also, more generally, to that substratum that corresponds to what we would probably call today the proletarian and plebeian masses born in the normal way to serve,
and that in India as in Rome were excluded from the bright cults characteristic of the
higher patrician, warrior, and priestly castes.

Buddhism can claim to be called Aryan in this more particular social sense also,
notwithstanding the attitude, of which we shall have more to say later, that it adopted
toward the castes of those times.

The man who was later known as the Awakened One, that is, the Buddha, was
the Prince Siddhattha. According to some, he was the son of a king; according to
others, at least of the most ancient warrior nobility of the Sākiya race, proverbial for
its pride: there was a saying, "Proud as a Sākiya."[5] This race claimed descent, like
the most illustrious and ancient Hindu dynasties, from the so-called solar race—
sūrya vaṁsa—and from the very ancient king Ikśvāku.[6] "He, of the solar race," one
reads of the Buddha.[7] He says so himself: "I am descended from the solar dynasty
and I was born a Sākiya,"[8] and by becoming an ascetic who has renounced the world
he vindicates his royal dignity, the dignity of an Aryan king.[9] Tradition has it that his
person appeared as "a form adorned with all the signs of beauty and surrounded by a
radiant aureole."[10] To a sovereign who meets him and does not know who he is, he
immediately gives the impression of an equal: "Thou hast a perfect body, thou art
resplendent, well born, of noble aspect, thou hast a golden colour and white teeth,
thou art strong. All the signs that thou art of noble birth are in thy form, all the marks
of a superior man."[11] The most fearsome bandit, meeting him, asks himself in amaze-
ment who might be "this ascetic who comes alone with no companions, like a

---

5. H. Oldenberg, *Buddha* (Stuttgart and Berlin, 1923), p. 101. Prince Siddhattha seems to retain his pride
even when he is the Buddha uttering such words as these: "In the world of angels, of demons and of gods,
among the ranks of ascetics and of priests, I do not see, O Brāhman, any one whom I should respectfully
salute nor before whom I should rise for him to be seated" (*Anguttara-nikāya*, 8.11).

6. *Suttanipāta*, 3.6.31. It is worth noting that Ikśvāku was conceived as the son of Manu, that is, of the
primordial legislator of the Indo-Aryan races, and that these references in Buddhism are significant: in
fact, the same royal and solar origin is attributed to the doctrine expounded in the *Bhagavadgītā* (4.1–2);
a doctrine that was revealed after a period of oblivion to a *kṣatriya*, that is, to an exponent of warrior
nobility, and that shows us how the path of detachment can also produce an unconditioned and irresistible
form of heroism; cf. *Revolt Against the Modern World*.

7. *Saṁyutt.*, 22.95.

8. *Suttanipāta*, 3.1.19.

9. Ibid., 3.7.7.

10. *Jātaka*, 1.

11. *Suttanipāta*, 3.7.1–2; 5–6.

conqueror."[12] And not only do we find in his body and bearing the characteristics of a *khattiya*, of a noble warrior of high lineage, but tradition has it that he was endowed with the "thirty-two attributes" that according to an ancient brahmanical doctrine were the mark of the "superior man"—*mahāpurisa-lakkhaṇa*—for whom "exist only two possibilities, without a third": either, to remain in the world and to become a *cakkavatti*, that is, a king of kings, a "universal sovereign," the Aryan prototype of the "Lord of the Earth," or else to renounce the world and to become perfectly awakened, the Sambuddha, "one who has removed the veil."[13] Legend tells us that in a prophetic vision of a whirling wheel an imperial destiny was foretold for Prince Siddhattha; a destiny that, however, he rejected in favor of the other path.[14] It is equally significant that, according to tradition, the Buddha directed that his funeral rite should not be that of an ascetic, but of an imperial sovereign, a *cakkavatti*.[15] In spite of the attitude of Buddhism toward the caste problem, it was generally held that the *bodhisatta*, those who may one day become awakened, are never born into a peasant or servile caste but into a warrior or Brāhman caste, that is to say, into the two purest and highest of the Aryan castes: indeed, in the conditions then prevailing, the warrior caste, the *khattiya*, was said to be the more favored.[16]

This Aryan nobility and this warrior spirit are reflected in the Doctrine of Awakening itself. Analogies between the Buddhist ascesis and war, between the qualities of an ascetic and the virtues of a warrior and of a hero recur frequently in the canonical texts: "a struggling ascetic with fighting breast," "an advance with a fighter's steps," "hero, victor of the battle," "supreme triumph of the battle," "favorable conditions for the combat," qualifies of "a warrior becoming to a king, well worthy of a king, attributes of a king," etc.[17]—and in such maxims as: "to die in battle is better than to live defeated."[18] As for "nobility," it is bound up here with aspiration toward superhumanly inspired liberty. "As a bull, I have broken every bond"—says Prince Siddhattha.[19] "Having laid aside the burden, he has destroyed the bonds of existence": this is a theme that continually recurs in the texts, and refers to one who follows the path they indicate. As "summits hard to climb, like solitary lions" the enlightened are described.[20] The Awakened One is "a proud saint who has climbed

12. *Majjh.*, 86.
13. *Suttanipāta*, 3.8; 5.1.25–28; *Majjh.*, 91; *Dīgha*, 3.1.5, etc.; *Suttanipāta*, 3.1.16, 19. A racial detail, not without interest, is that among the distinguishing marks included a dark blue color of the eyes.
14. *Jātaka*, intr. (W. 64).
15. *Dīgha*, 16.5.11; 17.1.8.
16. *Jātaka*, intr. (W. 40–41).
17. Cf. *Majjh.*, 53; 26; *Angutt.*, 4.181, 196; 5.90, 73 ff.
18. *Suttanipāta*, 3.2.16.
19. Ibid., 1.2.12.
20. *Majjh.*, 92; *Suttanipāta*, 3.7.25.

the most sublime mountain peaks, who has penetrated the remotest forests, who has descended into profound abysses."[21] He himself said, "I serve no man, I have no need to serve any man";[22] an idea that recalls the "autonomous and immaterial race," the race "without a king" *(ἀβασίλευτος)*—being itself kingly—a race that is also mentioned in the West.[23] He is "ascetic, pure, the knower, free, sovereign."[24]

These, which are frequent even in the oldest texts, are some of the attributes, not only of the Buddha, but also of those who travel along the same path. The natural exaggeration of some of these attributes does not alter their significance at least as symbols and indications of the nature of the path and ideal indicated by Prince Siddhattha, and of his spiritual race. The Buddha is an outstanding example of a royal ascetic; his natural counterpart in dignity is a sovereign who, like a Caesar, could claim that his race comprehended the majesty of kings as well as the sacredness of the gods who hold even the rulers of men in their power.[25] We have seen that the ancient tradition has this precise significance when it speaks of the essential nature of individuals who can only be either imperial or perfectly awakened. We are close to the summits of the Aryan spiritual world.

A particular characteristic of the Aryan-ness of the original Buddhist teaching is the absence of those proselytizing manias that exist, almost without exception, in direct proportion to the plebeian and anti-aristocratic character of a belief. An Aryan mind has too much respect for other people, and its sense of its own dignity is too pronounced to allow it to impose its own ideas upon others, even when it knows that its ideas are correct. Accordingly, in the original cycle of Aryan civilizations, both Eastern and Western, there is not the smallest trace of divine figures being so concerned with mankind as to come near to pursuing them in order to gain their adherence and to "save" them. The so-called salvationist religions—the *Erlösungsreligionen,* in German—make their appearance both in Europe and Asia at a later date, together with a lessening of the preceding spiritual tension, with a fall from Olympian consciousness and, not least, with influxes of inferior ethnic and social elements. That the divinities can do little for men, that man is fundamentally the artificer of his own destiny, even of his development beyond this world—this characteristic view held by original Buddhism demonstrates its difference from some later forms, especially of the Mahāyāna schools, into which infiltrated the idea of a

---

21. *Majjh.*, 50.
22. *Suttanipāta*, 1.2.8.
23. Zosimus, text in Berthelot, *Collection des alchimistes grecques* (Paris, 1887), vol. 2, p. 213.
24. *Majjh.*, 39.
25. Suetonius, *De vita Caesarum*, 6. The equivalence of the two types is indicated, for example, by *Angutt.* (2.44), where it is said that two beings appear in the world for the health of many, for the good of gods and men: the perfect Awakened One and the *cakkavatti* or "universal sovereign."

power from on high busying itself with mankind in order to lead each individual to salvation.

In point of method and teaching, in the original texts we see that the Buddha expounds the truth as he has discovered it, without imposing himself on anyone and without employing outside means to persuade or "convert." "He who has eyes will see"—is a much repeated saying of the texts. "Let an intelligent man come to me"—we read[26]—"a man without a tortuous mind, without hypocrisy, an upright man: I will instruct him, I will expound the doctrine. If he follows the instruction, after a short while he himself will recognize, he himself will see, that thus indeed one liberates oneself from the bonds, the bonds, that is, of ignorance." Here follows a simile of an infant freeing itself gradually from its early limitations; this image exactly corresponds to the Platonic simile of the expert midwife and the art of aiding births. Again: "I will not force you, as the potter his raw clay. By reproving I will instruct, and by urging you. He who is sound will endure."[27] Besides, the original intention of Prince Siddhattha was, having once achieved his knowledge of truth, to communicate it to no one, not from ill-mindedness, but because he realized its profundity and foresaw that few would understand it. Having then recognized the existence of a few individuals of a nobler nature with clearer vision, he expounded the doctrine out of compassion, maintaining, however, his distance, his detachment, and his dignity. Whether disciples come to him or not, whether or not they follow his ascetic precepts, "always he remains the same."[28] This is his manner: "Know persuasion and know dissuasion; knowing persuasion and knowing dissuasion, do not persuade and do not dissuade: expound only reality."[29] "It is wonderful"—says another text[30]—"it is astonishing that no one exalts his own teaching and no one despises the teaching of another in an order where there are so many guides to show the doctrine."

This, too, is typically Aryan. It is true that the spiritual power that the Buddha possessed could not but show itself sometimes almost automatically, demanding immediate recognition. We read, for example, of the incident described as "the first footprint of the elephant," where wise men and expert dialecticians wait for the Buddha at a ford seeking an opportunity to defeat him with their arguments, but when they see him they ask only to hear the doctrine;[31] or of another where, when the Buddha enters a discussion, his words destroy all opposition "like a furious elephant or a blazing fire."[32] There is the account of his former companions who, be-

26. *Majjh.*, 80.
27. Ibid., 122.
28. Ibid., 49; 137.
29. Ibid., 139.
30. Ibid., 76.
31. Ibid., 27.
32. Ibid., 35.

lieving him to have left the road of asceticism, propose among themselves not to greet him, but who when immediately they see him go to meet him; and there is the story of the fierce bandit Angulimāla who is awed by the Buddha's majestic figure. In any case, it is certain that the Buddha, in his Aryan superiority, always abstained from using indirect methods of persuasion and, in particular, never used any that appealed to the irrational, sentimental, or emotional element in a human being. This rule too is definite: "You must not, O disciples, show to laymen the miracle of the super-normal powers. He who does this is guilty of an offence of wrongdoing."[33] The individual is put on one side: "In truth, the noble sons declare their higher knowledge in such a manner, that they state the truth without any reference whatsoever to their own person."[34] "Why is this?"—says the Buddha to one who has eagerly waited for a long time to see him—"He who sees the law sees me and he who sees me sees the law. In truth, by seeing the law I am seen and by seeing me the law is seen."[35] Being himself awakened, the Buddha wishes only to encourage an awakening in those who are capable of it: an awakening, in the first place, of a sense of dignity and of vocation, and in the second, of intellectual intuition. A man who is incapable of intuition, it is said, cannot approve.[36] The noble miracle "conforming to the Aryan nature" *(ariya-iddhi)* as opposed to prodigies based on extranormal phenomena, and considered to be non-Aryan *(anariya-iddhi)* is concerned with this very point. The "miracle of the teaching" stirs the faculty of discernment and furnishes a new and accurate measure of all values;[37] the most typical of the canonical expressions for this is: "'There is this'—he understands—'There is the common and there is the excellent, and there is a higher escape beyond this perception of the senses.'"[38] Here is a characteristic passage describing the awakening of intuition: "His [the disciple's] heart suddenly feels pervaded with sacred enthusiasm and his whole mind is revealed pure, clear, shining as the luminous disc of the moon: and the truth appears to him in its completeness."[39] This is the foundation of the only "faith," of the only "right confidence" considered by the order of the Aryans, "an active confidence, rooted in insight, firm"; a confidence that "no penitent or priest, no god or devil, no angel nor anyone else in the world can destroy."[40]

Perhaps it is worth briefly discussing a final point. The fact that the Buddha, normally, does not appear in the Pāli texts as a supernatural being descended to

33. *Vinaya*, 2.112.
34. *Angutt.*, 6.49.
35. *Saṁyutt.*, 22.87.
36. *Majjh.*, 95.
37. *Dīgha*, 11.3–8.
38. *Majjh.*, 7.
39. *Mahāparinirv.*, 52–56.
40. *Majjh.*, 47.

earth to broadcast a "revelation," but as a man who expounds a truth that he himself has seen and who indicates a path that he himself has trodden, as a man who, having himself crossed by his own unaided efforts[41] to the other bank of the river, helps others to cross over[42]—this fact must not lead us to make the figure of the Buddha too human. Even if we omit the Bodhisatta theory that so often suffers from infiltration of fabulous elements and that only came into being at a later period, the concept in the early texts of what is known as *kolankola* makes us seek in the Buddha the reemergence of a luminous principle already kindled in preceding generations: this is an idea that agrees perfectly with what we are about to say on the historical significance of the Buddhist Doctrine of Awakening. In any case, whatever his antecedents, it is extremely difficult to draw a line between what is human and what is not, when we are dealing with a being who has inwardly attained deathlessness *(amata)* and who is presented as the living incarnation of a law bound up with that which is transcendental and that can be "confined" by nothing—*apariyā-panna*. The question of race comes in here, too. If a being feels himself remote from metaphysical reality, then he will imagine any strength that he may acquire as a "grace," knowledge will appear as "revelation" in its accepted meaning in the West since the time of the Hebrew prophets, and the announcer of a law may assume for him "divine" proportions rather than be justly regarded as one who has destroyed ignorance and who has become "awakened." This separation from metaphysical reality masks the dignity and the spiritual level of a teaching and wraps the person of the teacher himself in an impenetrable fog. One thing is certain: ideas of "revelations" and of men-gods can only sound foreign to an Aryan spirit and to a "noble son" *(kula-putta)*, particularly in periods when the mind of humanity had not yet entirely lost the memory of its own origins. This introduces us to the next chapter, where we shall say something of the meaning and of the function of the doctrine of Prince Siddhattha in the general setting of the ancient Indo-Aryan world.

41. Ibid., 26.
42. *Suttanipāta*, 3, 6.

3

༺ ✿ ༻

The Historical Context
of the Doctrine of Awakening

First, a word about method. From the "traditional" point of view that we follow in this work, the great historical traditions are to be considered neither as "original" nor as arbitrary. In every tradition worthy of the name, elements are always present, in one form or another, of a "knowledge" that, being rooted in a superindividual reality, is objective. Furthermore, each tradition contains its own special mode of interpretation and cannot be considered as arbitrary or as proceeding from extrinsic or purely human factors. This particular element tends to vary with the prevailing historical and spiritual climate; and we can find in it the reason for the existence of certain formulations, adaptations, or limitations of the one knowledge—and the nonexistence of others. No one individual, suddenly, and as if inspired haphazardly by some outside agency, ever proclaimed the theory of the *ātmā,* for example, or invented *nirvāṇa* or the Islamic theories. On the contrary, all traditions or doctrines obey, even without seeming to do so, a profound logic—discoverable by means of an adequate metaphysical interpretation of history. Accordingly, this shall be our standpoint when we deal with these aspects of Buddhism: this is also why we consider that critic to be fundamentally mistaken who tries at all costs to pin the label "original" on Buddhism or, indeed, on any great tradition, and who argues that "otherwise" such a tradition would in no way differ from others. A difference there is, as there is also an element in common with what has gone before; but both are determined—as we have said—by objective reasons, even though they may not always have been seen clearly by the individual exponents of particular historical trends.

Having said this, we must go back to the pre-Buddhist Indo-Aryan traditions in order to find the precise implications of the Buddhist doctrine, and in them we must distinguish between two fundamental phases: the Vedic and the *Brāhmaṇa Upaniṣad.*

With regard to the Vedas, which constitute the essential foundation of the entire tradition in question, it would not be correct to talk either of "religion" or of "philosophy." To begin with, the term *veda*—from the root *vid,* which is equivalent to the Greek ιδ (whence we have, for example, οίδα) and which means "I see," "I have seen"—refers to a doctrine based not on faith or "revelation," but on a higher knowledge attained through a process of seeing. The Vedas were "seen": they were seen by the *ṛshi,* by the "seers" of the earliest times. Throughout the tradition their essence has never been regarded as a "faith" but rather as a "sacred science."

Thus it is frivolous to see in the Vedas, as many people do, the expression of a "purely naturalistic religion." As in other great systems, impurities may be present, particularly where foreign matter has crept in, and very noticeably, for example, in the *Atharva Veda.* But what the essential and most ancient part of the Vedas reflects is a cosmic stage of the Indo-Aryan spirit. It is not a question of theories or of theologies, but of hymns containing a magnificent reflection of a consciousness that is still so harnessed to the cosmos and to metaphysical reality that the various "gods" of the Vedas are more than religious images; they are projections of the experience of significances and forces directly perceived in man, in nature, or beyond through a cosmic, heroic, and "sacrificial" concept, freely and almost "triumphantly."[1]

Although they were written considerably later, the fundamental thought contained in such epic poems as the *Mahābhārata* goes back to the same epoch. Men, heroes, and divine figures appear side by side; and as Kerényi said when referring to the Olympian-Homeric phase of the Aryo-Hellenic tradition, men could "see the gods and be seen by them," and could "stand with them in the original state of existence."[2] The Olympian element is reflected also in a typical group of Vedic divinities: in Dyaus (from *div,* "to shine"—a root that is also found in Zeus and Deus), for example, lord of the heavenly light, the origin of splendor, strength, and knowledge; in Varuṇa, also a symbol of celestial and regal power, and connected with the idea of *ṛta,* that is to say, of the cosmos, of a cosmic order, of a natural and supernatural law; while in Mitra there is, in addition, the idea of a god of the specifically Aryan virtues, truth and fidelity. We also have Sūrya, the flaming sun from whom, as from the Olympian νούς, nothing is hidden, who destroys every infirmity and who, in the form of Savitar, is the light that is exalted in the first daily rite of all the Aryan castes as the principle of awakening and intellectual animation; or there is Uṣas, the dawn, eternally young, who opens the way for the sun, who gives life and who is the "token of immortality." In Indra we find the incarnation of the heroic and metaphysical impulse of the first Hyperborean conquerors: Indra is "he, without whom men cannot win," he is the "son of force," the lightning god of war, valor, and victory, the annihi-

---

1. To some extent we can here refer to what K. Kerényi has written on the "sense of festivity" in *La religione antica nelle sue linee fondamentali* (Bologna, 1940), chap. 2.
2. Cf. ibid., chaps. 4 and 5.

lator of the enemies of the Aryans, of the black Dasyu, and, consequently, of all the tortuous and titanic forces that "attempt to climb the heavens"; while at the same time he appears as the consolidator, as "he who has consolidated the world." The same spirit is reflected, in varying degrees, in minor Vedic divinities, even in those tied to the most conditioned forms of existence.

In the Vedas we find that this cosmic experience is evoked through the agency of sacrificial action. The sacrifice rite extends human experience into the non-human, and provokes and establishes communion between the two worlds in such a manner that the sacrificer, a figure as austere and majestic as the Roman *flamen dialis,* assumes the traits of a god on earth *(bhū-deva, bhū-sura).* As for life after death, the Vedic solution is fully consonant with the oldest Aryo-Hellenic spirit: images of obscure hells are almost entirely absent from the most ancient parts of the Vedas: the crisis of death is hardly noticed as such—in the *Atharva Veda* it is even considered as the effect of a hostile and demoniacal force that, with suitable rites, can be repulsed. The dead pass into an existence of splendor that is also a "return," and in which they once again take up their form: "Having laid aside all defects, return home: full of splendour unite thyself to [thy] form"[3]—and again: "We drank the *soma* [symbol of a sacred enthusiasm], we became immortal, we reached the light."[4] The symbolic Vedic rite of "wiping out the tracks," so that the dead will not return among the living, well shows how the idea of reincarnation was almost totally absent in this period; such a possibility was ignored in the light of the high degree of heroical, sacrificial, and metaphysical tension belonging to that epoch. There is no trace in the Vedas of the later significance of Yama as god of death and hell; rather, he retains the outlines of his Irano-Aryan equivalent, Yima, sun king of the primordial age: son of the "Sun." Yama is the first of the mortals and he "who first found the road [to the hereafter]":[5] thus, broadly speaking, the Vedic "hereafter" is bound up in great measure with the idea of a reintegration of the primordial state.

About the tenth century B.C. new developments began: they found expression in the Brāhmaṇa texts on the one hand, and on the other in the Upaniṣad texts. Both go back to the tradition of the Vedas: yet there is a noteworthy change of perspective. We are slowly approaching "philosophy" and "theology."

The speculation of the Brāhmaṇa texts rests chiefly on that part of the Vedas that refers to ritual and sacrificial action. Ritual, in all the traditional civilizations, was conceived neither as an empty ceremony nor as a sentimental and, at the same time, formal act of praising and supplicating a God, but rather as an operation with real effects, as a process capable not only of establishing contacts with the

3. *Ṛg Veda,* 10.14.8.
4. Ibid., 8.48.3.
5. Ibid., 10.14.2.

transcendent world, but of imposing itself upon supersensible forces and, through their mediation, eventually influencing even the natural forces. As such, ritual presupposes not only knowledge of certain laws, but also, and more essentially, the existence of a power. The term *brahman* (in the neuter, not to be confused with Brahmā in the masculine, which designates the theistically conceived divinity) originally signified this particular energy, this kind of magic power, this fluid or life force, upon which the ritual rests.

In the Brāhmaṇa texts this ritual aspect of the Vedic tradition was enlarged and formalized. Ritual became the center of everything and the object of a fastidious science that often became a formalism destitute of any vital content. Oldenberg, referring to the period of Prince Siddhattha, talks in this connection of "an idiotic science knows everything and explains everything, and sits enthroned, satisfied, amongst its extravagant creations."[6] This judgment is excessive, but it is not entirely unjustified. In the Buddha's time there existed a caste of *theologi philosophantes* who administered the remnants of the ancient tradition, trying with all the means in their power to establish a prestige that did not always correspond to their human qualifications or to their race—if not their physical race, which was well cared for by the caste system, at least their spiritual race. We have used the word "theologists" since the concept of *brahman* in these circles gradually became generalized and, in a manner of speaking, substantialized, to such an extent that the *brahman* finally no longer signified the mysterious force that, fundamentally, only made sense in terms of ritual and magic experience; it came to mean the soul of the world, the supreme force-substance of the universe, the substratum, indeterminate in itself, of every being and of every phenomenon. It thus became an almost theological concept.

The Upaniṣads, on the other hand, concentrated mainly on the doctrine of the *ātmā*, which largely reflected the original cosmic and solar sentiment of the earliest Aryan consciousness, insofar as it stressed the reality of the "I" as the superindividual, unchanging, and immortal principle of the personality, as opposed to the multiple variety of the phenomena and forces of nature. The *ātmā* is defined by *neti neti* ("not so, not so"), that is to say, by the idea that it does not belong to nature or, more generally, to the conditioned world.

In India the speculative current of the Brāhmaṇa and that of the Upaniṣads gradually converged; this convergence resulted in the identification of the *brahman* with the *ātmā:* the "I," in its superindividual aspect, and the force-substance of the cosmos became one and the same thing. This was a turning point of the greatest importance in the spiritual history of the Indo-Aryan civilization. The doctrine of the identity of the *ātmā* with the *brahman* did, in fact, constitute a metaphysical achievement but, at the

6. Oldenberg, *Buddha*, p. 21.

same time, it initiated a process of breaking up and of spiritual dissolution. This process was bound to take place as shadows began to cloud the luminosity of the original heroic and cosmic experience of Vedic man and as foreign influences gained ground.

Originally the doctrine of the Upaniṣads was considered as "secret," as a knowledge to be transmitted only to the few—the term *Upaniṣad* itself conveyed this idea. But in point of fact the philosophical and speculative tendencies became uppermost. This resulted in divergencies of opinion even in the oldest Upaniṣad—the *Chāndogya*—and the *Bṛhadāraṇyaka Upaniṣad*—as to the plane of consciousness to be used as the reference point for the doctrine. Is the *ātmā* object of immediate experience or is it not? It is both one and the other at the same time. Its substantial identity with the "I" of the individual is affirmed but, at the same time, we often see the unity of the individual with the *ātmā-brahman* postponed till after death; and not only this, but conditions are postulated under which it will happen, and the case is considered in which the "I," or rather the elements of the person, may not leave the cycle of finite and mortal existences. In the ancient Upaniṣads, in fact, no precise solution is ever reached of the problem of the actual relationship existing between the individual "I" of which everyone can talk, and the *ātmā-brahman.* We do not consider that this was accidental: it was a circumstance that corresponded to an already uncertain state of consciousness, to the fact that, while for the adepts of the "secret doctrine" the "I" could be equated effectively with the *ātmā,* for the general consciousness the *ātmā* was becoming a simple speculative concept, an almost theological assumption, since the original spiritual level was beginning to be lost.

Furthermore, the danger of pantheistic confusions showed itself. This danger did not exist in theory since, in the Upaniṣads, following the Vedic concept, the supreme principle was not only conceived as the substance of the world and of all beings, but also as that which transcends them "by three quarters," existing as "the immortal in the heavens."[7] In the same Upaniṣads, however, prominence is also given to the identity of the *ātmā-brahman* with elements of all kinds in the naturalistic world, so that the practical possibility of a pantheistic deviation encouraged by the assimilation of the *ātmā* with the *brahman* was real: particularly so, if we take into account the process of man's gradual regression, of which we can find evidence in the teaching of all traditions, including the Indo-Aryan, where the theory of the four *yuga* corresponds exactly to the classical theory of the four ages and of man's descent to the last of them, the Iron Age, equivalent to the "Dark Age" *(kali-yuga)* of the Indo-Aryans. If, during the period of these speculations, the original cosmic and uranic consciousness of the Vedic origins had already suffered in this way a certain overclouding, then the formulation of the theory of the identity of the *ātmā* with the

---

7. *Ṛg Veda,* 10.90.3; *Chāndogya Upaniṣad,* 3.12.6.

brahman provided a dangerous incentive toward evasion, toward a confused self-identification with the spirituality of everything, at the very moment when a particularly energetic reaction by way of a tendency toward concentration, detachment, and awakening was needed.

Altogether, the germs of decadence, which were already showing themselves in the post-Vedic period and which were to become quite evident in the Buddha's day (sixth century B.C.), are as follows: above all, a stereotyped ritualism; then the demon of speculation, whose effect was that what ought to have remained "secret doctrine," *upaniṣad, rahasya,* became partly rationalized, with the result that there eventually appeared a tumultuous crowd of divergent theories, sects, and schools, which the Buddhist texts often vividly describe.[8] In the third place, we find a "religious" transformation of many divinities who, in the Vedic period were, as we have said, simply cosmically transfigured states of consciousness; these have now become objects of popular cults.[9] We have already spoken of the pantheistic danger. In addition to these points we have yet to consider the effect of foreign, non-Aryan influences, to which we believe are attributable in no small degree the formation and diffusion of the theory of reincarnation.

As we have said, there is no trace of this theory in the early Vedic period; this is because it is quite incompatible with an Olympian and heroic vision of the world, being as it is a "truth" of non-Aryan races that are tellurically and matriarchally adjusted in outlook. Reincarnation, in fact, is conceivable only by one who feels himself to be a "son of the earth," who has no knowledge of a reality transcending the naturalistic order; bound as he is to a female-maternal divinity found alike in the pre-Aryan Mediterranean world, and in the pre-Aryan Hindu civilization, such as the Dravidian and Kosalian. Into the source from which as an ephemeral being he has sprung, the individual, when he dies, must return, only to reappear in fresh terrestrial births, in an inescapable and interminable cycle. This is the ultimate sense of the theory of reincarnation, a theory that begins to infiltrate as early as the period of Upaniṣad speculations; it gives place gradually to mixed forms that we can use as a measure of the change in the original Aryan consciousness to which we have referred.

While in the Vedas only a single fate after death is considered, as in ancient Hellas, in the Brāhmaṇa texts the theory of the double way already appears: "[Only] he who knows and practices ritual action rises again in life and obtains immortal life;

---

8. Cf. *Dīgha,* 1.1.29 ff.; *Suttanipāta,* 4.12, 13.
9. It is essentially of these gods that we must think when we see them assume, in Buddhist texts, quite modest and subordinate parts, transforming themselves sometimes almost into quasi disciples who receive revelation of the doctrine from the Buddha. We are dealing, that is, with the degradation of the ancient gods: and the doctrine revealed by the Awakened One corresponds, basically, with what they once signified, but which at this period, had been forgotten.

the others who neither know nor practise ritual action will continue to be born anew, as nourishment for death."[10] In the Upaniṣads, however, as the relationship between the real "I" and the *ātmā* oscillates, so does their teaching of what happens after death. They speak of the "dyke, beyond which even night becomes day, since the world of the *brahman* is unchangeable light"; a dyke constituted by the *ātmā* against which neither decay, nor death, nor pain, nor good action, nor bad action can prevail.[11] They speak of the "way of the gods" *(deva-yāna)* that leads one after death to the unconditioned whence "there is no return." But at the same time another road is considered, the *pitṛ-yāna*, along which "one returns," the individual after death being little by little "sacrificed" to various divinities for whom he becomes "food," finally to reappear on the earth.[12] In the oldest texts the possibility of a liberation is not considered for those who go on this second road: they speak instead of the "causal law," of the *karma*, which determines a man's subsequent existence on the basis of what he has done in the preceding one. We have now arrived at what we shall call the saṁsāric consciousness (from *saṁsāra*), which is the keystone of the Buddhist vision of life: the secret knowledge, confided privately by the wise Yājñavalkya to the king Ārtabhāga, is that after death the individual elements of man dissolve in the corresponding cosmic elements, including the *ātmā,* which returns to the "ether," and that which is left is only the *karma,* that is, the action, the impersonal force, bound to the life of one being, that will go on to determine a new being.[13]

In all this can be seen, then, more than just the effect of "free" metaphysical speculation: it is, rather, a sign of a consciousness that begins to consider itself terrestrial or, at the most, pantheistically cosmic, and that now centers itself on that part of the human being that may really be concerned with death and rebirth and indefinite wandering across various forms of conditioned existence; we say "various" since the horizons gradually widened and it was even thought that one might re-arise in this or that world of gods, according to one's actions. In any case, in the epoch in which Buddhism appeared the theories of reincarnation and of transmigration were already an integral part of the ideas acquired by the predominant mentality. Sometimes, and even in the Upaniṣads, different outlooks became indiscriminately combined so that on the one side was conceived an *ātmā* that, although divorced from any concrete experience, was supposed to be permanently and intangibly present in everyone, and on the other side there was the interminable wandering of man in various lives.

It is on these lines that practical and realistic currents gradually established

10. *Śatapatha Brāhmaṇa,* 10.4.3, 10.
11. *Chāndogya Upaniṣad,* 8.4.1–2.
12. Ibid., 3–10; *Bṛhadāraṇyaka Upaniṣad,* 6.2.9–16.
13. *Bṛhadāraṇyaka Upaniṣad,* 3.2.13.

themselves in opposition to the speculative currents. We can include Sāṃkhya, which opposed to the pantheistic danger a rigid dualism and in which the reality of the "I" or *ātmā*—called here *puruṣa*—as the supernatural, intangible, and unalterable principle is opposed to all the forms, forces, and phenomena of a natural and material order. But more important in this respect are the trends of yoga. Based both on Sāṃkhya and on ascetic tendencies already coming to the fore in opposition to ritualistic and speculative Brahmanism, these recognized more or less explicitly the new state of affairs, which was that in speaking of "I" one could no longer concretely understand the *ātmā*, the unconditioned principle; that it appeared no longer as direct consciousness; and that therefore, apart from speculation, it could only be considered as an end, as the limit of a process of reintegration with action as its basis. As the immediate real datum there was substituted instead what we call "saṃsāric" consciousness and existence, consciousness bound to the "current"—and the term *saṃsāra* (which thus only makes a relatively late appearance) means precisely "current"—it is the current of becoming.

It is not out of place to consider another point. The *brāhmaṇa* caste is habitually thought of in the West as a "sacerdotal" caste. This is true only up to a certain point. In the Vedic origins the type of Brāhman or "sacrificer" bears little resemblance to that of the "priest" as our contemporaries think of him: he was, rather, a figure both virile and awful and, as we have said, a kind of visible incarnation in the human world of the superhuman *(bhū-deva)*. Furthermore, we often find in the early texts a point where the distinction between the *brāhman*—the "sacerdotal" caste—and the *kṣatram* or *rājam*—the warrior or regal caste—did not exist; a feature that we see in the earliest stages of all traditional civilizations, including the Greek, Roman, and German. The two types only began to differ in a later period, this being another aspect of the process of regression that we have mentioned. Besides, there are many who maintain that in Aryan India the doctrine of the *ātmā* was originally confined almost exclusively to the warrior caste, and that the doctrine of *brahman* as an undifferentiated cosmic force was formulated mainly by the sacerdotal caste. There is probably some truth in this view. In any case, it is a fact that in many texts we see a king or a *kṣatriya* (a member of the warrior nobility) vying in knowledge with and sometimes even instructing members of the Brāhman caste; and that, according to tradition, primordial knowledge was handed down, starting from Ikśvāku, in regal succession;[14] the same "solar dynasty" *(sūrya-vaṃsa)* that we mentioned in connection with the Buddha's family, also figures here. We should have the following picture: in the Indo-Aryan post-Vedic world, while the warrior caste held a more realistic and virile view and put emphasis on the doctrine of the *ātmā* as the unchangeable and immortal principle of human personality, the Brāhman caste was becoming,

14. Cf. *Bhagavadgītā*, 4.1–2.

little by little, "sacerdotal" and, instead of facing the reality, was moving among ritual and stereotyped exegeses and speculations. Simultaneously, in another way, the character of the first Vedic period was becoming overgrown with a tropical and chaotic vegetation of myths and popular religious images, even of semidevotional practices seeking the attainment of this, that, or the other divine "rebirth" on the basis of views on reincarnation and transmigration that, as we have said, had already infiltrated into the less illuminated Indo-Aryan mentalities. Leaving yoga apart, it is worth noting that it was the warrior nobility—the *kṣatram*—that furnished the principal support not only of the Sāṁkhya system, which is regarded as representing a clear reaction against speculative "idealism," but also of Jainism, the so-called doctrine of the conquerors (from *jina*, "conqueror"), which laid emphasis, though with a tendency to extremism, on necessity for ascetic action.

All this is necessary for our understanding of the historical place of Buddhism and of the reasons of its most characteristic views.

From the point of view of universal history, Buddhism arose in a period marked by a crisis running through a whole series of traditional civilizations. This crisis sometimes resolved itself positively thanks to opportune reforms and revisions, and sometimes negatively with the effect of inducing further phases of regression or spiritual decadence. This period, called by some the "climacteric" of civilization, falls approximately between the eighth and the fifth centuries B.C. It is in this period that the doctrines of Lao-tzu and Kung Fu-tzu (Confucius) were taking root in China, representing a renewal of elements of the most ancient tradition on the metaphysical plane on the one hand, and on the ethical-social on the other. In the same period it is said that "Zarathustra" appeared, through whom a similar return took place in the Persian tradition. And in India the same function was performed by Buddhism, also representing a reaction and, at the same time, a re-elevation. On the other hand, as we have often pointed out elsewhere, it seems that in the West processes of decadence mainly prevailed. The period of which we are now talking is, in fact, that in which the ancient aristocratic and hieratic Hellas declined; in which the religion of Isis along with other popular and spurious forms of mysticism superseded the solar and regal Egyptian civilization; it is that in which Israelite prophetism started the most dangerous ferments of corruption and subversion in the Mediterranean world. The only positive counterpart in the West seems in fact to have been Rome, which was born in that period and which for a certain cycle was a creation of universal importance, animated in high measure by an Olympian and heroic spirit.[15]

Coming to Buddhism, it was not conceived, as many who unilaterally take the Brāhman point of view like to claim, as an antitraditional revolution, similar, in its

---

15. On this significance of Rome as a "rebirth" of a primordial Aryan heritage cf. our *Revolt Against the Modern World*, part 2.

own way, to what the Lutheran heresy was to Catholicism;[16] and still less as a "new" doctrine, the result of an isolated speculation that succeeded in taking root. It represented, rather, a particular adaptation of the original Indo-Aryan tradition, an adaptation that kept in mind the prevailing conditions and limited itself accordingly, while freshly and differently formulating preexistent teachings: at the same time Buddhism closely adhered to the *kṣatriya* (in Pāli, *khattiya*) spirit, the spirit of the warrior caste. We have already seen that the Buddha was born of the most ancient Aryan nobility; but this is not the end of the matter, as a text informs us of the particular aversion nourished by his people for the Brāhman caste: "The *Sākiya*" (Skt.: *Śākya*)—we read[17]—"do not esteem the priests, they do not respect the priests, they do not honour the priests, they do not venerate the priests, they do not hold the priests of account." The same tendency is maintained by Prince Siddhattha, but with the aim of restoring, of reaffirming, the pure will for the unconditioned, to which in the most recent times the "regal" line had often been more faithful than the priestly caste that was already divided within itself.

There are, besides, many signs that the Buddhist doctrine laid no claim to originality but regarded itself as being, in a way, universal and having a traditional character in a superior sense. The Buddha himself says, for example: "Thus it is: those who, in times past, were saints, Perfect Awakened Ones, these sublime men also have rightly directed their disciples to such an end, as now disciples are rightly directly here by me; and those who in future times will be saints, Perfect Awakened Ones, also these sublime men will rightly direct their disciples, as now disciples are rightly directed here by me."[18] The same is repeated in regard to purification of thought, word, and action;[19] it is repeated about right knowledge of decay and death, of their origin, of their cessation and of the way that leads to their cessation; and it is repeated about the doctrine of the "void" or "emptiness," *suññatā*.[20] The doctrine and the "divine life" proclaimed by Prince Siddhattha are repeatedly called "timeless," *akāliko*.[21] "Ancient saints, Perfect Awakened Ones" are spoken of,[22] and a traditional theme occurs in connection with a place (here called "the Gorge of the Seer") where a

---

16. This is the point of view held by R. Guénon, *L'Homme et son devenir selon le Vêdânta* (Paris, 1925), p. 111 ff., with which we cannot—"according to truth"—agree [(English trans.: *Man and His Becoming According to the Vedānta*, [London, 1945)]. More correct are the views of A. K. Coomaraswamy, *Hinduism and Buddhism* (New York, 1941), although in this book is apparent the tendency to emphasize only what in Buddhism is valuable from the *brāhmaṇa* standpoint, with disregard of the specific functional meaning he possesses as compared to Hindu tradition.
17. *Dīgha*, 3.1.12.
18. *Majjh.*, 51.
19. Ibid., 61.
20. *Saṁyutt.*, 12.33.
21. *Majjh.*, 7.
22. *Ibid.*, 75; cf. 81.

whole series of Paccekabuddhas are supposed to have vanished in the past, a series, that is, of beings who, by their own unaided and isolated efforts, have reached the superhuman state and the same perfect awakening as did Prince Siddhattha himself.[23] Those who are "without faith, without devotion, without tradition"[24] are reproached. A repeated saying is: "What for the world of the sages is not, of that I say: 'It is not', and what for the world of sages is, of that I say: 'It is.'"[25] An interesting point is the mention in a text of "extinction," the aim of the Buddhist ascesis, as something that "leads back to the origins."[26] This is supported by the symbolism of a great forest where "an ancient path, a path of men of olden times" is discovered. Following it, the Buddha finds a royal city; and he asks that it should be restored.[27] In another text the significance of this is explained by the Buddha in a most explicit way: "I have seen the ancient path, the path trodden by all the Perfected Awakened Ones of olden times. This is the path I follow."[28]

It is quite clear, then, that in Buddhism we are not dealing with a negation of the principle of spiritual authority but rather with a revolt against a caste that claimed to monopolize this authority while its representatives no longer preserved its dignity and had lost their qualifications. The Brāhmans, against whom Prince Siddhattha turns, are those who say they know, but who know nothing,[29] who for many generations have lost the faculty of direct vision, without which they cannot even say: "Only this is truth, foolishness is the rest,"[30] and who now resemble "a file of blind men, in which the first cannot see, the one in the middle cannot see and the last cannot see."[31] Very different from the men of the original period—from the *brāhmaṇa* who remembered the ancient rule, who guarded the door of the senses, who had entirely controlled their impulses, and who were ascetics, rich only in knowledge, inviolable and invincible, made strong by truth *(dhamma)*—were their worldly successors, who were wrapped up in ritualism or intent on vain fasting and who had abandoned the ancient laws.[32] Of these "there is not one who has seen Brahmā face to face," whence it is impossible that "these *brāhmaṇa*, versed in the science of the threefold Vedas,

23. Ibid., 116; cf. 123.
24. Ibid., 102.
25. *Saṁyutt.*, 22.94.
26. *Mahāparinirv.*, 52–53 (this is from the Chinese version of the text, however).
27. *Saṁyutt.*, 12.65.
28. Ibid., 3.106. It is interesting that according to the myth, Buddha attained the awakening under the Tree of Life placed in the navel of the earth where also all the previous Buddhas reached transcendent knowledge. This is a reference to the "Center of the World," which is to be considered, in its way, as a chrism of traditionality and initiatic of orthodoxy whenever a contact with the origins was restored.
29. *Majjh.*, 93.
30. Ibid., 95.
31. *Dīgha*, 13.15; *Majjh.*, 95; 99.
32. *Suttanipāta*, 2.7.1–16.

are capable of indicating the way to a state of companionship with that which they neither know nor have seen."[33] The Buddha is opposed to one who knows "only by hearsay," to one who knows "the truth only by repetition, and who, with this traditionally heard truth, as a coffer handed down from hand to hand, transmits the doctrine," the integrity of which, however, it is impossible to guarantee in such circumstances.[34] A distinction is therefore made between the ascetics and Brāhmans who "only by their own creed profess to have reached the highest perfection of knowledge of the world: such are the reasoners and the disputers," and other ascetics and Brāhmans who, "in things never before heard, recognise clearly in themselves the truth, and profess to have reached the highest perfection of knowledge of the world."

It is to these latter that Prince Siddhattha claims to belong, and this is the type that he indicates to his disciples:[35] "only when he knows does he say that he knows, only when he has seen does he say that he has seen."[36] Regarded from this standpoint Buddhism does not deny the concept of *brāhmaṇa;* on the contrary the texts use the word frequently and call the ascetic life *brahmacariya,* their intention being simply to indicate the fundamental qualities in virtue of which the dignity of the true *brāhmaṇa* can be confirmed.[37]

Here, with the aim being essentially one of reintegration, the qualities of the true *brāhmaṇa* and of the ascetic become identified. These notions had previously been distinct, particularly when the Asrama teaching of the Aryan code, according to which a man of Brāhman caste was obliged to graduate to a completely detached life, *vānaprashta* or *yati,* had practically and with but few exceptions disappeared. By understanding this point we can also understand the Buddha's true attitude to the problem of caste. Even in the preceding tradition ascetic achievement had been considered as above all caste and free from obligations to any of them. This is the Buddha's point of view, expressed in a simile: as one who desires fire does not ask the type of wood that in fact produces it, so from any caste may arise an ascetic or an Awakened One.[38] The castes appeared to Prince Siddhattha, as they did to every traditional mind, as perfectly natural and furthermore, justified transcendentally, since in following the doctrine of the Upaniṣads he understood that birth in one caste or another and inequality in general were not accidental but the effect of a particular preceding action. Thus he was never concerned with upsetting the caste system on the ethnic, political, or social plane; on the contrary, it is laid down that a man should not omit any of the obligations inherent in his station in life,[39] and it is never said that

35. *Majjh.,* 100.
36. Ibid., 77.
37. Ibid., 48; *Dhammapada,* 383 ff.; *Suttanipāta,* 3.4, passim; 9.27, passim; 1.7.
38. *Majjh.,* 93; 90.
39. *Mahāparinirv.,* 6–11.

a servant—*sudda* (Skt.: *śūdra*)—or a *vessa* (Skt.: *vaiśya*) should not obey higher Aryan castes. The problem only concerns the spiritual apex of the Aryan hierarchy, where historical conditions required discrimination and revision of the matter: it was necessary that the "lists" should be reviewed and reconstructed, with the traditional dignities being considered real only on "the merits of the individual cases."[40] The decisive point was the identification of the true Brāhman with the ascetic and, thence, the emphasis placed on what in fact is evidenced by action. Thus the principle was proclaimed: "Not by caste is one a pariah, not by caste is one a *brāhmaṇa;* by actions is one a pariah, by actions is one a *brāhmaṇa.*"[41] In respect of the "flame that is sustained by virtue, and lighted by training," as in respect of liberation, the four castes are equal.[42] And again: as it is not to be expected in answer to a man's invocations, prayers, and praises, so it is not to be expected that the *brāhmaṇa* who, although they are instructed in the triple Veda yet "omit the practise of those qualities that make a man a true *brāhmaṇa* can, by calling upon Indra, Soma, Varuṇa and other gods, acquire those qualities that really make a man a non-*brāhmaṇa.*"[43] If they have not destroyed desire for the five stems of sense experience, they can as little expect to unite themselves after death with Brahmā as a man, swimming, can expect to reach the other bank with his arms tied to his body.[44] To unite himself with Brahmā a man must develop in himself qualities similar to Brahmā.[45] This, however, in no way prevents the consideration in the texts of the ideal *brāhmaṇa,* in whom the purity of the Aryan lineage is joined with qualities which make him like a god or a divine being;[46] and the texts even go so far as to reprove the contemporary Brāhmans not only for their desertion of ancient customs and for their interest in gold and riches, but also for their betrayal of the laws of marriage within the caste, for they are accused of frequenting non-Brāhman women at all times from mere desire "like dogs."[47] The general principle of any right hierarchy is confirmed with these words: "In serving a man, if for this service one becomes worse, not better, this man, I say, one ought not to serve. In serving a man, on the other hand, if for this service one becomes better, not worse, this man, I say, one ought to serve."[48]

This shows that there is no question here of equalitarian subversion under spiritual pretexts, but of rectification and epuration of the existing hierarchy. Prince

---

40. *Majjh.*, 84.
41. *Suttanipāta*, 1.7.21.
42. *Majjh.*, 90.
43. *Dīgha*, 13.24–25.
44. Ibid., 13.26, 28; *Suttanipāta*, 2.2.11.
45. *Dīgha*, 13.33–38.
46. *Angutt.*, 5.192.
47. Ibid., 5.191 (vol. 3, p. 221 f.).
48. *Majjh.*, 96.

Siddhattha has so little sympathy for the masses that in one of the oldest texts he speaks of the "common crowd" as a "heap of rubbish," where there takes place the miraculous flowering of the Awakened One.[49] Beyond the ancient division into castes, Buddhism affirms another that, deeper and more intimate, *mutatis mutandis,* is not unlike the one that originally existed between the Aryans, those "twice-born" *(dvīja)* and other beings: on one side stand the Ariya and the "noble sons moved by confidence," to whom the Doctrine of Awakening is accessible; on the other, "the common men, without understanding for what is saintly, remote from the saintly doctrine, not accessible to the saintly doctrine; without understanding for what is noble, remote from the doctrine of the noble ones, not accessible by the doctrine of the noble ones."[50] If, on the one hand, as rivers "when they reach the ocean lose their former names and are reckoned only as ocean, so the members of the four castes, when they take up the law of the Buddha, lose their former characteristics"—yet on the other they form a well-defined company, the "sons of the Sākiya's son."[51] We can see that the effective aim of Buddhism was to discriminate between different natures, for which the touchstone was the Doctrine of Awakening itself: a discrimination that could not do other than stimulate the spiritual bases that originally had themselves been the sole justification of the Aryan hierarchy. In confirmation of this is the fact that the establishment and diffusion of Buddhism never in later centuries caused dissolution of the caste system—even today in Ceylon this system continues undisturbed side by side with Buddhism; while, in Japan, Buddhism lives in harmony with hierarchical, traditional, national, and warrior concepts. Only in certain Western misconceptions is Buddhism—considered in later and corrupted forms—presented as a doctrine of universal compassion encouraging humanitarianism and democratic equality.

The only point we must take with a grain of salt in the texts is the affirmation that in individuals of all castes all possible potentialities, both positive and negative, exist in equal measure.[52] But the Buddhist theory of *sankhāra,* that is, of prenatal predispositions, is enough to rectify this point. The exclusiveness of caste, race, and tradition in a hierarchical system results in the individual possessing hereditary predispositions for his development in a particular direction; this ensures an organic and harmonious character in his development, as opposed to the cases in which an attempt is made to reach the same point with a kind of violence, by starting from a naturally unfavorable base. Four ways are considered in some Buddhist texts,[53] in

49. *Dhammapada,* 58–59.
50. *Majjh.,* 1.
51. *Angutt.,* 8.19, §14; 10.96.
52. *Majjh.,* 96.
53. *Angutt.,* 4.162.

three of which either the road or the achievement of knowledge is difficult, or both are difficult; the fourth way offers an easy road and easy attainment of knowledge; this way is called the "path of the elect," and it is reserved for those who enjoy the advantages bestowed by a good birth. At least it would have been so had circumstances been normal. But, let us repeat, Buddhism appeared in abnormal conditions in a particular traditional civilization: it is for this reason that Buddhism placed emphasis on the aspect of action and of individual achievement; and it is also for this reason that the support offered by tradition, in its most restricted sense, was held of little account. Prince Siddhattha stated that he himself had attained knowledge through his own efforts, without a master to show him the way; so, in the original Doctrine of Awakening, each individual has to rely on himself, and on his own exertions, just as a soldier who is lost must rely on himself alone to rejoin the marching army.

Thus Buddhism, if a comparison of various traditions were being made, could legitimately take its place with the race that elsewhere we have called heroic, in the sense of the Hesiodic teaching on the "Four Ages."[54] We mean a type of man in which the spirituality belonging to the primordial state is no longer taken for granted as something natural, for this tradition is no longer itself an adequate foundation. Spirituality has become an aim to him, the object of a reconquest, the final limit of a reintegration to be carried out by one's own virile efforts.

This ends our account of the historical place of Buddhism, an essential prerequisite for understanding the meaning of its principal teachings and the reasons for their existence.

Before going on to discuss the doctrine and the practise we must return to a point we have already mentioned, that is, that Buddhism belongs to a cycle that modern man can also comprehend.

Although in the epoch in which Prince Siddhattha lived there was already a certain clouding over of spiritual consciousness and of metaphysical vision of the world such as was possessed by ancient Indo-Aryan man, the later course of history—and particularly of Western history—has produced an increasing amount of regression, materialism, and individualism together with a corresponding loss of direct contact with metaphysical and, generally speaking, supersensible reality. With the "modern" world we have come to a point beyond which it would be difficult to go. The object of direct knowledge for modern man is exclusively the material world, with its counterpart, the purely psychological sphere of his subjectivity. His philosophical speculations and his religion stand apart, the first are purely cerebral creations, the second is based essentially on faith.

It is not entirely a case of Western religion, as opposed to the highest traditions

54. Cf. *Revolt Against the Modern World*, chap. 22.

of the most ancient time, having centered itself on faith, thereby hoping to save what yet could be saved. It is, rather, a counsel of despair: a man who has long since lost all direct contact with the metaphysical world can only adopt one possible form of *religio*, of reconnection, namely, that provided by belief or faith. It is in this way that we can also come to understand the real significance of Protestantism as compared with Catholicism. Protestantism took root in a period when humanism and naturalism were ushering in a phase of "secularization" of European man, a process that went much further than the normal regression of the epoch in which Christianity in general arose; and at the same time decadence and corruption appeared among the representatives of the Catholic tradition, to whom had been entrusted the task of support and mediation. These being the real circumstances and the rift having thus grown wider, the principle of the pure faith was emphasized and opposed to any hierarchical organization and mediation; a distrust of "works" (even the Christian monastic asceticism was included in this) was nourished; these are tendencies that are characteristic of Protestantism.

The present crisis of Western religions based on "belief" is known to all, and we need not point out the completely secular, materialistic and saṁsāric character of the mentality predominant in our contemporaries. We are entitled to ask ourselves, under these circumstances, what a system, based rigorously on knowledge, free from elements of both faith and intellectualism, not tied to local organized tradition, but in reality directed toward the unconditioned, may have to offer. It is evident that this path is only suited to a very small minority, gifted with exceptional interior strength. Original Buddhism, in this respect, can be recommended as can few other doctrines, particularly because when it was formulated the condition of mankind, although still far from the straits of Western materialism and the subsequent eclipse of any living traditional knowledge, nevertheless manifested some of these signs and symptoms. Nor must we forget that Buddhism, as we have said, is a practical and realistic adaptation of traditional ideas, an adaptation that is mainly in the spirit of the *kṣatriya,* of the Aryan warrior caste; it should be remembered especially since Western man's line of development has been warlike rather than a sacerdotal, while his inclination for clarity, for realism, and for exact knowledge, applied on the material plane, has produced the most typical achievements of his civilization.

Other metaphysical and ascetic systems might appear more attractive than Buddhism and might offer a deeper gratification for a mind anxiously trying to penetrate the mysteries of the world and of existence. Yet they tend proportionately to provide modern man with opportunities for illusions and misconceptions; the reason being that genuinely traditional systems, such as the Vedānta, if they are to be fully understood and realized, presuppose a degree of spirituality that has disappeared long ago in the vast majority of men. Buddhism, on the other hand, poses a total problem, without any loopholes. As someone has rightly said, it is "no milk for babies,"[55] nor does it provide metaphysical feasts for lovers of intellectual speculation.[56] It states: "Man, this is what you have become and this is what your experience has become. Know it. There is a Way which leads beyond. This is its direction, these are its milestones, these are the means for following it. It rests with you to discover your true vocation and to measure your strength." "Do not persuade, do not dissuade; knowing persuasion, knowing dissuasion, neither persuade, nor dissuade, expound only reality"—we have already seen that this is the fundamental precept of the Awakened Ones.

Thus, in describing the historical place of Buddhism, we have also explained the last of the reasons we adopted to justify the choice of Buddhism as a basis for a study of a complete and virile ascesis, formulated with regard to the cycle that also includes contemporary man.

---

55. [In English in the original.—Trans.].
56. Rhys Davids, Early *Buddhism* (London, 1908), p. 7.

4

Destruction
of the Demon of Dialectics

The premise from which the Buddhist Doctrine of Awakening starts is the destruction of the demon of dialectics; the renunciation of the various constructions of thought and speculation, which are simply an expression of opinion, and of the profusion of theories, which are projections of a fundamental restlessness in which a mind that has not yet found in itself its own principle seeks for support.

This applies not only to cosmological speculation, but also to problems concerned with man, his nature and destiny, and even to any conceptual determination of the ultimate aim of asceticism. "Have I ever existed in past epochs? Or have I never existed? What was I in past epochs? And how did I come to be what I was? Shall I exist in future epochs? Or shall I not exist? What shall I be in future epochs? And how shall I become what I shall be? And even the present fills [the common man] with doubts: Do I indeed exist? Or do I not exist? What am I? And how am I? This being here, whence has it really come? And whither will it go?" All these for Buddhism are but "vain thoughts": "This is called the blind alley of opinions, the gorge of opinions, the bramble of opinions, the thicket of opinions, the net of opinions," caught up and lost in which "the ignorant worldling cannot free himself from birth, decay and death."[1] And again: "'I am' is an opinion; 'I am this' is an opinion; 'I shall be' is an opinion; 'I shall not be' is an opinion; 'I shall be in the worlds of [pure] form' is an opinion; 'I shall be in the worlds free from form' is an opinion; 'Conscious, I shall be' is an opinion; 'Unconscious, I shall be' is an opinion; 'Neither conscious nor unconscious, I shall be' is an opinion. Opinion, O disciples, is a disease; opinion is a tumour; opinion is a sore. He who has overcome all opinion, O disciples, is called a saint, one who knows."[2]

1. *Majjh.*, 2.38.
2. Ibid., 140.

It is the same with the cosmological order: "'The world is eternal,' 'The world is not eternal,' 'The world is finite,' 'The world is infinite,' 'The life-principle and the body are the same,' 'The life-principle is one thing, the body another,' 'The Accomplished One is after death,' 'The Accomplished One is not after death,' 'The Accomplished One both is and is not after death,' 'The Accomplished One neither is nor is not after death'—this is a blind alley of opinions, a thicket of opinions, a wood of opinions, a tangle of opinions, a labyrinth of opinions, painful, desperate, tortuous, not leading to detachment, not leading to progress, not leading to vision, not leading to awakening, not leading to extinction."[3] The doctrine of the Accomplished Ones is described as that which "destroys to the foundations every attachment to and satisfaction in false theories, dogmas and systems" and which therefore cuts off both fear and hope.[4] The reply to the question asked of the Buddha: "Perhaps Lord Gotama [this is the Prince Siddhattha's family name] has some opinion?" is categorical: "Opinion: that is remote from the Accomplished One. The Accomplished One has seen."[5]

This reply indicates the fundamental point. It is not that Buddhism intended to exclude the possibility of obtaining some answer to these problems—for by doing so it would fall into contradiction, since the texts offer, where necessary, fairly precise teachings with regard to certain of them. It has, rather, wished to oppose the demon of dialectics and has rejected every "truth" that is based only on discursive intellect—*vitakka*—and that can only have the value of "opinion," of $\delta\delta\xi\alpha$. It keeps its distance from "reasoners and disputers" for they "can reason well and reason badly, they can say thus and they can also say otherwise,"[6] and they deal with theories that are only their own excogitations. And the $\ddot{\alpha}\phi\eta\lambda\varepsilon$ $\pi\dot{\alpha}\nu\tau\alpha$, the "take away all" of the Buddhist ascesis is by no means a *sacrificium intellectus* in favor of faith, as in some forms of Christian mysticism. It is, rather, a preliminary catharsis, an *opus purgationis* justified by a superior type or criterion of certainty, which is rooted in an actual knowledge, acquired—as in the early Vedic tradition—by immediate vision. It is a criterion of direct experience. Once "cut off from faith, from inclinations, from hearsay, from scholastic arguments, from ratiocinations and from reasoning, from pleasure in speculation," the same criterion serves the Buddha when deciding the existence or nonexistence of a thing, as it serves a man who judges the existence of pleasure, pain, or delusion on the basis of having himself experienced these states.[7] Besides, much knowledge, discursive knowledge that is, leaves an individual as he is: it does not contribute at all to the removal of the "triple bond" necessary to

3. Ibid., 72.
4. Ibid., 22.
5. Ibid., 72.
6. Ibid., 76.
7. *Saṁyutt.*, 35.152.

advance toward superior knowledge.[8] Already master in fact of "deep psychology," the Buddha recognized that vain speculation and the posing of numberless problems reflect a state or restlessness and anguish, that is, the very state that must first be put behind him by one going along the "path of the *ariya*." That is why, in the parable of the hunter,[9] the inclination of a disciple at a certain point in his development to set himself the usual problems concerning the soul and the world is considered as a step backward: it is one of the baits laid down by the Enemy and any man who feeds on it falls back into his power.

"To know by seeing, to become cognition, to become truth, to become vision"— this is the ideal: knowing-seeing in conformity to reality—*yathā-bhūta-ñāṇa-dassana:* direct intellectual intuition, far beyond all discussion and closely bound up with ascetic realization. "Recognizing the poverty of philosophical opinions, not adhering to any of them, seeking the truth, *I saw.*"[10] A recurring passage in the Pāli canon is: "He [the Accomplished One] shows this world with its angels, its good and bad spirits, its ranks of ascetics and Brāhmans, of gods and men, after he himself has known and apprehended it," etc. There are even more radical expressions. "I affirm," says Prince Siddhattha,[11] "that I can expound the law concerning this or that region in such a manner that he who acts in conformity therewith will recognise the existing as existing and the not-existing as not-existing, the vulgar as vulgar and the noble as noble, the superable as superable and the insuperable as insuperable, the possible as possible and the impossible as impossible; that he will know, understand and apprehend this exactly as it is to be known, understood and apprehended. *The supreme form of knowledge is knowledge conforming to reality.* A higher and more sublime knowledge does not exist, I say." And again: "'A perfect Awakened One you call yourself, it is true; but these things you have not known': that an ascetic or a Brāhman, a god or a demon, Brahmā or anyone else in the world can thus accuse me justly, this possibility," says Prince Siddhattha, "does not exist."[12] The wise man, the Ariya, is not a follower of systems, he does not recognise dogmas, and having penetrated the opinions current among the people and being indifferent in face of speculation, he leaves it to others, he remains calm among the agitated, he does not take part in the verbal battles of those who maintain: "This only is the truth," he does not consider himself equal to others, nor superior, nor inferior.[13] In the canonical texts, after a description of the morass of contemporary philosophical opinions, we meet with this passage: "The Accomplished One knows other things well beyond [such speculations] and having such knowledge he does not

8. *Majjh.*, 113; cf. *Suttanipāta*, 5.8.2.
9. *Majjh.*, 25; cf. *Saṁyutt.*, 35.207.
10. *Suttanipāta*, 4.9.3.
11. *Angutt.*, 9.22.
12. Ibid., 4.8; *Majjh.*, 12.
13. *Suttanipāta*, 4.5.4; 13.10–19.

become proud, he remains impassive, he realizes in his mind the path that leads beyond. . . . There are, O disciples, other things, profound things, things difficult to apprehend, hard to understand, but that beget calm; joyful things, things not to be grasped simply by discursive thought, things that only the wise man can understand. These things are expounded by the Accomplished One, after he himself has known them, *after he himself has seen them.*"[14]

We already know that the title Buddha, given to Prince Siddhattha and then extended to all those who have followed his path, means "awakened." It takes us to the same point, to the same criterion of certainty. The doctrine of the Ariya is called "beyond imagination"[15] and not susceptible of assimilation by any process of ratiocination. The term *atakkāvacara* often recurs, a term that means just that which cannot be apprehended by logic. Instead the doctrine is presented in an "awakening" and as an "awakening." One can see at once the correspondence between this mode of knowing and Plato's view of anamnesis, "reminiscence" or "recollection" overcoming the state of oblivion; exactly as Buddhism aims to overcome the state produced by the *āsava*, by the "intoxicants," by the manias, by the fever. These terms, "reminiscence" and "awakening," however, should not represent more than the manner in which knowledge appears, than recognition and appraisal of something as directly evident, like a man who remembers or who wakes and sees something. This is the reason for the recurrence in later Buddhist literature of the term *sphoṭa*, which has a similar meaning: it is knowledge manifested as in an unveiling—as if an eye, after undergoing an operation, were to reopen and see. *Dhamma-Cakkhu,* the "eye of truth" or of "reality," *cakkhumant,* "to be gifted with the eye" are normal Buddhist expressions, just as the technical term for "conversion" is: "his eye of truth opened." Where the Buddha speaks of his own experiences we often find references to the pure presentation of knowledge, either directly or "in similes never before heard or thought of."[16] Here is another *leitmotiv* of the texts: "As something never heard of before, vision arose in me, knowledge arose in me, intuition arose in me, wisdom arose in me, light arose in me";[17] this is called "the true excellence, conforming with the *ariya* quality of knowledge." This recalls the qualities of the voῦς, of the Olympian mind, a mind that, according to the most ancient Aryo-Hellenic tradition, is strictly related to "being" and that is manifested in a "knowledge by seeing": the voῦς is proof against deception, is "firm and tranquil as a mirror, it discovers everything without seeking, or rather, everything discovers itself in it," whereas the Titanic spirit is "restless, inventive and always in search of something, cunning and curious."[18] Vision conceived as

14. *Dīgha,* 1.1.28–37.
15. *Majjh.,* 26.
16. E.g., *Majjh.,* 85.
17. *Saṁyutt.,* 36.24; 12.10.
18. Cf. Kerényi, *La religionae antica* pp. 104, 167.

"transparency" is the Buddhist ideal: "as one sees through limpid water, the sand, the gravel, and the color of the pebbles, simply by reason of its transparency, so one who seeks the path of liberation must have just such a limpid mind."[19] The image that illustrates the manner in which an ascetic apprehends the four truths of the Ariya is this: "If at the edge of an alpine lake of clear, transparent and pure water there were to stand a man with keen sight looking at the shells and shellfish, the gravel and the sand and the fish, watching how they swim and how they rest; this thought would come to him: 'This alpine lake is clear, transparent, and pure; I see the shells and shellfish, the gravel, the sand and the fish, how they swim and rest.'" In this same manner an ascetic apprehends "in conformity with truth" the supreme object of the doctrine.[20] The formula "in conformity with truth" or "with reality" *(yathābhūtaṁ)* is a recurrent theme in the texts, like the attributes, "eye of the world," or "become eye," or "become knowledge," of the Awakened Ones.

This is naturally an achievement only through a gradual process. "As an ocean deepens gradually, declines gradually, shelves gradually without sudden precipices, so in this law and discipline there is a gradual training, a gradual action, a gradual unfolding, and no sudden apprehension of supreme knowledge."[21] Again: "One cannot, I say, attain supreme knowledge all at once; only by a gradual training, a gradual action, a gradual unfolding, does one attain perfect knowledge. In what manner? A man comes, moved by confidence; having come, he joins [the order of the Ariya]; having joined, he listens; listening, he receives the doctrine; having received the doctrine, he remembers it; he examines the sense of the things remembered; from examining the sense, the things are approved of; having approved, desire is born; he ponders; pondering, he eagerly trains himself; and eagerly training himself, he mentally realizes the highest truth itself and, penetrating it by means of wisdom, *he sees.*"[22] These are the milestones of the development. It is hardly worth saying that the placing of "confidence" at the beginning of the series does not signify a falling back into "belief": in the first place, the texts always consider that confidence is prompted by the inspiring stature and the example of a master;[23] in the second place, as we can see clearly from the development of the series, it is a matter of a provisional admission only; the real adherence comes when, with examination and practice, the faculty of direct apprehension, of intellectual intuition, absolutely independent of its antecedents, has become possible. Therefore it is said: "He who cannot strenuously train himself, cannot achieve truth; through strenuous training (an ascetic) achieves truth: there-

19. *Angutt.*, 1.5; *Mahāparinirv.*, 64.
20. *Majjh.*, 39.
21. *Angutt.*, 8.19.
22. *Majjh.*, 70.
23. Ibid., 95.

fore strenuous training is the most important thing for the achieving of truth."[24]

Naturally, there is here an implicit assumption, which we shall discuss before long in detail, an assumption, that is to say, that the men to whom the doctrine was directed were not entirely in the state of brute beasts; that they recognised, not as an intellectual opinion, but through a natural and innate sense, the existence of a reality superior to that of the senses. For the "common man," one who thinks in his heart: "There is no giving, no offering, no alms, there is no result of good and bad actions, there is no this world, there is no other world, there is no spiritual rebirth, there are not in the world ascetics or Brāhmans who are perfect and fulfilled and who, having with their own understanding comprehended, and realised this world and the other world, make known their knowledge"—for such the doctrine was not considered to have been expounded, since they lack the elementary quality of "confidence" that defines the "noble son" and that is the first member of the series we have mentioned. Such men, according to an apt textual illustration,[25] are as "arrows shot by night."

As for the preeminence accorded, in a pragmatic and anti-intellectualistic spirit, to action in the Doctrine of Awakening, we quote another Buddhist simile. A man struck by a poisoned arrow, for whom his friends and companions wish to fetch a surgeon, refuses to have the arrow extracted before learning who struck him, what his name might be, who his people are, what his appearance, if his bow was great or small, of what wood it was made, with what it was strung, and so on. This man would not succeed in learning enough to satisfy him before he died. Just so—says the text[26]—would a man behave who followed the Sublime One only on the condition that the latter gave him answers to various speculative problems, telling him if the world was eternal or not, if body and the life-principle are distinct or not, what happens to the Accomplished One after death, and so on. None of this—says the Buddha—has been explained by me. "And why has it not been explained by me? Because this is not salutary, it is not truly ascetic, it does not lead to disgust, it does not lead to detachment, it does not lead to dispassion, it does not lead to calmness, it does not lead to contemplation, it does not lead to awakening, it does not lead to extinction: therefore has this not been explained by me."[27]

In the opposing theories regarding the world and regarding man, characteristically reminiscent of the Kantian antinomies, either one opposite or the other might be true. One thing is certain, however: the state in which man actually finds himself, and the possibility of his training himself, during his lifetime, to achieve the destruction of this state.[28]

24. Ibid.
25. *Dhammapada*, 304.
26. *Majjh.*, 63.
27. *Dīgha*, 9.28; *Majjh.*, 63.
28. *Majjh.*, 63.

5

The Flame
and Saṁsāric Consciousness

In order to understand the Buddhist teaching we must start from the idea that to the man it had in mind the *ātmā-brahman,* the immortal and immutable "I" identical with the supreme essence of the universe, would not be a concept "conforming to reality" *(yathā-bhūtaṁ),* based, that is to say, on the actual evidence of experience, but rather that it would be only a speculation, a creation of philosophy or theology. The Doctrine of Awakening aims at being entirely realistic. From the realistic point of view, the immediate evidence for such a man is what we have already called "saṁsāric consciousness." Buddhism proceeds to analyze this consciousness and to determine the "truth" corresponding to it, summarized in the theory of universal impermanence and insubstantiality *(anattā).*

In previous speculation, the first term of the binomial *ātmā-saṁsāra*—that is, the immutable, transcendent "I" and the current of becoming—stood in the foreground. In the teaching that serves as the point of departure for the Buddhist ascesis emphasis is placed instead almost exclusively on the second term, *saṁsāra,* and the consciousness associated with it. This second term, however, is considered in all those aspects of contingency, relativity, and irrationality that can only proceed from a comparison with the metaphysical reality already directly intuited. This reality itself therefore remains tacitly presupposed, even if, for practical reasons, it is not mentioned in the argument.

The world of "becoming" is thus, in a manner of speaking, the truth Buddhism uses from the start. In the becoming nothing remains identical, there is nothing substantial, and nothing permanent. It is the becoming of experience itself, consuming itself in its own momentary content. Ceaseless and limitless, it is also conceived as nothing more than a succession of states that give place one to another according to an impersonal law, as in an eternal circle. We can here see an exact parallel of the

44

Hellenic concept of the "cycle of generation" κύκλος τῆς γενέσεως, and the "wheel of necessity," κύκλος τῆς εἱμαρμένης.

The Buddhist term designating a particular reality or individual life or phenomenon is *khandha* or *santāna*. *Khandha* literally means "a group," "a heap"—to be understood as a bundle or aggregation—and *santāna* means "current." In the flux of becoming there form vortices or currents of psychophysical elements and of allied states—called *dhammā*—which persist as long as the conditions and the force remain that have made them come together and pile up. After this they dissolve and, in their becoming (*saṁsāra*) they form similar conglomerations elsewhere, no less contingent than the preceding ones. Thus it is said: "All the elements of existence are transitory"—"All things are without individuality or substance *(sabbe dhammā anattā 'ti).*[1] The law of saṁsāric consciousness is expressed by this formula: *suññaṁ idam attena va attaniyena vā ti*—void of "I" or of anything that resembles "I," void of substance. Another expression: everything is "compounded" *(saṅkhata)*, "compounded" being the equivalent here of "conditioned."[2] In *saṁsāra* there are only conditioned states of existence and consciousness.

This view is valid both for external and internal experience. We must emphasize that the *dhammā*, the primary elements of existence, are considered by Buddhism—and particularly its later forms—to be simple contents of consciousness, and not abstract explanatory principles created by thought, as, for example, the atoms of the ancient schools of physics. Thus we shall find that the doctrine of *anattā*, of insubstantiality, when applied to external experience will tend more and more toward pure empiricism. As the external world directly appears, so it is. We should not say "this object *has* this form, this color, this taste, etc.," but: "this object *is* this form, this color, this taste, etc."—there is nothing behind sensible evidence to which it must be referred.[3] As we would say in modern terms, there only exists and is real the *continuum* of lived experience.

The same point of view is adopted with coherence—we might even say, with surgical directness—toward internal and personal experience. As the legitimacy of speaking "in conformity with reality" of a permanent substance behind individual phenomena—and even behind all nature, as the Brahmanical theory had it—is contested by Buddhism, so it challenges the idea of a substantial, immortal, and unchangeable principle of the person, such as the *ātmā* of the Upaniṣads. Even the person—*sakkāya*—is *khandha* and *santāna*, an aggregate and a current of elements and of impermanent, "compounded," and conditioned states. It is also *sankhata*. Its

---

1. *Dhammapada*, 277, 279.
2. *Dhamma-saṅgani*, 185.
3. Cf. T. Stcherbatsky, *The Central Conception of Buddhism* (London, 1923), pp. 26–27.

unity and reality are purely nominal, at the most "functional." It is said: as the word "wagon" is used when the various parts of a wagon are found together, so when the various elements making up human individuality are present, we speak of a "person." "As the joining together of the various parts makes up the concept of a wagon, so the aggregation or series of states gives name to a living being."[4] The wagon is a functional unity of elements, not a substance; so with the person and the "mind"—"in the same way the words 'living being' and 'I' are only a way of speaking of the fivefold stem of attachment."[5] When the conditions that have determined the combination of elements and states in that stem are no longer effective, the person as such—that is, as the particular person—dissolves. But even while he endures, the person is not a "being" but a flowing, a "current" *(santāna)* or rather a *section* of a "current," since *santāna* is thought of as something that is neither started by birth nor interrupted by death.[6]

The positive basis of this view—not very encouraging for our everyday "spiritualists"—is that the only consciousness of which the overwhelming majority of modern men can speak truthfully, *yathā-bhūtaṁ,* is "become" and "formed" consciousness: consciousness determined and conditioned by content, which are, however, impermanent. Consciousness and perception are inseparable: "these two things are joined, not separate, and it is impossible to dissociate them so as to differentiate between them: since of what one has a perception of that one is conscious and that of which one is conscious, of that one has a perception."[7] As it is meaningless to talk of fire in general, since a fire is only of logs, dung, faggots, or grass, and so on, so we cannot talk of consciousness in general, but only of a consciousness that is visual, or aural, or olfactive, or gustative, or tactile, or mental—according to the case in question.[8] "Through the eye, the object and visual consciousness, sight originates; so for hearing, so for smelling, taste, and touch; and so through the mind and mental states, thought originates. These sensory states, then, derive their origins from other causes and can claim no substantial beginning."[9] "It is in relation to body that the idea 'I am' arises, and not otherwise. And similarly with feeling, perception, the formations, and consciousness—in relation to such causes the idea 'I am' arises, and not otherwise"; but these causes are, however, impermanent.[10] Looking at things in this manner, it

---

4. *Milindapañha,* 28.
5. *Visuddhi-magga,* 8.
6. The notion of "current" appears as early as *Dīgha,* 3.105, and *Saṁyutt.,* 3.143: "This current is like a phantasmagoria void of substance": beyond it the ascetic, going as "one whose head is on fire," seeks "the unshakable abode."
7. *Majjh.,* 43.
8. Ibid., 38.
9. *Milindapañha,* 54–57.
10. *Saṁyutt.,* 22.83.

becomes quite evident that the idea of an *ātmā*, of a substantial unconditioned "I" cannot be accepted. Consciousness is thus "void of 'I'," since consciousness always arises in the presence of any sensory or psychic content.[11] More generally, the real "I" experienced by everyone, not the theoretical "I" of the philosophers, is conditioned by "name-and-form." This expression, taken by Buddhism from the Vedic tradition, designates the psychophysical individual: "that part of this aggregate, which is gross and material"—it is said[12]—"is form; that part which is subtle and mental is name," and between the one and the other there is an interdependent relationship. Bound to "name-and-form," the "soul" follows its fated changes, and for this reason as we shall see, anguish and trepidation belong to the deepest stratum of every human and, more generally, samsaric life.[13] Finally, individual consciousness and "name-and-form" condition each other. One cannot stand without the other as, according to a textual simile, two planks cannot stand without one leaning against the other. This is the same as saying that person is considered as a "functional" whole to which the becoming is not accidental but is his very substance. "One state ends and another begins: and the succession is such that it is almost possible to say that nothing precedes and nothing follows."[14]

All this can be considered as a general introduction to the theory of the "four truths of the Ariya" *(cattāri ariya-saccāni)* and of "conditioned genesis" *(paticca-samuppāda)*. The view of insubstantiality, as already discussed, does not go beyond a phenomenalistic consideration of the inward and outward world. To go further, we must adopt a different point of view in order to discover—in terms of direct experience—the deeper meaning and the law of this flowing, of this succession of states. The first two truths of the Ariya corresponding to the terms *dukkha* and *taṇhā*, then appear.

Already at this point of our investigations we have to undertake the task of separating the core of the Buddhist teaching from its accessory elements and from its popular adaptations; and, furthermore, we have to contend with a terminology whose precise significance is extremely difficult to formulate in Western languages, particularly as the meaning of a term often changes even in the course of a single text. While the terms of modern Western languages have strictly precise meanings, due to their being based for the most part on verbal and conceptual abstractions, the terms of Indo-Aryan languages have, on the other hand, essentially

---

11. Ibid, 35.193.

12. *Milindapañha*, 49.

13. Ibid., 49; cf. *Visuddhi-magga*, 17 (W., 184). The same idea is expressed with the following simile: if the oil and the wick of a light are impermanent, then it cannot be thought that the light is permanent or eternal (*Majjh.*, 146).

14. *Milindapañha*, 40–41.

variable meanings as they have to express the richness of direct experience.

The term *dukkha* is frequently translated as "pain," whence the stereotyped notion that the essence of Buddhist teaching is simply that the world is pain. But this is the most popular and, we might almost say, profane interpretation of the Buddhist doctrine. It is quite true that *dukkha* in the texts also refers to such things as growing old, being ill, undergoing what one wishes to avoid and being deprived of what one desires, and so on; all of which can in general be considered as pain or suffering. Yet, for example, the idea that birth itself is *dukkha* should make us pause, and particularly as the same term refers to nonhuman, "celestial" or "divine" states of consciousness that certainly cannot be considered as subject to "pain" in the ordinary sense of the word. The deeper, doctrinal, and nonpopular significance of the term *dukkha* is a state of agitation, of restlessness, or of "commotion"[15] rather than "suffering." We can describe it as the lived counterpart of what is expressed in the theory of universal impermanence and insubstantiality, of *anicca* and of *anattā*. And it is for this reason that, in the texts, *dukkha*, *anicca*, and *anattā* when they do not actually appear as synonyms,[16] are always found in close relationship. This interpretation is confirmed if we consider *dukkha* in the light of its opposite, that is, of the states of "liberation": *dukkha* now appears as the antithesis of unshakable calm, which is superior not only to pain, but also to pleasure; as the opposite of the "incomparable safety," the state in which there is no more "restless wandering," no more "coming and going," and where fear and anguish are destroyed. In order really to understand the implications of *dukkha*, the first truth of the Ariya, and therefore to grasp the deepest significance of saṁsāric existence, we must associate the notion of "anguish" with that of "commotion" and "agitation." The Buddha saw in the world: "A race which trembles"—men trembling, attached to their persons, "like fish in a stream that is almost dry."[17] "This world is fallen into agitation" is the thought that came to him while he was still striving to achieve illumination,[18] "in truth, this world has been overcome by agitation. We are born, we die, we pass away from one state, we arise in another. And from this sorrow, from this decay and death, no one knows the escape."[19] Therefore it is a question of something far deeper and larger than anything the usual notion of pain can designate.

We now come to the second truth of the Ariya, which deals with *samudaya*, that is, with origin. From what does this experience of ours, which manifests itself as *dukkha*, as agitation, as anguished becoming, originate; from where does it draw nourishment

15. Cf. Stcherbatsky, *Central Conception*, p. 48.
16. Jansink, *Mistica del buddismo*, p. 95.
17. *Suttanipāta*, 4.2.5–6.
18. *Saṁyutt.*, 12.10.
19. *Dīgha*, 14.2.18.

and what maintains it? The answer is *taṇhā* (Skt.: *tṛṣṇā*), that is to say, craving or thirst: "thirst for life for ever renewing itself, which, when it is joined to the pleasure of satisfaction and gratifies itself here and there, is thirst for sensual pleasure, thirst for existence, thirst for becoming." This is the central force of samsaric existence, this is the principle that determines the *anattā,* that is, the nonaseity of any thing and any life whatsoever and that endows all life with alteration and death. Thirst, craving, burning, according to the Buddhist teaching, stand not only at the root of all states of mind, but also of experience in general, of the forms of feeling, perception, and observation that are most nearly considered to be neutral and mechanical. Thus we get the suggestive symbolism of the "burning world." "The whole world is in flames, the whole world is consumed by fire, the whole world trembles."[20] "All is in flames. And what is the all that is in flames? The eye is burning, what is visible is burning, consciousness of the visible is burning, contact of the eye with what is visible is burning, the feeling—be it pleasure or pain, or neither pain nor pleasure—which arises from the contact with what is visible is burning. And with what is it burning? With the fire of desire, with the fire of aversion, with the fire of delusion"—and the same theme is repeated separately for what is heard, for what is tasted, touched, and smelled, and for what is thought;[21] and again there is the same theme for the *pañcakkhandhā,* the fivefold stem of the personality: materiality, feeling, perception, the formations, consciousness.[22] This flame burns not only in desire, aversion, and delusion, but also in birth and death, in decay, in every kind of pain and suffering.[23]

Such is the second truth of the Ariya, the truth about "origin." To understand it we must go beyond the most superficial plane of consciousness: since although everyone will probably concede that desire is the root of a large number of human actions, practically none will ever understand intuitively that it is the substance of his own bodily form, the root of his very individuality, the base of his every experience, even of that of a color or a sound, to which he is indifferent. This holds good to a certain extent for the first truth also, since it is most improbable that everyone will understand that beneath his joy lies *dukkha,* that is, agitation, suffering, and restlessness. The fact is that these two truths are already, in a certain measure, related to the "other shore," being directly evident only to those who have already crossed over and can comprehend objectively and fully the nature of the state in which they previously found themselves.[24] In this particular connection the texts provide an

---

20. *Saṁyutt.,* 1.133.
21. *Mahāvagga (Vinaya),* 1.21.2–3; *Saṁyutt.,* 35.28.
22. *Saṁyutt.,* 22.61.
23. Ibid., 35.28; *Mahāvagga (Vin.),* 1.21.2–3.
24. In *Majjh.,* 80, it is, in fact, explicitly stated that only those who have arrived at the goal, have laid aside the burden, have done what was to be done, and who have freed themselves from the bonds of existence, can understand what craving and thirst for craving are.

illuminating simile, that of the leper. Those who, "driven by desire, consumed by the thirst of desire, burned by the fever of desire, delight in desire," are like those lepers, their bodies covered with sores, ulcerated, eaten by worms, who, in scratching their sores and scorching their limbs, feel a morbid delight. But one who frees himself from leprosy, feels cured, healthy, and independent, "master of where he would go"; this man would then understand "according to reality" the morbid delight of the leper, and should anyone attempt to drag him by force toward the fire in which he formerly found delight, he would struggle in every manner possible to withdraw his body.[25]

Apart from this, the symbolism of the flame and of the fire is enough to help us to understand approximately the law of conditioned existence and of becoming as "craving" or "thirst." Besides, let us take as an illustration physical thirst or, in general, nourishment. Instinct induces an organism to satisfy itself by assimilating and consuming something for maintenance. Maintenance, however, implies that there is later a fresh feeling of hunger or thirst, because of the law of the organism that has been strengthened through the very satisfaction of the need. It is stated thus in the Gospels: "Whosoever drinketh of this water shall thirst again. But whosoever drinketh of the water that I shall give him shall never thirst; but the water that I shall give him shall be in him a well of water springing up into everlasting life."[26] Still more appropriate is the symbolism of the flame and of the processes of combustion. We owe to Dahlke an account of it that allows us to penetrate into the secret of saṁsāric life. Having likened craving to a fire, every living being appears, not as an "I," but as a process of combustion since, at the level on which we are talking, we cannot say that a being *has* craving, but rather that he himself *is* craving. There is then—latent in everyone—a will to burn, to become a flame consuming some particular material. The fuel stimulates this will and starts the fire in a process of combustion that, however, results in a greater degree of heat, that is, in a fresh will to burn, thus starting a new combustion, and so on, endlessly. From this point of view it is a process that generates and sustains itself; and at each instant the flame represents a particular degree of heat that, as such, is the potentiality for a new combustion as soon as contact is made with some fresh inflammable material.[27] In this way the text we have been following considers every contact, every perception, vision, or thought as a species of "burning." The fire is the craving that the will induces toward this or that contact, in which it spreads and sharpens itself, feeding itself, in a manner of speaking, on itself and provoking itself in the very act of satisfaction and of consuming its fuel. The "I" as *santāna*, or "current," is none other than the continuity of this fire that

25. *Majjh.*, 75.

26. John, 4:13–14.

27. Dahlke, *Buddhismus als Weltanschauung*, pp. 50–57 [*Buddhism and Science*, pp. 47–56]; *Buddhismus als Religion und Moral*, pp. 102 ff.

dies down and smolders among the ashes when the supply of material grows short, yet ready to blaze forth at every fresh contact. The process of saṁsāric life is thought of as a flame attached to burning material or rather as a flame that is itself its own material. The contacts develop through attachment, *upādāna*. This occurs above all in the fivefold stem that makes up the person in general: materiality, feeling, perception, formations, individuated consciousness. Burning potentially in this stem, thirst develops in each one of its five parts through the series of contacts furnished by the outside world; the world itself appears to the will to burn and to be burning as a kind of varied fuel, a fuel that incites greater combustion in proportion to the delusive satisfaction it affords this will. The theory of *anattā*, of "not-I," thus has this meaning: the "I" does not exist outside the process of burning, it *is* this very process—were a halt really made, the "I," the illusion of being "I" would collapse. Here, then, is the reason for the anguish and for the primordial "agitation" of which we have already spoken, here is the profound source of the "triple fire of sensuality, hate, and delusion" and of the will that "causes the search for other worlds." The saṁsāric "I" has its foundation in craving, without which it would collapse.[28] Even in suffering and in pain there works a variety of this profound fire, of the will of conditioned beings for existence, which involves a fundamental abdication.

On this basis the Buddhist theory of *saṁsāra* has been able to develop as far as the theory of "instantaneousness" or "instantaneous existence," *khaṇa*. If existence and the sense of "I" are conditioned by contacts, this existence must resolve itself into the point series of these same contacts. In this sense, strictly speaking, life is instantaneous, just as, in the Buddhist image of the wheel of a wagon whose movement is continuous, but which, moving or at rest, touches the ground at only one point. "In the same way the life of beings has only the duration of a thought: the being of the past moment has lived, but does not live and will not live; the being of the future moment will live, but does not live and has not lived; the being of the present moment lives, but has not lived and will not live."[29]

This is the *coup de grâce* delivered to the Brahmanical theory of *ātmā*. And even if we ignore the later and more extreme expressions of the theory of "instantaneous existence," however coherent, this way of thinking is enough to destroy the theory of reincarnation that we considered to be largely in Hinduism the effect of foreign influences. In fact, we have already seen that the preoccupation with knowledge of what one was and of what one will be beyond this life is considered by the Buddha to be an opining and a rambling that is a disease, a thorn, a sore, a forest, a tumor, a labyrinth. In any case, the idea that "this consciousness persists

---

28. Thus in *Angutt.*, 5.69 he who destroys *taṇhā*, craving, is called "he who destroys the support."
29. *Visuddhi-magga*, 8 (W., 150).

unchangeable through the cycle of changing existences" is expressly stated to be "false opinion, not spoken of by the Buddha," the idea of "a fool,"[30] a judgment in which the order of disciples, after questioning by Prince Siddhattha, agrees.[31] The fundamental argument here is that it is impossible in practice to refer the possibility of having already existed to any evidence of consciousness,[32] and in the second place, that "the nature of consciousness is conditioned"[33]—conditioned above all by "name-and-form"; a real continuity of consciousness is inconceivable where "name-and-form" is liable to change, where new *khandha*, new and different psychophysical aggregates may be produced in the current. In fact, "it is not the same name-and-form that re-arises."[34] When, with the cessation of a life, "name-and-form," that is to say individuality, ceases, it does not go on to exist elsewhere as the same aggregate. We must imagine it, rather, as the sound of a lute that comes into being without ever having existed elsewhere and that does not pass on to another place when the musician has ceased playing.[35] A continuity does indeed exist, but it is impersonal, it is the continuity of craving, of the "current," of the will to burn in order to be; when this force has exhausted, like fuel, one life it leaps like a flame to attach itself to another stem and to blaze forth in it. According to one text,[36] it remains in the intermediate stages as a flame that consumes itself, that is, as pure calorific potential. Strictly speaking we should here refer to a continuum from which both absolute diversity and absolute identity are excluded. A simile used in this connection is that of the flames of the three watches of the night: the torch of the first watch, which, when it is about to die out, lights another torch, and this in its turn, lights a third. These three flames cannot be called either the same or different. One has lighted another, one has the fire of another, but they are all different from each other, and the flame is in each case the flame (life, consciousness) of a different torch. Another simile is that of milk that turns into curd and then into butter and then into cheese. We are dealing with the same substance, but any change of state makes the use of the same name improper, and we cannot say that curd is milk or that butter is curd.[37] In changing the

30. *Majjh.*, 38.

31. Ibid.

32. Ibid., 101.

33. Ibid., 38.

34. *Milindapañha*, 46.

35. *Visuddhi-magga*, 20 (W., 186). In Tantric Buddhism *(vajra-yāna)*, a bell and a scepter are the two symbolic objects used in magical operations. The bell *(ghantā)* is the symbol of "knowledge" of the phenomenal world, where every reality, as the sound of a bell, is perceptible but evanescent; the scepter, on the other hand, symbolizes the male principle of the *vajra*, of the diamond-lightning, of which the spirit of every "Awakened One" is composed.

36. *Saṁyutt.*, 44.9. The text, in fact, says this: "as fuel is necessary for the flame, so a new existence needs a substance." It is asked, however, what is the substance when the flame is carried by the wind. The Buddha's reply is: the wind itself. It is then asked: when a being leaves one body and arises in another, what is the fuel indicated by the Lord Gotama? The reply is: "In this case, in truth, the fuel is the craving itself."

37. *Milindapañha*, 40–41.

state—in having a different "name-and-form" (philosophically we might say: a different *principium individuationis*)—it is well to change also the denomination.

The only real continuity is a causal connection, a kind of impersonal heredity. The flame that, in a given being, is the life of that being, assumes in the course of that life a certain quality, a certain *habitus* that will last and manifest itself in successive combustions. From this we derive the notion of what are called the *sankhārā* (the formations) that correspond to the directions adopted by desire and that constitute one of the five groups of the personality; while for the general determining law whereby this fundamental force gathers together its particular group of *dhammā*, or the elements, when manifesting itself, the Upaniṣad term *karma* (Pāli: *kamma*) is used, especially in later Buddhist texts. Thus *kamma* is spoken of as a "matrix of beings"—*kammayoni*—and the principle is formulated that "according to the actions of a being, there arises fresh becoming; what one does causes one to become again. Re-become, contacts touch one [that is, the new process of combustion is started]. Beings, then, are the heirs of actions."[38] From this kind of concept, however, we must not again presume the continuity of an individual substratum, of an "I"; we should bear in mind, rather, the idea of a flame that moves from one branch (of a tree) to another, and we should take into special account only the particular quality assumed by the fire in the one combustion that transfers itself to the next. This is why there is no answer in the texts to the question: Is it the same individual who feels the effects of a preceding existence or is it another individual? The only answer we can give is to refer to "conditioned genesis," that is, to the process that, in general, leads to samsāric consciousness.[39] To the question: Is it the same name-and-form that arises in a new existence? the answer is: "It is not the same name-and-form that arises in the next existence; but with this name-and-form good or bad actions are done, by means of which a new name-and-form arises in a future existence."[40] The text concludes: "The effects arise in a series from which both absolute identity and absolute diversity are excluded, whence one cannot say if they are created by the same being or by something different."[41] More radically, we could give the illustration of the billiard ball that moves after receiving both force and direction from another billiard ball, distinct, of course, from the first one—had not this same animated world of ours already provided us with a perfect analogy in the phenomenon of generation and biological heredity: for although distinct from his parent, in the new animal we find the life, the tendencies, the instincts, and often even the blemishes of his forebears.

---

38. *Majjh.*, 57.
39. *Saṁyutt.*, 12.17, 24.
40. *Milindapañha*, 46.6–9. Also in *Saṁyutt.*, 12.37, where it is said that this body is considered neither as one's own, nor as someone else's, but as determined by a preceding action, that is, by the energy produced by preceding actions, either mental or physical.
41. *Milindapañha*, 46–49; *Visuddhi-magga*, 17 (W. 238–40).

However, we deem that one should think less of a linear continuity of individual existences, than of so many appearances of a single stem of craving. This, while in the process of combustion, *is* every single life, every single individual; it is the desire that composes that life, that individual, but that at the same time transcends it and, after returning to a latent state, moves on to emerge elsewhere and to establish itself mainly according to the force and the direction that it has already given itself in its preceding life (or lives).

With this doctrine the compromise inherent in the Upaniṣadic concept—oscillating between truth relative to *ātmā* consciousness and truth relative to saṁsāric consciousness—is overcome, and at the same time a severely realistic point of view is established, void of "idealisms" and attenuations. The result is certainly not a consoling view. The Buddha, in a manner of speaking, by speeding up the rhythm has set forth what amounts to the limiting-form of the fall or regression, because it is only in this way that a total reaction can be provoked and the necessity for the ascesis demanded by the path of Awakening understood.

Here it will be well to add the following consideration. We have already said that the first two truths of the Ariya, with particular reference to the doctrine of thirst and of fire, may not be directly evident to modern man. He may be able to understand them fully only in special or critical moments, because the life he normally leads is as if outside himself; half sleepwalking, he moves between psychological reflexes and images that hide from him the deepest and most fearful substance of existence. Only in particular circumstances is the veil of what is, fundamentally, a providential illusion torn aside. For example, in all moments of sudden danger, on the point of being threatened either by the vanishing of ground from under one's feet through the opening of a chasm or glacier crevasse, or in touching inadvertently a glowing coal or an electrified object, an instantaneous reaction takes place. This reaction does not proceed from the "will," consciousness, nor from the "I," since this part follows only after the initial reaction is complete; in the first moment it is preceded by something more profound, more rapid, and more absolute. During extreme hunger, panic, fear, sensual craving, or extreme pain and terror the same force again shows itself—and he who can comprehend it directly in these moments likewise creates for himself the faculty of perceiving it gradually as the invisible substratum of all waking life. The subterranean roots of inclinations, faiths, atavisms, of invincible and irrational convictions, habits, and character, all that lives as animality, as biological race, all the urges of the body—all this goes back to the same principle. Compared with it, the "will of the 'I'" has, normally, a liberty equivalent to that of a dog tied to a fairly long chain that he does not notice until he has passed a certain limit. If one goes beyond that limit, the profound force is not slow to awaken, either to supplant the "I" or to mislead it, making it believe that it wills that which, in fact, the force itself wills. The wild force of imagination and of suggestion takes us to the same point: to that where according to the so-called law of "converse effort," one does something the more strongly the more one "wills" against it—as sleep eludes one the more one "wills" it, or as the suggestion that one will fall into an abyss will certainly cause one to fall if one "wills" against it.

This force, which is connected with the emotive and irrational energies, gradually identifies itself as the very force that rules the profound functions of physical life, over which the "will," the "mind," and the "I" have very little influence, to which they are external and on which they live parasitically, extracting the essential fluids yet without having to go down for them into the heart of the trunk. Thus one must ask oneself: What, of this "my" body, can be justifiably thought of as subject to "my" will? Do "I" will "my" breath or the mixtures of the digestive juices by which food is digested? Do "I" will my form, my flesh, or my being this man who is conditioned thus and not otherwise? Can he who asks himself this not go on even further and ask himself: My "will" itself, my consciousness, my "I"—do I will these, or simply is it that they are?

We shall see that the Doctrine of Awakening actually asks questions of this kind. And he who is strong enough to force himself, in this sense, to go beyond illusion, cannot help arriving at this disconcerting conclusion: "You are not life in yourself. You do not exist. You cannot say 'mine' of anything. You do not possess life—it is life that possesses you. You suffer it. And the possibility of immortal survival of this phantom 'I' at the dissolution of the body is only a mirage, since everything tells you that its correlation with this body is essential to you and a trauma, an indisposition, a fainting fit, or any kind of accident has a definite influence over all its faculties, however 'spiritual' and 'superior' they may be."

There are some who, at certain moments, are able to become detached from themselves, get beneath the surface, down into the dark depths of the force that rules their body, and where this force loses name and identity. They have the sensation of this force expanding and including "I" and "not-I," pervading all nature, substantiating time, supporting myriad beings as if they were drunk or hallucinated, reestablishing itself in a thousand forms, irresistible, untamed, inexhaustible, ceaseless, limitless, burning with eternal insufficiency and hunger. He who reaches this fearful perception, like an abyss suddenly opening, grasps the mystery of saṁsāra and of saṁsāric consciousness and understands and fully lives anattā, the doctrine of nonaseity, of "not-I." The passage from purely individual consciousness to this saṁsāric consciousness that includes indefinite possibilities of existence, both "infernal" and celestial—this, fundamentally, is the basis of the whole Doctrine of Awakening. We are not dealing here with a "philosophy" but with an experience that, to tell the truth, is not the sole property of Buddhism. Traces and echoes of it are also to be found in other traditions, both Eastern and Western: in the West, particularly in terms of secret knowledge and of initiatory experience. The theory of universal pain, of life as pain, does not represent, in this respect, anything other than something completely external and, as we have already said, profane. Where it has been widely diffused it refers only to the forms of a popular exposition.

From the point of view of Western mentality, as a general outlook, two forms or degrees of existence and saṁsāric consciousness can be distinguished: one is truly saṁsāric, the other is limited to the time and the space of a single individual existence. The consciousness prevalent in the modern West is this second one. But this only represents a part, a section of a consciousness or a saṁsāric existence that stretches out across time, and that, as we have just pointed out, may also include states free from the temporal law that we know. In the ancient Eastern world there still existed, in great measure, this much vaster saṁsāric consciousness. And the initiatory-ascetic path considered as an essential first phase the passage from the particular consciousness that is bound to a single life and defined by the illusion of the individual "I" to truly saṁsāric consciousness: a concept to which the notion of *santāna*, of the "I" as flux, current or indefinite series of insubstantial states determined by *dukkha*, also corresponds. Only after mastering this phase can a passage be found to what is really unconditioned and extra-saṁsāric. But, as we shall soon see when we speak of the vocations, it is very rare in the West to find anyone who does not confuse the unconditioned, the absolute, with what are only higher states of saṁsāric consciousness.

6

❦

Conditioned Genesis

The problem of "origin," corresponding to the second truth of the Ariya, is investigated more deeply in what is known as doctrine of dependent origination or "conditioned genesis" *(paṭicca-samuppāda)*, which makes a separate study of the stages and states by which conditioned existence is arrived at. "Profound, hard to perceive, hard to understand, peaceful, elevated, not reducible to discursive thought, subtle, accessible (only) to the wise" this doctrine is called.[1] It seems that it may have been due to the common man's difficulties in understanding it, that Prince Siddhattha at first hesitated to reveal it: "a doctrine that leads on against the current, internal and profound, it will be invisible to those who are ensnared by craving, wrapped up in the shadow of ignorance."[2] This should be borne in mind by all who, in this matter, like to advance a *"caveat* against reading profound metaphysical concepts into this old series."[3] Indeed, we are dealing here with the results of a transcendental investigation, realized—according to tradition—in states of consciousness corresponding to the three watches of the night, during which Prince Siddhattha's spiritual activity brought him to superrational illumination, to *bodhi.*[4] We must therefore also anticipate the objection that this discourse on transcendental states, in spite of the declared ostracism of all speculation, is based on simple philosophical hypotheses. Buddhism belongs to a civilization that accepted as a principle the possibility of insight "with which not only this world but also the world beyond is seen"[5] and thence the possibility of discovering in certain conditions, both the states that precede the appearance

1. *Saṁyutt.,* 6.1.
2. *Majjh.,* 26.
3. C. A. F. Rhys Davids in the introduction to *Kindred Sayings* (the translation of *Saṁyutta-nikāya* [London, 1922]), vol. 2, p. 6.
4. *Mahāvagga (Vin.),* 1.1.2; *Majjh.,* 4.
5. *Dīgha,* 19.15; *Majjh.,* 34.

57

of a man in a bodily existence and those that occur when this form of manifestation is exhausted.[6] The horizons of our contemporaries are naturally very different, and for this reason the impression that we are dealing here simply with theories cannot be entirely eliminated.

However, in one way or another, it is still necessary to penetrate this knowledge, since it is fundamental both for the doctrinal and the practical part of the Buddhist teaching. "He who sees conditioned genesis"—it is said[7]—"sees the truth *(dhamma)* and he who sees the truth sees conditioned genesis." And again: "Of all things which proceed from cause, the Accomplished One has explained the cause and also its destruction. This is the doctrine of the great ascetic."[8] It serves as the immediate basis for practical action, and it is the generator of "tranquillity" (the opposite state to *dukkha*), because its meaning is this: "If that is, this comes of it; with the origin of that this originates; if that is not, this does not come of it; with the end of that this ends."[9] By knowing what are the causes in virtue of which we come to a state of saṁsāric existence, we also know that their removal also removes this same state of saṁsāric existence. For this reason the doctrine of *paṭicca-samuppāda* constitutes the premise for the two remaining truths of the Ariya: namely, the third truth concerning *nirodha,* that is, the possibility of the destruction of the state marked by *dukkha;* and the fourth truth concerning *magga,* or the methods to be followed in order to achieve such a destruction.

The *paṭicca-samuppāda*—which literally means "conditioned genesis" or "formation"—considers a series of twelve conditioned states. The term used is *paccaya,* condition, and not *hetu,* cause: it is a question of conditionality and not of true causality. We may here return to the simile of a substance that, in being transformed, passes through various states, each of which contains the potentiality of giving place, in appropriate circumstances, to the next, or, if neutralized, of suspending the next. On what level does this causal series develop?

Oriental commentators and, naturally, still more, European Orientalists have often held discordant opinions on this point. This is due to their not having realized that the same series is susceptible of two different interpretations, neither of which excludes or contradicts the other since each refers to a distinct plane. According to the first interpretation—followed unanimously by those on guard against "metaphysics"—the entire series develops on the plane of saṁsāric existence and provides a

6. For this second form of knowledge, cf. *Bardo Thödol (The Tibetan Book of the Dead),* trans W. Y. Evans-Wentz [London, 1927]. Cf. also *Majjh.,* 136, where it is said that through *cetosamādhi* the ascetic perceives the posthumous destiny of beings.
7. *Majjh.,* 28.
8. *Mahāvagga (Vin.),* 1.23.10.
9. *Saṁyutt.,* 12.21, 41.

detailed account of the process, which is one developing in time—let us say: in a horizontal direction. Accordingly, a single finite existence is determined by others preceding it, while it, in its turn, determines a successive existence or a number of successive existences. It is thus at the same time an effect in one respect and a cause in another.

But above and beyond this there is a much more profound interpretation, which really concerns the origins and which is a higher form of knowledge than the "four truths."

According to this interpretation, the series is not only to be considered in temporal terms, but also in transcendental terms; it develops, that is to say, not horizontally but essentially in a vertical manner, starting from preindividual and prenatal states and finishing on the plane of saṁsāric existence, in which the "horizontal" series considered by the first interpretation develops. Since in the texts these *nidāna* or causal "nexuses" are quite obviously considered now from one point of view and now from the other, there has been opportunity for confusion and for divergent interpretations wherever general doctrine principles have been left out of account.

Here we have particularly to consider the *paṭicca-samuppāda* in the sense of a transcendental, vertical, and descending series that even if it finishes by entering time, is not in itself temporal.

1. The basic element of the whole series is *avijjā*, that is to say, "ignorance," unawareness. The significance of this term in Buddhism is not essentially different from its significance in other branches of the Indo-Aryan tradition, the *Sāṁkhya* or the *Vedānta* doctrines, for example, and where it might be figuratively illustrated by saying: man is a god who is unaware that he is such—it is his unawareness *(avijjā)* alone that makes him a man. It is a question, then, of a state of "oblivion," of deliquescence, by which the primary motive for identification with one or other form of finite and conditioned existence is determined. We must not therefore think of an abstract discernible condition, but rather of something that also includes a disposition, a tendency, a virtual movement. Thus we can think of this state simultaneously as "infatuation," "intoxication," "mania"—and, in fact, we find in some texts that "ignorance" and "mania" condition each other; it is said, for example: "the origin of ignorance determines the origin of mania" and, at the same time, "the origin of mania determines the origin of ignorance"—mania here being considered as tripartite, that is, as "mania of desire, mania of existence, mania of ignorance—*kāmāsava, bhavāsava, avijjāsava.*"[10] Following Neumann and de Lorenzo, we have translated the term *āsava* as "mania." It has been rendered by Orientalists in various ways: sometimes as "passions" (Nyanatiloka), sometimes as "toxins"—deadly floods, intoxicants (Rhys Davids) or as

10. *Majjh.,* 9.

"depravities" (Warren) or "drugs"[11] (Woodward), ferments or stupefacients—or by effluvia, impure emanations, suppurations—*unreine Ausflüsse* (Walleser), etc. The literal sense is exactly the idea of an intoxicant drug that can alter and pervade an entire organism with a disturbance or a "mania." We must imagine a state of drunkenness that makes a man forget himself and, at the same time, makes an irrational action possible. The close relation of *avijjā*, ignorance, to *āsava*, mania, is confirmed not only by the fact that, as we have seen, this same ignorance is described as an *āsava*—*avijjāsava*—but still more by the fact that the state of intuitive knowledge or wisdom, *paññā*, as opposed to that of ignorance, is very frequently said to be attained when the *āsavā* have been neutralized or destroyed.

Here we must touch on the problem of the degree in which "ignorance" can be considered as something absolutely original. Various views are possible, according to the point of reference. In itself, the Buddhist teaching does *not* go back beyond *avijjā*. And, for all practical ascetic purposes, it is not even necessary to go further back than the transcendental fact, the mysterious crisis that in the mythological form of an original "fall" or "descent" or "fault" or "alteration" appears to some extent in the teachings of all peoples. Doctrinally, however, things are somewhat different. It is stated that "an anterior limit, in which ignorance has not been in some degree, but only after which ignorance has been, it is not possible to find"[12]; this idea refers, however, not to the transcendental series, but to the horizontal and temporal series of saṁsāric existence, about which it is, in fact, stated in the same text: "Saṁsāra does not lead towards what is free from death. And it is not possible to chart the first point of the journey of beings who are hindered by ignorance and bound by craving."[13] It would, indeed, be an absurdity to attempt, as some do, to make ignorance the absolute *prius* in the order of conditioned genesis: it would certainly endow Buddhism with an "originality," but only to condemn it to every form of contradiction and incoherence. Craving might possibly be conceived as something absolutely fundamental; but certainty not ignorance that already, as such, presupposes knowledge. Nor would it be sensible to talk of an awakening, for obviously one cannot awake if one has not been sleeping, and if there is nothing that shines beyond the cloud of oblivion. And, finally, the very substance of the Buddhist doctrine, that is, the ascesis, would be fundamentally prejudiced; for it would not be possible to understand whence one derives the impetus for resisting, for detaching oneself from saṁsāra, for destroying the whole chain of the *nidāna* by following it in reverse or backward, and for extinguishing mania without leaving any residue, unless ignorance signified something additional: an intoxication, a darkness, and a drunkenness that, however profound,

11. [These terms in English in the original.—Trans.].
12. *Saṁyutt.*, 15.1.
13. Ibid., 15.3.

yet still presuppose an antecedent state, and that are not capable of irretrievably paralyzing all energy connected with this state. That the Buddhist teaching agrees with this point of view can be seen in this passage: "There is, O disciples, an unborn, not become, not compounded, not constructed. If there were not this unborn, not become, not compounded, not constructed, no escape could be seen here from that which is born, become, compounded, constructed. But since there is an unborn, not become, not compounded, not constructed, so an escape is possible from what is born, become, compounded, constructed."[14]

In the view of the most celebrated commentator on the texts,[15] moreover, ignorance is, and at the same time is not the prime cause; "it is the principal element, but not the beginning." It is not the beginning from the point of view of saṃsāric existence, of which it is said that there never was a time in which ignorance was not, since this existence has ignorance and craving as its double root and coessential substratum. But it is the beginning from the higher point of view of the origins. According to this view, it seems that the āsava themselves are conditioned by ignorance and that it is because of this that they lead to a determined form of existence on the subhuman, human, or "divine" plane.[16] On the saṃsāric plane, and therefore according to the temporal interpretation, an ignorant man is described as one who, having descended into birth, cannot apprehend that the law of the world is dukkha, cannot see its origin, nor deliverance from it nor the path by which this deliverance is obtained: ignorance is thus ignorance of the four truths of the ariyan. Having been determined by the āsava, by intoxication or mania, this particular ignorance establishes the saṃsāric state of existence and determines the substratum (upadhi) that protracts it.

2. In the connected series, after avijjā follow the sankhāra. This term also has been variously interpreted. Literally, sankhāra means a formation or predisposition in regard to a particular aim. We are dealing, that is to say, with a state in which the potential motion of the first nidāna has already assumed a certain direction and has entered on the path that later development will follow. To translate sankhāra by "distinctions" (Neumann) is, to some extent, exact, seeing that we cannot choose a direction without first having defined it and thus distinguished it from other possible directions. We must, however, bear in mind the volitional and active factor (sankhāra as kamma-cetanā) and the "conceptional" factor. In this connection, Burnouf recorded the exegesis according to which sankhāra is "the passion which includes desire, aversion, fear and joy," noting, however, that the terms desire and passion are here too much restricted. In a commentary quoted by Hodgson, we read: "The belief of a sensible incorporeal principle in the reality of that which is only a mirage, is accompanied

14. *Udāna,* 8.1–3.
15. *Visuddhi-magga,* 17 (W., 171–75).
16. *Angutt.,* 6.63.

by a desire for this mirage and by a conviction of its value and reality: this desire is called *sankhāra*."[17] To which Burnouf added: "The *sankhāra* are thus the things *quae fingit animus*, that is, which the spirit creates, makes, imagines *(sankharoti)*; they are, in a word, the products of the faculty which it has of conceiving, of imagining."[18] It is in such terms that the object of the "mania" begins to manifest itself and that a particular current, *santāna*, begins to define itself in the descent toward saṁsāric existence. We can, moreover, relate the *sankhārā* to *kamma* (Skt.: *karma*) in a double sense: in the vertical chain, by taking *kamma* in the general meaning of action and as the general principle accounting for the difference of beings;[19] and in the saṁsāric, temporal, and horizontal chain, by seeking in *kamma*, rather, the roots of the character, the predispositions, the innate tendencies, as well as all fresh ones that develop and which, when they are established and incorporated in the body of craving, pass from being to being. In this second sense we shall see that the *sankhāra* are considered to be one of the five groups making up the personality. But, ultimately, the root of these *sankhāra* on the conditioned, saṁsāric plane, goes back, in everyone, to the *sankhāra* that make up the second *nidāna* of the vertical series.

3. The *sankhārā*, through the distinction or individuation that they imply, give place to the third *nidāna*, to *viññāna* or "consciousness," understood as distinctive consciousness. That is to say, it is the germ of all that will eventually appear as individuality, as individual consciousness or consciousness of "I," in the general sense of the Sanskrit term *ahamkāra*, and which also includes forms of individuality differing from what is usually understood as human individuality.

4. The fourth *nidāna* is *nāma-rūpa* or "name-and-form." This has already been discussed in some detail. All that is necessary here is to extend the concept once again, thinking of the general combination of both material elements ("matter") and immaterial or mental elements ("mind") that *viññāna*, or individual consciousness in general, needs as a base. On the level of the fourth *nidāna* occurs the meeting of the vertical direction with the horizontal, and which leads to the conception and the generation of a being. At this point the transcendental dispositions are incorporated in the elements of saṁsāric heredity that, whenever the series turns toward a human birth, show themselves, to a large extent, in the material of the biological heredity of the parents.

To orient ourselves on this point we must consider Buddhism in the light of a

---

17. Cf. *Corpus Hermeticum*, 1.1: "Seeing his own form in the water, he conceived a desire for it and wished to possess it. The act accompanied the desire and the irrational form was conceived. Nature took possession of her lover, surrounded him and they joined in mutual love. This is why, alone amongst the beings that live on the earth, man is twofold, mortal in the body, immortal in essence . . . Superior to sleep (= *avijjā*), he is dominated by sleep."

18. E. Burnouf, *Introduction à l'histoire du bouddhisme indien* (Paris, 1876), pp. 448–49.

19. Cf. *Visuddhi-magga*, 17.

more general teaching. Three factors come together in the birth of a human being. The first is of a transcendental nature and is connected with the first three *nidāna:* "ignorance," mania, and *sankhāra* must, in the first place, have determined a darkening and a descending current that, through the second *nidāna*, has already been given its direction, and through the third, already tends toward an individuated form having an "I"-consciousness. The second factor, on the other hand, is connected with forces and influences that are already organized, with a will that is already determined, thus corresponding to one of those processes of "combustion" that constitute *samsāra*, and of which we have already spoken. These influences and this will can be considered comprehensively as a form of entity *sui generis,* which we may call "samsāric entity" or entity of craving." It is a "life" that does not exhaust itself within the limits of the individual but which is thought of, rather, as the "life" of this life and which is associated with the notions of "daemon," "double," and "genius," of *kā, fravashi,* and *fylgya,* etc., which occur in other traditions and which, in the Indo-Aryan tradition, already existed as, for example, the *liṅga-śarīra* or "subtle body" of Sāṁkhya, or as that entity—*gandharva* (Pāli: *gandhabba*)—whose presence a text of the earliest Buddhist canon records as necessary, in addition to the parents, for a birth to occur.[20] In the *Abhidharmakośa,* that is to say, in the theoretical system of Buddhism, this entity receives the name of *antarābhava;* it is thought that it has a pre- and internatal existence; nourished by "desire" and carried by impulses fed by other lives, it seeks to manifest itself in a new existence.[21] This, then, is the second factor, already potentially corresponding to a largely predetermined "name-and-form." On the level of this *nidāna*—*nāma-rūpa*—occurs the meeting of the principle that is obscured by ignorance with the *antarābhava*, or samsāric daemon, or entity of craving: the first, in a manner of speaking, joins with the second, inserting itself in this way into a particular group of samsāric heredity.

We have now to consider the third factor. In one of the texts we have just mentioned it says that the supersensible eye sees the daemon wandering about until an opportunity for a new "combustion" presents itself on the occasion of the meeting of a man and a woman who may be suitable as its father and mother, that is to say, who may present it with a heredity in accordance with its cravings. A thing then occurs, with reference to which the doctrine in question is singularly in agreement with what "psychoanalysis"—even with its various deformations and exaggerations—has presented to our modern eyes in the guise of theories of the *libido* and of the "Oedipus" or "Electra complex." The doctrine speaks, in fact, of a desire that this entity may conceive either for the future mother or for the future father, according to the sex to

---

20. *Majjh.*, 38; *Jātaka*, 330; *Milindapañha*, 123.
21. *Abhidharmakośa*, 3.12; cf. L. de la Vallée-Poussin, *Nirvāṇa* (Paris, 1925), p. 28.

which it belonged in its previous and now exhausted life, and of a corresponding aversion for the other parent.[22] An identification follows through the infatuation and delight of the pair, by means of which the entity enters the womb and conception takes place. Immediately the various *khandhā*, the germinal chain of factors that will form the basis of the personality, condense around it, and from this point there follows that physiological process of embryonic development that, in its exterior aspects, is known to contemporary medicine. Its internal development is determined by the various remaining *nidāna*, of which we yet have to speak.[23]

Thus, finally, there are present in the human being three principles or entities, which are called in *Sāṃkhya, kāraṇa, liṅga,* and *sthūla-śarīra*. These are also known to the ancient Western traditions as *nous, psyche,* and *soma,* or as *mens, anima,* and *corpus*. In connection with these last, we should remember the strict relationship that was conceived between the spirit as daemon or double, and the "genius" as life and memory of a particular blood and a particular stock; a concept which, in its turn goes back to the Upaniṣadic "way of the fathers"—*pitṛ-yāna,* to the path that continually leads back to birth according to the law of craving and the nature of saṃsāric existence. The *anima,* according to the original concept, belongs to this very plane, it combines more or less with the "daemon" as an irrational entity; and even in the Buddhist texts dealing with the *prajñā-pāramitā,* the person or *anima (pudgala)* is often confused with this preformed principle that takes on existence as the life of a determined life, and holds together its elements; a principle that yet maintains itself as a separate energy, not bound to these elements, and that transmits itself through various lives.

In the texts of the oldest Buddhist canon (which is in Pāli), things are often presented in such a manner that the daemon or saṃsāric entity seems to be equivalent to *viññāṇa,* that is, to "consciousness," the third *nidāna*. In reality, the two things, as we have said, are quite distinct: the identification is explained by the fact that, through what we may call an elective affinity or a convergence, an identification is made between the force from above that is carried down by ignorance, and this entity made of desire: this identification is entirely analogous to the identification of the same entity with the material that the future parents offer for its new manifestation of craving. "Consciousness," *viññāṇa,* is not the "daemon"; it meets the "daemon," however, and identifies and joins itself with it at the moment when it achieves one of its individuations and incarnations; this requires, in fact, an already specified life-force and its craving. Thus, in the human compound there certainly exists a "daemon" that is the seat of a more than individual saṃsāric consciousness and to which

---

22. It was, moreover, already a Vedic idea (*Ṛg Veda,* 10.85.40) that the *gandharva,* the genius or double, found the wife before the husband.
23. L. de la Vallée-Poussin, *Bouddhisme: Études et matériaux* (Paris, 1909), pp. 25 ff.

there may also be attached memories, instincts, and causes of remote origin and this is the signification of the so-called *ālayaviññāṇa,* the "containing-consciousness" that receives all impressions both conscious and unconscious of a certain stock or current; yet there also exists in the human being a higher principle, but which ignorance and the *āsavā* have bewildered and obscured. This is a fundamental point, and if it is not kept in mind, large parts of the Buddhist ascesis will remain unintelligible.

It is said that at the point when the *antarābhava,* the daemon, enters the womb, and when the regrouping and solidification of the material elements begins around it, it "dies."[24] By this we must understand the cessation of the continuity of consciousness, and this means that one does not in the ordinary way remember prenatal and preconceptional states either saṁsāric or transcendental. It is a kind of rupture, for, starting from this point, the fourth *nidāna,* the interdependent correlation between consciousness and the psychophysical unity *(nāma-rūpa)* that individuates it, is established. For if consciousness, *viññāṇa,* must enter the mother's womb in order that "name-and-form" can originate, then there must, at the same time, be "name-and-form" so that consciousness can exist.[25]

In the texts we find the following simile for the relationship existing between the three principles: the seed is *viññāṇa,* consciousness, the earth is *kamma,* and the water that makes the seed grow into a plant is thirst. *Kamma* here is the force, already determined by the *sankhārā,* that corresponds to the "saṁsāric entity," into which the descending principle (seed) enters and is brought to a fresh existence because there is craving. Only in cases of exceptional "descents," "fatidic" in nature, of beings who, having removed ignorance to a certain degree, are in their substance mainly composed of "illumination" (*bodhi*—this is the literal sense of the expression *bodhisattva*), is the "vehicle" they use in place of the *antarābhava* or entity of craving, a "celestial body" or "body of splendor" *(tusita-kāya).* In these cases birth takes place without any dissolution of the continuity of consciousness; the individual is in perfect possession of himself, he is imperturbable and has vision; and for his nativity he has a choice of the place, the time, and the mother.[26]

Such views naturally reduce the implications of earthly biological heredity to merely relative importance. Heredity is considered here as something much vaster: as not only that which one inherits from one's ancestors, but also as that which comes from oneself and from antecedent identifications. Indeed, taking heredity comprehensively, only the latter is essential as far as the core of the human personality is concerned. From a higher point of view, to leave this heredity out of account would

---

24. Cf. G. Tucci, *Il buddhismo* (Foligno, 1926), p. 75.
25. Cf. *Dīgha,* 15.21–22.
26. Cf., e.g., *Majjh.,* 123; *Dīgha,* 14.1.17; *Bardo Thödol,* p. 191; *Angutt.,* 8.70.

be as absurd as thinking that chicks of different species are born only from eggs, without a corresponding animal heredity.[27] Returning to the symbolism of burning: if we wish to find the origin of the fire that burns with some particular log, it would be absurd to trace the origin of the log to the tree from which it came, and that to the forest to which it belonged, and so on—at the most we could only discover the quality of the fuel. The origin of the fire must, instead, be sought in the nature of the fire itself, not in that of the wood, by tracing the spark that lit the flame, and then the flame from which the spark came, and so on. Equally, the most essential and truly "direct" heredity of a being is not found in the genealogy of its earthly parents. For beings are heirs and sons of action and not of father and mother.[28] Besides one's own heredity of body and *soma*, there is saṁsāric heredity and, finally, there is one's heredity that is the principle "from above" clouded by "ignorance."

5. Returning to the chain of conditioned genesis, the states or *nidāna* that follow "name-and-form" refer to the internal side of embryonic development. As the fifth link of the series we have *ṣaḍ-āyatana*, that is (the assumption of) the sixfold base. By this is meant the sensory fields or strands in which, through "contact," the various sense impressions and the various images of the mind will burn. In the Indo-Aryan tradition there are always considered to be six senses, the five that we know, with the addition of *mano* (Skt.: *manas*), mind or thought. Far from being synonymous with "spirit," as many of our contemporaries believe, thought, subjective thought tied to the brain, is here considered as a sense *sui generis*, ranking more or less with the others. While it is not limited to coordinating and organizing the impressions derived from the senses, it is held that thought originates from special and subtle forms of "contact."

6–7. With the sixth *nidāna*, *phassa*, we pass from potentiality to actuality. *Phassa* literally means "contact" or "touch." It refers to all experience that, under particular stimuli, begins to burn or blaze up in each of the six sensory fields we have mentioned. For this reason the next *nidāna* is *vedanā*, feeling, the affective coloring of the perceptions, sensation as a whole. Here a new development begins, which we may regard as the manifestation, the igniting, of the, so to speak, transcendental mania that appears in the guise of that particular desire or attachment forming the substratum of a given being's experience in given surroundings.

8. The *nidāna* that immediately follows feeling is therefore thirst, *taṇhā*. This awakens in the various sensory fields, and is nourished by contact, exactly like the flame that—according to a text we have quoted—burns in every sense and includes the object, the sense organ, the contact, and the impression that follows from it, even when it is neither pleasurable nor painful but neutral.

27. Cf. H. C. Warren, *Buddhism in Translations* (Cambridge, Mass., 1909), p. 212.
28. Dahlke, *Buddh. als Weltansch.*, p. 61 [*Buddhism and Science*, p. 55].

9. And as "to burn" on this level is the same as "to be," but since the flame, in order to burn, needs material and depends on material and must have material, there follows the ninth *nidāna, upādāna.* The term, literally, means "to embrace": it is an acceptance, a coming into possession in the sense of attachment or dependence. Thus many have translated the word by "will" or by "affirmation" *(anunayo),* which is the opposite of detachment or rejection *(vinayo).* Therefore, just at this point the *ahamkāra,* the general category of the "belonging to self," *adhyātmika* (Pāli: *ajjhattika),* arises and comes into being: there arises the feeling of "I" or of the "person" *(sakkāya)* defined, by reference to this or that object, by the formula "this is mine, I am this, this is my self": here, then, take place the aggregations, the formation of the personality based on the five groups, which are once again: the group of materiality *(rūpa),* including all that falls under the dominion of the senses; the group of feeling *(vedanā);* the group of perceptions or representations or mental forms *(saññā);* the group of formations, tendencies, and, in general, volition *(sankhāra);* finally, the group of consciousness itself, in so far as it is determined, conditioned, and individuated *(viññāna).* It is said: "Attachment *(upādāna)* is not the same as the five groups of attachment; and neither is attachment outside the five groups of attachment. That which, in the five groups, is the cause of will, is affirmation, that is attachment."[29] Thus samsāric personality is not made up of these five groups, but of that which in them is "craving of will,"[30] of that which proceeds as the result of the fundamental element of the whole process, namely, thirst. This now joins with the craving of the "daemon," and, at the moment of satisfying itself through the contacts, determines dependence; while from dependence, in turn, proceed the anguish, the restlessness, and the fundamental fear of those who have not in themselves their own principle and who desperately cling to *sakkāya,* to the person, to the "I." On the subject of "attachment," there is said to exist a kind of brooding and watch over the feelings that are experienced, be they pleasant, unpleasant, or neither unpleasant nor pleasant, and a clinging to them. With this brooding and watch over the feelings and with this adherence to them, there arises satisfaction (in a special, transcendental sense for, as we have seen, the feelings may be entirely neutral); this satisfying of the feelings is attachment. Through this attachment originates "becoming."[31]

10. In fact, all the necessary conditions for the establishment of the person are

29. *Majjh.,* 109.
30. Ibid., 44.
31. Ibid., 38. In this connection we may here explain two important Buddhist notions: that of *sāsavā* and that of *prāpti* (Skt.). *Sāsavā,* from *āsava,* means the co-intoxicant, or everything that lends itself to a development of "mania" or original "intoxication"; it is extended to include both "good" and "bad" states, and only "that which is not included" and is not cointoxicant, and has the nature of pure transcendency (cf. *Dhammasang.,* 1103, 1104). As for *prāpti,* this signifies assumption or incorporation: it is the primary adhesion by which a tendency that one has acquired exists potentially, only awaiting the opportunity for appearing again, even when, through satisfaction, it seemed to have disappeared. Cf. below, p. 197–98.

now present, and with its actual becoming there occurs the act of synthesis for its definite solidification as an individual being, and of its "existence" in a literal sense: to stand or come out in an exteriorized existence. This constitutes the tenth *nidāna*, *bhava*, which literally means "becoming" and which has as its counterpart the next *nidāna*.

11. Birth, *jāti*, is often thought of also as a "descent."[32] From the fifth to the tenth *nidāna* we are concerned with states that develop in a complementary manner to embryonic life, starting from conception, with the determination of what in modern philosophy would be called the a priori categories of experience, that is, the modes in which this experience develops in space and time or in other conditions of existence. It is noteworthy that the doctrine in question does not limit itself to the case of human and terrestrial birth. Although it is evident that Buddhism has formulated the theory of conditioned genesis for this case in particular, yet, in general, the possibility of a birth—*jāti*, the eleventh *nidāna*—must be considered not only on the plane of animal generation, but also on that of "pure forms" *(rūpa)* or on the plane "free from form" *(arūpa)*.[33] In dealing with these cases, however, a modification of the preceding exposition is necessary here and there so as to conform to the different circumstances. It must be emphasized, however, that the Buddhist doctrine, like every really metaphysical teaching, goes far beyond the singular narrowness of outlook prevalent in the West, and considers that the human being is only one of many possible states of conditioned existence, just as individual human existence is only one of many possible forms of individual existence and, in itself, is simply a section of a current, of a *santāna*.

12. The last *nidāna* is *jarāmaraṇa*, that is, decay *(jarā* in this particular case meaning "old age") and death *(maraṇa)*. The inseparable complement to birth *(jāti)* is decay and death. *Omnia orta occidunt et aucta senescunt:* "becoming generates, the become grows old and dies."[34] According to the texts, not theoretically, but by direct experience, by an absolute liberating vision, the "clear, immaculate eye of truth" apprehends at a particular moment the meaning hidden in these words: "All that has origin has also an end."[35]

The chain of conditioned genesis has now gradually brought us to the world of contingency, of eternal impermanence, of agitation, of individuality, which is an illusion and purely a name, of life, which is mixed with death and which is parched by anguish and by radical privation or insufficiency; to the world in which there is no liberty, in which beings, in the grip of craving, either "leap hither and thither like

32. *Samyutt.,* 12.2.
33. Cf., e.g., *Majjh.,* 9.
34. Ibid., 1.
35. Ibid., 56; 74; *Dīgha,* 21.2.10.

hares caught in a snare,"[36] or are lost, as "arrows shot by night." In these terms, he who declared that he was able to "explain all life from its foundations"[37] has expressed the teaching that comprises the first two truths of the Ariya, that is *dukkha*, agitation as the root of all suffering, and its underlying *taṇhā*, craving or desire.

Now that we have referred to the various possibilities of "birth," we must emphasize that while Buddhism recognizes the existence of another world, or rather, of other worlds, of other conditions of existence beyond this world, these celestial worlds are also considered subject to *dukkha*. Divine entities *(deva)* exist in their hierarchies like those of the angels of Western theology, but they are not immortal beings. Although their existence may be indefinitely long compared with the life of a man *(devā dīghāyukā)* yet even for them there will be *jarāmaraṇa*, decline and dying. This is to be understood in the sense of the general Hindu teaching on the cyclical laws of the cosmic periods in which was put forward the alternate reabsorption and emanation of all manifested forms, including the highest, into the unmanifested principle, superior and anterior to them all. We know also that the ancient Western traditions, with their doctrine of the aeons, of the *saecula* and of the cosmic years, were acquainted with similar views.

In passing, it is worth mentioning that there occurs in Buddhism a personification of the *princeps hujus mundi* in the shape of Māra. If Māra is etymologically derived from Mṛtyu, the ancient god of death, here he appears as the power that stands at the root of the whole saṁsāric existence, asserting himself wherever there is passive identification, attachment, bond of desire, satisfaction, on whatever plane of existence or in whatever "world," even, therefore, in the spiritual world.[38] Māra, who has three daughters—Taṇhā, Rati, and Arati, that is, craving, love, and hate—is he who sows the pastures where beings, once enticed, satisfy themselves; but in the moment of their satisfaction they fall into his power[39] and, paralyzed by mania, reenter without rest the flux of transient existence.[40] Māra is also an incarnation of the ephemeral character of saṁsāric existence, and therefore, as the god of death, when the moment comes he surprises people and carries them off, while they are busy with this or that, "like the inundation of a sleeping village."[41] Māra is closely related to "ignorance." He can act so long as he remains unknown. "This man knows me not"—this is the condition under which he works. The moment the unclouded eye perceives him, however, his power becomes paralyzed.[42]

---

36. *Dhammapada*, 342.
37. *Majjh.*, 11.
38. *Saṁyutt.*, 22.63; 35.114; *Mahāvagga (Vin.)*, 1.11.
39. *Itivuttaka*, 14.
40. *Majjh.*, 25.
41. *Dhammapada*, 287.
42. *Mahāvagga (Vin.)*, 1.11.2; 1.13.2; *Majjh.*, 49, etc.

The great practical significance of the doctrine of *paticca-samuppāda* lies in the fact that, through it we see that the conditioned and contingent world does not exist as something absolute, but is itself, in its turn, conditioned, contingent; it is the effect of a process in which extraneous causes do not figure; a change, therefore, or a removal or a destruction is always possible.[43] Created by deeds, the conditioned forms of existence can be dissolved by deeds. Buddhist teaching considers, besides the descending series of the "formations" from ignorance—called the "false road"—the ascending series of the dissolutions, called the "right road."[44] While in the first series, resulting from ignorance the *sankhāra* are formed, and from these, "consciousness," from consciousness, "name-and-form," and so on to birth, decline, suffering, and death—in the second series, when "ignorance" is destroyed, the *sankhāra* are destroyed; when the *sankhāra* are destroyed, "consciousness" is destroyed, and so on to the conditioned removal of the ultimate effects, that is, of birth, decline, suffering, and death, or in other words, the law of samsāric existence.[45]

It can now be understood why the attainment of the truth of conditioned genesis by Prince Siddhattha—the truth, that is, that *samsāra* "is" not, but "is become"—was conceived of by him as a liberating illumination: "'It is become, it is become': as something never heard before, this knowledge arose in me, vision arose in me, intuition arose in me, wisdom arose in me, light arose in me." And it was also said on this same occasion: "When the real nature of things is made clear to the ardent, meditating ascetic, then all his doubts fall away, having realized what this nature is and what is it cause."[46] And again: "When the real nature of things is made clear to the ardent, meditating ascetic, he arises and scatters the ranks of Māra, like the sun which lights the sky."[47] At this point the samsāric demonism comes to an end.

Now that the descending chain of the twelve *nidāna* has taken us to the plane of samsāric existence lived by a finite being, we can consider the other interpretation of these same *nidāna* that we have called "horizontal." We must now subdivide the twelve *nidāna* into four groups and refer them to more than one individual existence. The first group will then consist of the first two *nidāna* (*avijjā* and *sankhāra*), which correspond to a samsāric heredity come to a particular being from another life. Avijjā, unawareness, then refers to the "four truths," and it means the unawareness both of the contingency of the world and of the way out of it, while the *sankhāra* are the predispositions created in a previous life lived in this ignorance. The second group refers, instead, to present existence and includes the three *nidāna*, "consciousness,"

---

43. *Samyutt.*, 12.1ff, 20.
44. Ibid., 12.3.
45. *Mahāvagga (Vin.)*, 1.1.2.
46. Ibid., 1.1.3.
47. Ibid., 1.1.7.

"name-and-form," and "base of the six senses," all connected with the formation and development of the new life that takes on this heredity. The third group consists of the four *nidāna:* "contact," "sensations," "thirst," and "attachment" and refers to the normal life of the average man insofar as this confirms the saṁsāric state of existence by nourishing the preexisting craving on further craving and by generating, through thoughts and actions, energies that will appear in a new life. Finally, the last three *nidāna:* "(new) becoming," "birth," and "decay and death" refer to this new life being, as it were, effects.[48] In regard to this interpretation, individual explanations of some of the *nidāna* are as follows: ignorance is ignorance of the four truths; the *sankhāra* are the formations or predispositions manifesting in the three fields of deed, word, and thought; consciousness—*viññāna*—is the consciousness that relates to the sixfold base (to the six senses); "name-and-form" is the psychophysical whole of the living man; contacts and feeling again refer to sensory experience; finally, *upādāna* is attachment to desire, or opinions, or belief in the "I," or belief in the miraculous efficacy of rules and rites.[49]

Although this "horizontal" interpretation should be kept in mind in order to clarify certain canonical contexts, it must be remembered that in character it is lower and more external than the other vertical and transcendental interpretation, since it refers exclusively to the saṁsāric plane; nor can it claim to be completely coherent. For example, it is difficult to see why "becoming," "birth," and "decay and death" are not included in the middle group, which refers to present existence, but apply instead to a successive existence, almost as if they were not valid either for the present life or for that in which ignorance and the *sankhāra* are placed; as if the successive existence did not again contain ignorance and the *sankhāra*, consciousness, sixfold base, etc., that is, the *nidāna* that are referred only to a previous existence or to the present existence that takes its heredity from the previous existence. The fact that the majority of Orientalists, in spite of this, have halted at this second interpretation without becoming aware of these incoherencies, only shows the superficiality of their minds and their complete lack of metaphysical sensibility.

Once the doctrine of *paticca-samuppāda* has been understood as indicating the conditioned nature of saṁsāric existence, then, as we have said, the third and fourth truths of the Ariya follow directly. The third postulates the possibility of destroying the state generated through the twelve *nidāna;* and the fourth concerns the method by which this possibility can be realized and leads up to the achievement of awakening and illumination.

As a practical ascetic presupposition, the principle of immanence is valid here.

48. This is the interpretation mainly followed by Nyāṇatiloka in his edition of the *Anguttara-nikāya*, vol. 1, p. 291.
49. *Saṁyutt.*, 12.2.

It is suggestively expressed in an allegorical story about the "world's end." One of the Buddha's interlocutors says that he was once carried—with magical rapidity—further and further on without succeeding in reaching the end of the world. The Buddha replies: "One can not, by walking, reach the end of the world"—and immediately passes to the symbolical significance by adding: "where there is no birth nor decadence nor death nor rising nor perishing." By walking, by going—that is, along *samsāra*—one does not find the end of the world. For it is in oneself. The world ends when the intoxications or manias, the *āsava*, are destroyed. And here the principle is stated: "In this fathom-length body, furnished with perception and consciousness, there is contained the world, the arising of the world the end of the world, and the path which leads to the end of the world."[50] The body taken as a whole is the concrete center of the samsāric experience of the world, yet both in its physical and in its invisible, hidden sides all the *nidāna* are immanent. We can, however, find the roots of this experience and, furthermore, the powers that can eventually cut off these roots, and are thus enabled to transform one mode of being into another.

In this connection the power of the "mind" is often emphasized; mind, that is, in a general sense, and not just psychological faculties. "What we are is the result of our thoughts mind is the foundation of all our conditions; they are mind-made."[51] "The world is guided by consciousness, drawn along by consciousness, subject to the power of consciousness that has arisen."[52] It is the mind that "deceives man and kills his body." Because of it, there "exists all that has a form." "The mind, our destiny, and our life, these three things are closely connected. The mind directs and guides, and determines our destiny here below, on which depends our life: thus, in a mutual perennial succession."[53] But the mind depends on the man: it may lead him to the world of agitation and impermanence, yet to it Prince Siddhattha owed his awakening, his becoming a Buddha.[54]

We have now discussed all the necessary assumptions for the Buddhist ascesis, both as ascesis in general and as the Ariyan Doctrine of Awakening.

---

50. *Angutt.*, 4.45; 4.46; 9.38.
51. *Dhammapada*, 1.
52. *Angutt.*, 4.186; *Saṁyutt.*, 1.7.
53. *Mahāparinirv.*, 64.
54. Ibid.

7

❧

Determination of the Vocations

The Buddhist Way, as a whole, is signposted by *samatha* and *vipassanā*. *Samatha* must be understood as an unshakable calm, which is gained with the help of various disciplines, particularly of mental concentration and control of thought and conduct; in attaining it, we still remain in the domain of an ascesis which, as we have said, need not in itself imply any transcendental realization and which, therefore, may also be regarded as a form of mastery and as an acquisition of strength for one who remains and acts in the world. *Vipassanā*, on the other hand, indicates "knowledge"— clear perception, making for detachment, of the essence of saṁsāric life and of its contingency and irrationality: the noble, penetrating knowledge "which perceives rise and fall." If to this "knowledge" is added the calm and the control of *samatha*, then its development is assured and transfigured, and the result is the ascesis that leads to awakening. In any case, these two factors are such that they reciprocally integrate each other.[1] *Vipassanā* is the indispensable condition for liberation.

The point of departure therefore consists in arousing this "knowledge" to some extent. In this connection we can speak of a real and positive determination of vocations. It is a widely held opinion that Buddhist "preaching" had a "universal" character. This is an error—it may be true superficially, and of later and altered forms of the doctrine, but not of essentials. Buddhism is essentially aristocratic. We can see this in the legendary story in the canonical texts where the divinity Brahmā Sahampati, in order to induce Prince Siddhattha not to keep to himself the knowledge he had obtained, points out to him the existence of "beings of a nobler kind" capable of understanding it. The Buddha himself finally recognizes this, in these terms: "And I saw, looking at the world with the awakened eye, beings of noble kind and of common kind, acute of mind and obtuse of mind, well endowed and ill endowed, quick to

1. Cf. *Angutt.*, 5.92–94.

73

understand and slow to understand, and many who consider that enthusiasm for other worlds is bad." There follows a simile: as some lotus flowers grow in deep, muddy water, as others push up toward the surface of the water, yet others "emerge from the water and stand up, free from the water"—thus there are, in contrast to the mass of people, beings of a nobler kind.[2] They are, in other words, those who hold fast, who have not been entirely blinded by "ignorance," but who preserve a memory of the origins. Water, moreover, is a general traditional symbol of inferior nature that is bound to passion and becoming—whence, be it noted in passing, is derived the symbolism used by Buddhism of the man who walks on the "waters" without sinking down in them, or of the man who crosses the waters.

It is, then to an elite that Buddhism originally addressed its Doctrine of Awakening; a doctrine that is, in fact, a touchstone. Only the "noble natures," the "noble sons" react positively. This is now the place to discuss the problem of the "vocations."

Let us consider first the idea of "renunciation," which is, in some ways, the key to the whole ascesis. "Renunciation" may have many different meanings, depending on circumstances. There is a renunciation of an inferior kind, which is the one that—as we said at the beginning—recurs in the ascetic forms that have developed in the West since the decline of the ancient classical and Aryan world. This renunciation signifies "mortification"; it means painful separation from things and pleasures that are still desired; it is a kind of masochism, of taste for suffering not entirely unmixed with an ill-concealed resentment against all forms of health, strength, wisdom, and virility. This kind of renunciation, in fact, has often been the strength, born of necessity, of the world's disinherited, of those who do not fit in with their surroundings or with their own body or with their own race or tradition and who hope, by means of renunciation, to assure for themselves a future world where, to use a Nietzschean expression, the inversion of all values will occur. In other cases, the motive for renunciation is mainly supplied by a religious vision: the "love of God" induces renunciation and detachment from the joys of the world; a detachment that even here keeps, in the most favorable circumstances, its painful and almost violent character with regard to all that one would naturally tend to wish and desire. The fact that asceticism is generally associated, in the West, with such attitudes is one of the many consequences of the low level to which, as we have already mentioned, the "Dark Age," *kali-yuga*, had fallen.

The Ariya type of renunciation, presupposed by the Buddhist Doctrine of Awakening, is of a very different character. Even the term normally used—*paviveka, viveka*—means detachment, scission, separation, aloofness, without any particular

---

2. *Majjh.*, 26; *Mahāvagga (Vin.)*, 1.5.2–12; *Angutt.*, 4.36, where the simile is applied to the Awakened One himself and is continued with the following addition: "Thus I also, born in the world, grown up in the world, have overcome the world and stand, untouched by the world."

affective tone.[3] Apart from this, the example of the Buddha himself is decisive. He left the world and took to the ascetic road, not as one forced to reject the world through necessity, indigence, or dangers[4], but as the son of a king, a prince, "in the first flower of life," healthy, endowed with "happy youth," possessing all that he could desire.[5] Neither religious visions of any description, nor hopes of a hereafter played any part in his decision: it came inevitably from the firm reaction of a "noble spirit" to the lived experience of saṁsāric existence. One text, here, is quite definite: it says that, on the path of the Ariya renunciation is not made by reason of the "four misfortunes": disease, disasters, old age, or the loss of dear ones—but by reason of the knowledge that the world is contingent, that one is alone and without help in it, that it is not one's own, and finally, that it is in the grip of an eternal insufficiency, unsated and burning with thirst.[6]

It is now easy to see how exoteric and popular are some of the views ascribed to the doctrine. Such views have led some Westerners to the conclusion that Buddhism begins and ends by showing that "the world is pain" and hence appealing to man's natural tendency to flee pain until he is induced to prefer the "nothing." For the same reason the legend of the four meetings—according to which Prince Siddhattha was persuaded to renounce the world after seeing a newborn baby, a sick man, an old man, and a dead man—is to be taken with great reserve. Causes such as these can only occasionally produce a reaction, which in any case will eventually transcend them. And the same must be said of the more general theme of the "divine messengers"—consisting likewise of new-birth, disease, old age, and death: through failure to understand their message one would be destined to the "infernal regions."[7]

This is only superstructure. The essential, rather, is to confront a man with a relentless analysis of himself, of the conditioned nature of common existence in this world, or any other world, and to ask him: "Can you say: this am I? Can you really identify yourself with this? Is it this that you wish?" This is the moment of fundamental testing, this is the touchstone for distinguishing the "noble beings" from average

---

3. Cf. *Angutt.*, 3.92. It should be noted in this passage how detachment occurs as a result of the presence of a *positive* element—it states: since one's own conduct is right, false conduct is got rid of; since one possesses true understanding, false understanding is got rid of; since the manias are shut out, the manias are got rid of.

4. *Majjh.*, 68.

5. Ibid.; this describes all that Prince Siddhattha is supposed to have enjoyed, although with an intentional exaggeration, cf. *Angutt.*, 3.38.

6. *Majjh.*, 75; 82.

7. *Majjh.*, 130; *Angutt.*, 3.35. It is easy to see that the references to the infernal regions that are found in these texts are simply popular references, without logical connection with the central ideas expressed there. The "divine messengers" can only impress on the mind that terrestrial life is finite and contingent; one cannot see why those who either do not see the messengers or who limit themselves to taking note of that truth without deducing any special consequence, that is, by accepting contingent life as such, should be punished with all sorts of fantastic torments hereafter.

beings; it is here that they are separated according to their natures; it is thus that their vocations are decided. The test in Buddhism has various stages: from the most immediate forms of experience the disciple proceeds to higher levels, to supersensible horizons, to universality, to celestial worlds,[8] where the question is repeated: Are you this? Can you identify yourself with this? Can you satisfy yourself in this? Is this all that you wish? The noble being always ends by answering in the negative. And then the "revolution" occurs. The disciple leaves his home, renounces the world, and takes the ascetic path.

This clearly shows the significance of the other renunciation, the Ariya renunciation. This is based on "knowledge" and is accompanied by a gesture of disdain and a feeling of transcendental dignity; it is qualified by the superior man's will for the unconditioned, by the will, that is, of a man of a quite special "race of spirit." Such a man, then, does not reject life—life that is interwoven with death—for "mortification," thereby doing violence to his own being, but because it is too little for him, and when he remembers himself, he feels it to be inadequate to his real nature. At such a moment it is *natural* to renounce, to cut oneself off, to stop taking part in the game. The only feeling there can be is one of scorn, when a man becomes aware that he has been deceived and finally discovers the author of the deception: it is like the blind man who, while seeking a clean white cloak, but, being unable to see, is given and accepts a discolored and filthy one, and who, when his eyes are opened, is horrified and turns against the man who had made him wear it and who had profited by his blindness. "For a long time, indeed, I was deluded, deceived, and defrauded by my heart."[9] On the path of awakening, the point of departure is *positive:* it is not the forcible bending of a human being who is only conscious of being a man, aided and abetted by religious images and apocalyptic, messianic, or superterrestrial visions; it is rather, an impulse that springs from the supernatural element in oneself that— although it has been obscured during the passage of time—still survives in "noble beings" beyond their saṁsāric nature, like the lotus that, poised above the water, is free from the water. These are the beings who, according to a text, gradually realize that the world unveiled by ascesis is their natural place, "the land of their fathers," and that the other world—this world—is, instead, a foreign land to them.[10]

A short time ago we referred to a "quite special race of spirit." We must explain this point and, together with it, the specific place of the Ariya. The touchstone, as we have said, is the vision of universal impermanence, of *dukkha* and *anattā*. Now, it is *not* said that the realization that something is impermanent is *eo ipso* a motive for detachment from and renunciation of it. This depends, rather, on what we have else-

---

8. For the series of objects of possible identification see *Majjh.*, 1.

9. *Majjh.*, 75; *Dhammapada*, 153–54.

10. *Jātaka*, 168.

where called the "race of the spirit," which is at least as important as that of the body.[11] Here are some examples. A "telluric" spirit may consider as quite natural a dark self-identification with becoming and with its elementary forces, to such an extent that it does not even become aware of its tragic aspect—as sometimes occurs among the Negroes, savage peoples, and even among certain Slavs. A "Dionysian" spirit may consider universal impermanence of little account, opposing to it *carpe diem*, the joy of the moment, the rapture of a corruptible being who enjoys from instant to instant corruptible things, a joy so much the more acute in that—as the well-known song of the Renaissance has it—*"di doman non v'è certezza."* A "lunar" spirit, religiously inclined, may in its turn see in the contingency of life an atonement or a test, in face of which it should behave with humility and resignation, having faith in the impenetrable divine will and maintaining the feeling of being a "creature" created by it out of nothing. By others still this death of ours is considered as a completely natural and final phenomenon, the thought of which should not for a moment disturb a life turned toward earthly aspirations. Finally, a "Faustian," "titanic," or Nietzschean spirit may profess "tragic heroism," may *desire* becoming, and may even desire the "eternal return." And so on. From these examples, it is easily seen that "knowledge" produces "detachment" only in the case of a particular race of spirit, of that which in a special sense we have called "heroic" and which is not unconnected with the theory of the *bodhisatta*. Only in those in whom this race survives and who *wish* it, can the spectacle of universal contingency be the principle of awakening, can it determine the choice of the vocations, can it arouse the reaction that follows from "No, I want no more of it," from "This does not belong to me, I am not this, this is not my self" extended to all states of saṁsāric existence. The work, then, has one single justification: it must be done, that is to say, for the noble and heroic spirit there is no other alternative. *Katam karaṇīyam*—"that which has to be done has been done"—this is the universally recurring formula that refers to the Ariya who have destroyed the *āsava* and achieved awakening.

At this point *anattā*, the doctrine that denies the reality of the "I," shows us a further aspect. The meaning of this doctrine here is simply that in the "current" and in the contingent aggregation of states and functions which are normally considered as "I," it is impossible to recognize the true self, the supersensible *ātmā* of the preceding Upaniṣadic speculation; this true self is considered as practically nonexistent for the common man. Buddhism does not say: the "I" does not exist—but rather: one thing only is certain, that nothing belonging to saṁsāric existence and personality has the nature of "I." This is explicitly stated in the texts.

---

11. On the theory of the "races of the spirit," see our *Sintesi di dottrina della razza* (Milan, 1941), pp. 113–70 from which is taken the terminology of the phrases to follow.

This is the scheme. The Buddha repeatedly makes his questioner recognize that the bases of common personality—materiality, feeling, perception, the formations, consciousness—are changeable, impermanent, and nonsubstantial. After which, the question is asked: Can what is impermanent, changeable, and nonsubstantial be considered thus: this is mine, this am I, this is my self? The answer is always the same— as if it were perfectly natural and obvious—Certainly not, Lord. The conclusion is then more or less of this type: "All matter, all feeling, all perception, all formations, all consciousness, past, present, or future, internal or external, gross or subtle, low or high, far or near, all should be considered, in conformity with reality and with perfect wisdom, thus: 'This is not mine, this am I not, this is not my self.' Thus considering, the wise, noble disciple does not identify himself with materiality, does not identify himself with feeling, does not identify himself with perception, does not identify himself with the formations, does not identify himself with consciousness. Not identifying himself, he is detached. Being detached, he is freed."[12] The same theme has several variations in the canon, but the sense and the scheme are always the same. It is quite clear: that all the probative force of reason is a function of this implicit presmise: that by "I" we can only understand the unconditioned, that is to say, something that has nothing whatsoever to do with saṁsāric consciousness or with its formations. Only then do the texts become clear and logical. Only then can it be seen, for example, how it is that what is impermanent should always appear also as painful, and how this latter correlation is established: "That which is painful is void of 'I'; that which is void of 'I,' I am not, it is not mine, it is not my self—thus it is apprehended, in conformity with reality and with perfect wisdom."[13] Only in this way can we understand the passage from the ascertainment to a reaction and an imperative: recognizing the impermanence of the elements, of the groups of craving, of the senses, being convinced that they are not "I," being convinced that "they are in flames," the "wise Ariyan disciple" feels disgust; disgusted, he becomes detached; being detached, he is freed: he has had enough of form, of finite consciousness, of feelings, of the other *khandha,* of objects, of contacts, of the emotive states that proceed from them, whether they are pleasant, painful, or neutral; he becomes indifferent in face of them and he seeks their ending.[14] Here is a saying: What is impermanent, what is *anattā,* what is compounded and conditioned, this does not belong to you, you should not desire it, you should put it away—"the putting away of it will be greatly to your benefit, will lead to your well being": there can be no joy in it nor desire for it.[15] It is clear that all this will not be sufficient evidence for everyone. The tacit but indis-

12. *Majjh.,* 22; 109.
13. *Saṁyutt.,* 22.15; cf. 16 and 17, 49, 59, 76; 35.2, 3.
14. Ibid., 22.61, 9; 35.3, 12; *Mahāvagga (Vin.),* 1.21.4.
15. *Saṁyutt.,* 22.33; 23.25–33.

pensable prerequisite is a higher consciousness. When this dawns, then in an entirely natural manner, not from painful renunciation or "mortification," but almost accompanied by an Olympian bearing of the spirit, there occurs *viveka*, detachment.[16] Realizing this higher consciousness, it is said that one who attempts to find an "I" or something similar to the "I" *(attena vā attaniyena)* in the sphere of the senses is like a man who, when looking for heartwood, approaches a large tree and cuts it down but who, although not taking the trunk or new wood or branches, takes only the bark where there is no core and certainly none of the hard wood that he is seeking.[17] The "I," then, is like this hard primordial essential substance, and *this* "I" is the fundamental point of reference for Buddhism.

There is more to it than this. In speaking of "Olympian bearing" and of detachment we should not think of something like the indifference of a badly understood Stoicism. The Ariyan "renunciation" is fundamentally based on a will for the unconditioned considered also as liberty and power. This is apparent from the texts. The Buddha, while challenging the opinion that the stems of ordinary personality are self, asks his interlocutor if a powerful sovereign wishing to execute or proscribe one of his subjects could do so. The answer is naturally, yes. Then the Buddha asks: "You who say: 'materiality is my self,' do you now think that you have this power over materiality: 'Thus let my materiality be, thus let my materiality not be'?"—and the question is repeated for the other elements of the personality. The interlocutor is forced to answer no, and thus this view that the "I" is materiality, feeling, and so on comes to be confuted.[18] The basic idea is in no doubt here: not only the simple fact that body, feeling, consciousness, etc., are changeable, but that this changeability is independent of the "I," that it is such that, in the normal way, in saṁsāric existence, the "I" has little or no control over it—it is this fact that demands the statement "I am not this, this is not mine, this is not my self." On this is based the saying: "Renounce what does not belong to you."[19] This argument recurs in other passages. In particular it occurs in the second exposition of the doctrine given by Prince Siddhattha at Benares: "If materiality were the 'I,' it would not be subject to disease, and regarding it one could say: 'Let my materiality be thus, let my materiality not be thus.' But since materiality is subject to disease, and since one cannot say regarding it: 'Let my materiality be thus, let my materiality not be thus,' therefore materiality is not the 'I'";[20] and the same formula is repeated for the other *khandhā*. Elsewhere we find the attributes "powerless," "falling," "feeble," "infirm" associated with impermanence, *anicca*. It is by

16. Cf. *Majjh.,* 106.
17. Ibid., 29.
18. *Majjh.,* 35.
19. Ibid., 22.
20. *Mahāvagga (Vin.)* 1.6.38, 39–41; *Saṁyutt.,* 22.59.

considering these particular characteristics that attachment vanishes and the identification provoked by mania is interrupted.[21]

The correspondence of the Buddhist view with that of archaic Greece should be noted here. It is the eternal "privation" *(στέ ησις)*, the eternal impotence of things that become, that "are and are not," that brings about renunciation. "By recognizing that matter is impotent, unsatisfied, miserable, and that so are feeling, perception, the formations, and consciousness, by perceiving that in them that determines the clinging tendencies of the mind: by reflecting, destroying, abandoning it and by becoming detached from it, I know that the mind is liberated"—so says the ascetic.[22] One who considers materiality as self or materiality as belonging to self, or self as in materiality, or materiality as in self—continues the text—is like a man, carried off by a powerful alpine torrent, who believes he can save himself by grasping the grass or weak rushes on the banks.[23] He will be dragged away.

On these grounds we can speak, in connection with Buddhist realization, of a will not only for liberation, but also for liberty, unconditionedness and unbreakability. One of the more common descriptions of an ascetic is that he is a man who, having broken each and every bond, is free. The ascetic is one who avoids the snare, as does a wild beast, and so does not fall into the power of the hunter, but "can go where he will"—while the others, those who are subject to craving, "can be called lost, ruined, fallen into the power of harm."[24] The ascetic is one who has gained mastery over himself, who "has his heart in his power, and is not himself in the power of his heart."[25] He is the master of his thoughts. "Whatever thought he desires, that thought will he think, whatever thought he does not desire, that thought will he not think."[26] As a perfectly tamed elephant, led by his mahout, will go in any direction; as an expert charioteer, with a chariot ready on good ground at a crossroad and harnessed to a thoroughbred team, can guide the chariot where he wishes; or as a king or a prince with a chest full of clothes, may freely choose the garment that most pleases him for the morning, the afternoon, or the evening—so the ascetic can direct his mind and his being toward one state or another with perfect freedom.[27] Here are a few more similes: the ascetic is like a man burdened with debts, yet he not only pays them off but manages to gain a surplus on which to build his own life; or he is like a man enfeebled by disease, his body without strength, but who succeeds in removing the disease and regaining his strength; or, he is like a slave, dependent on others, but

21. Cf. *Majjh.*, 75; 74.
22. *Majjh.*, 112.
23. *Saṁyutt.*, 22.93.
24. *Majjh.*, 25.
25. Ibid., 32.
26. *Angutt.*, 4.35; *Majjh.*, 20.
27. *Majjh.*, 119; 32.

who is able to free himself from his slavery and feel master of himself, independent of others, a free man who can go where he will; or, again, he is like a man traveling through desert places, full of snares and dangers, who yet arrives safe and sound at his destination without losing anything.[28] To complete the list of what a noble spirit regards as valuable, let us remember these other epithets of the Awakened One: "he who has laid down the burden," the "unshackled one," the "unhooked one," the "escaped one," the "unhinger," the "remover of the arrow," the "leveller of the trench," "he who escapes from the whirlwind." The whirlwind is a synonym for the faculties of craving;[29] the arrow should be understood as the burning, the thirst for living, which has deeply wounded and poisoned the higher principle; the trench is *saṁsāra,* which appears here with the same meaning that "becoming" and "matter" possessed in the ancient Hellenic concept: Penia, perennial insufficiency and "privation," inability of self-fulfillment, or, in the symbolism of Oknos: a cord that while being woven is continually consumed.[30]

It is thus that "the noble sons moved by confidence" recognize their vocation and come to apprehend the "Ariyan quest": "Thus, O disciples, a man, himself subject to birth, observing the misery of this law of nature, seeks that which is without birth, the incomparable safety, extinction; himself subject to decay, observing the misery of this law of nature, seeks that which is without decay, the incomparable safety, extinction; himself subject to death, observing the misery of this law of nature, seeks that which is without death, the incomparable safety, extinction; himself subject to pain and to agitation, observing the misery of this law of nature, seeks that which is without pain, the without-agitation, the incomparable safety, extinction; himself subject to stain, observing the misery of this law of nature, seeks that which is without stain, the incomparable safety, extinction. This, O disciples, in the Ariyan quest."[31]

Returning to the problem of the determination of the vocations, we have said that the touchstone consists in the identification or nonidentification of oneself with a whole hierarchy of modes of being, and the point of departure—*anattā*—has already been implicitly indicated. Nonidentification of oneself not only with materiality, with feeling, with perception, with the formations, but nonidentification also with consciousness itself, if regarded as individuated consciousness—that is to say, the overcoming of the belief in "personality," *attānudiṭṭhi,* and in its persistency—this is the first test put to the noble nature.[32] To remain in this belief is a sign of a form of "ignorance" (the "ignorance" whose transcendental base, in the conditioned

28. Ibid., 39.
29. *Saṁyutt.,* 25.200.
30. *Majjh.,* 22.
31. Ibid., 26.
32. *Majjh.,* 44; 64.

genesis, is *viññāṇa*) and of being subject to one of the "five lower fetters."[33] One places oneself at a distance until there is a feeling that one's own person is a simple instrument of expression, something contingent that in due course will dissolve and disappear in the saṁsāric current, without the supermundane, Olympian nucleus in ourselves being in the slightest degree prejudiced. The doctrine of the inessentiality of the person, of the psychological and passional "I," must then result in a mind that becomes pacified, serene, uplifted, clarified.[34] It should not be a cause of dismay, but a source of superior strength. It is said that only the man who has experienced this doctrine has strength enough to cross the eddying current and to reach the further shore in safety; a weak man, who is incapable of this, is one whose mind has not been liberated by the working of the doctrine.[35] Therefore: consciousness must not be considered as one's self, nor one's self as possessed of consciousness, nor consciousness as in one's self, nor one's self as in consciousness—any more than one should so consider the other *khandhā:* feeling, perception, and the formations.[36]

Second point: The road toward any pantheistic promiscuity, any naturalistic mysticism, any confusion with the universe, any variety of immanency, must be resolutely barred. The aim of this further test of the noble spirit is to set it definitely at a distance from the confused spiritual world that is characteristic of many Western minds, decayed from all that is classical, clear, Doric, virile. It is a singular fact that, in the modern world, this pantheistic disintegration, this return of man to a state of mind confused by total reality or by "Life," is habitually considered to be a characteristic of the Eastern mentality, particularly of the Hindu. The fact of the existence and diffusion in the East of the Buddhist Doctrine of Awakening is sufficient to confute this opinion. Even if in pre-Buddhist India—and particularly with the later speculation on the Brāhman—this false development was to a certain degree prevalent (and it occurs again, later, in some popular forms of Hinduism)—yet it is to be considered as an anomaly, against which Buddhism together with Sāṁkhya afforded a salutary reaction. Similar phenomena occur, moreover, in the ancient Mediterranean world with the decline of the earlier Olympian and heroic traditions. This is a general phenomenon, and talk of "Oriental pantheism" should be left either to the uninstructed or to people of bad faith.

Therefore: antipantheism. "To take nature as nature, to think nature, to think of nature, to think 'nature is mine'" is to exult in it; to take unity or multiplicity, this or that cosmic or elemental force, and finally to take all as all, to think all, to think of all, to think "all is mine" is to exult in it—this pantheistic identification is, for Buddhism,

---

33. Ibid., 64.
34. *Saṁyutt.*, 22.45.
35. *Majjh.*, 64.
36. Ibid., 44.

yet another sign of "ignorance," a mark of one who "has known nothing," of one who is "a common man, without understanding for the doctrine of the Ariya, inaccessible by the doctrine of the Ariya."[37]

On this basis we can say more generally that the Buddhist Doctrine of Awakening demands an antimystical vocation. It is true that the term *mystikos*—from μυηῖν, "to close," "to lock" (in particular, the lips)—originally referred to the Mysteries and alluded to what is secret, hidden, not to be spoken. The current sense of the term is, however, quite different: today mysticism is used for the tendency toward confused identifications, with emphasis on the moment of feeling and with none on the element of "knowledge" and "clarity"; "experience" is certainly accentuated (usually in the face of dogma and tradition), but here it is prevalently an experience in which the sidereal and absolute nucleus in the being is dissolved, submerged, or "transported." For this reason, mystical ineffability, far from being connected with a really transcendental knowledge, is of those who—to use Schelling's apt expression—in their confused identification with one state or another, not only do not explain experience, but become themselves subjects in need of explanation. Thus, the mystical element, rather than being superrational, is often subrational. We are in the playground of the spiritual adventures that take place on the borders either of the devotional religions or of pantheistic evasions, whose manner is the opposite of that of a strict ascesis and of the path of awakening of the Ariya.

Third point: In the modern world, those who fight the doctrines of immanence and who conceive themselves "defenders of the West" against "Oriental pantheism," normally take "transcendency" as their point of reference and as their watchword. Their transcendency is, however, very relative, as it proceeds from the predominant theological-theistic concept. Even in this Buddhism finds a touchstone for the vocations. We have already seen that Prince Siddhattha was induced to divulge his knowledge after recognizing that, side by side with common beings, there are nobler ones and "many who consider that enthusiasm for other worlds is bad." The Doctrine of Awakening is presented as a doctrine that teaches men to make themselves free not only of the material "I," but also of the immaterial and spiritual "I."[38] Any form of moral conduct and any practice or rite whose motive is hope in a posthumous continuation of the personality is considered to be another of the lower fetters.[39] Thus, beyond a rabble of faint-hearted, restless, obtuse, and unvirile penitents,[40] the texts speak of ascetics and priests who "through fear of existence, through hate of existence, go round and round existence, almost as a dog, tied with a leash to

---

37. *Majjh.,* 1.
38. *Dīgha,* 9.41–43.
39. *Majjh.,* 16.
40. Ibid., 107.

a solid column or attached to a post, goes round and round this column or post."[41] The words become stronger when they deal with those ascetics or priests who "profess attachment to the hereafter" and who think: "Thus shall we be after death, thus shall we not be after death," just as a merchant, going to market, thinks: "From this I shall get that, with this I shall gain that."[42] Plotinus, speaking against moralistic concept, said: "Not to be a good man, but to become a god—this is the aim,"[43] but the Doctrine of Awakening goes still further.

Beyond the human bond is the divine bond, attachment to this or that state, to a state that is no longer human, corporeal, or terrestrial, but that is still conditioned existence. These states in the Hindu tradition are personified in the various gods and in their seats; they are equivalent to the seraphic and angelic hierarchies of Judeo-Christian theology, therefore, to what, in a more popular concept, is called "paradise." The Doctrine of Awakening aims at surmounting these states: it tests the vocations by asking at what point one can apprehend that these very states are inadequate in the face of a will for the unconditioned, and that to have them as the extreme point of reference and as the supreme justification of existence is still a bond, an insufficiency, a thirst, a mania. Thus, in the canon, these words appear: "You should feel shame and indignation if ascetics of other schools ask you if it is in order to arise in a divine world that ascetic life is practiced under the ascetic Gotama."[44]

Nor is this all. The very notion of "existence" is attacked, the stronghold of all theistic theology. Here, as we have said, Buddhism is no more than faithful to the purely metaphysical, superreligious teachings of the preceding Indo-Aryan tradition. In this, the personal god, as pure existence, himself belongs to manifestation and cannot therefore be called absolutely unconditioned. Existence has as its correlative nonexistence. For this reason only that which is beyond both existence and nonexistence, which is above and outside these two transcendental categories, can be understood as really unconditioned. So also for Buddhism this is the extreme point of reference, not the belief in existence, not the belief in nonexistence. Attachment to one or other of these is a bond, a limitation. "By contemplating, according to reality, the origination and cessation of both of these" one must be capable of overcoming both.[45] Even "universal consciousness" belongs, in the Buddhist teaching, to the saṁsāric world; it is a variety of saṁsāric consciousness.

This view is well illustrated in the texts by means of various similes. There is, for example, the story of one who, wishing to know where the elements are com-

---

41. Ibid., 102.
42. Ibid.
43. Plotinus, *Enneads*, 1.2.4, 7.
44. *Angutt.*, 3.18.
45. *Majjh.*, 11.

pletely annihilated, goes to the gods and passes from one hierarchy to another, finally reaching the world of the great Brahmā, the supreme god of being. But it is not in the power of Brahmā to answer him. He sends the ascetic to the Buddha, telling him, in addition, that he has done ill to have left the Sublime One and to have asked this knowledge of another. It is the Buddha and not Brahmā who gives the answer. He indicates the spiritual state of the *arahant,* invisible, endless, resplendent: here the elements have nowhere to plant their roots, here "name-and-form" ceases without leaving residue.[46] But there is a much more striking story, molded with the power of a Michelangelo. It is called the "visit to Brahmā."[47] The Buddha arrives in the kingdom of Brahmā, of which it is said: "Here is the eternal, here is the persistent, here is the everlasting, here is indissolubility and immutability: here there is no birth nor old age, nor death, nor passing away and reappearance; and another, higher liberation than this there is not." To Brahmā, who affirms this, the Buddha says that Brahmā himself is the victim of illusion and infatuation. But here Māra the malign, the god of craving and of death, intervenes; he enters into one of the celestial beings in Brahmā's retinue and from here speaks to the Buddha:

> O monk, beware of him. He is Brahmā, the omnipotent, the invincible, the all-seeing, the sovereign, the lord, the creator, the preserver, the father of all that has been and of all that will be. Long before you there were in the world ascetics and priests who were enemies of the elements, of nature, of the gods, of the lord of generation, of Brahmā; these, at the dissolution of the body, when their vital strength was exhausted, came to abject forms of existence. And therefore I counsel you, O ascetic: beware, O worthy one! What Brahmā has said to you, accept it, lest you contradict the word of Brahmā. Should you, O ascetic, contradict the word of Brahmā, it would be as though a man were to approach a rock and beat on it with a stick, or as though a man, O ascetic, were to fall into an infernal abyss and to seek to grasp the earth with his hands and feet: thus, O monk, would it befall you.

And Brahmā joins with Māra the malign, repeating:

> I, O worthy one, hold as eternal that which is truly eternal, as persistent, as perennial, as indissoluble, as immutable that which is truly so; and where there is no birth and decay, nor death, nor passing away and reappearance, of this I say: here truly there is no birth, nor decay and death, nor passing away and reappearance; and since there is no other,

46. *Dīgha,* 11.67–85.
47. *Majjh.,* 49; cf. also *Saṁyutt.,* 1.4.

higher liberation, therefore I say: there is no other, higher liberation. Therefore, O monk, speak if you will: you will certainly not discover another, higher liberation, try as you will. If you take the earth, if you take the elements as your standpoint, then you have taken me as your standpoint, you have taken me as your basis, you must obey me, you must yield to me; if you take, O monk, nature, the gods, the lord of generation as your standpoint, then you have taken me as your standpoint, you have taken me as your basis, you must obey me, you must yield to me; if you take, O monk, Brahmā as your standpoint, then you have taken me as your standpoint, you have taken me as your basis, you must obey me, you must yield to me.

At this point the antitheses build up to a cosmic and titanic grandeur ending with the most paradoxical reversal of the point of view that is prevalent in Western religions. In fact, while the desire of surpassing the very Lord of creation, from this point of view, appears as something diabolical, the Buddha, instead, finds a diabolical plot in the exact opposite, that is in the attempt to stop him in the region of being, to make this region an insuperable limit, beyond which it is both absurd and mad to seek a higher liberation. Here it is the Malign One in person who urges the belief that the personal God, the God of being, is the supreme reality, and who threatens the Buddha with the damnation that is supposed already to have claimed other ascetics. And in another text[48] his temptation consists of inducing the Buddha to confine himself to the path of good works, rites and sacrifices—to the path of theistic religions. But the Buddha discovers the plot, and speaks thus to Māra: "Well I know you, Malign One, abandon your hope: 'He knows me not'; you are Māra, the Malign. And this Brahmā here, O Malign One, these gods of Brahmā: they are all in your hand, they are all in your power. You, O Malign One, certainly think: 'He also must be in my hand, in my power!' I, however, O Malign One, am not in your hand, I am not in your power."

There follows a symbolical test. The personal God, the Hebraic "I am that I am," the God of being, whose essence is his existence, as such, cannot not be, that is, he is bound to being, he is passive with respect to being. He has not the power to go beyond being. It is here that the test occurs. Who can "disappear"? That is, who is lord both of being and of nonbeing? Who rests neither on the one nor on the other? Brahmā *cannot* disappear. Instead, the Buddha disappears. All the world of Brahmā is amazed and recognizes "the high power, the high might of the ascetic Gotama." Limitation is removed. The dignity of the *atideva*, of one who goes beyond the world of existence itself, not to mention the "celestial" worlds, is demonstrated. It is only

48. *Suttanipāta*, 3.2.3–4.
49. *Majjh.*, 49.

left to Māra the malign to try in vain to dissuade the Buddha from spreading the doctrine.[49]

Here, then, is one of the extreme points in the test of the vocations: not to crave "even the highest of all lives"—not only to pass from this shore to the other, but to apprehend that which lies beyond both.[50] The words of the Awakened One are: "Nature, the gods, the lord of generation, Brahmā, the Resplendent Ones, the Powerful Ones, the Ultrapowerful Ones, all things, I have known, how unsatisfying are all things: this have I recognized and I have renounced all things, abdicated from all things, detached myself from all things, forsworn all things, disdained all things. And in this, O Brahmā, not only am I your equal in knowledge, not only am I not less than you, but I am far greater than you."[51] And the words: "This is not mine, This am I not, this is not my self" must be said by the "noble son" for the whole of that world too.[52] It is still *"saṁsāra."*

Is a higher limit than this conceivable? For the Ariya it is conceivable. Attachment, dependence, and enjoyment are to be eradicated also in respect of the supreme goal of the Buddhist ascesis, that is to say, of extinction. Here is the final temptation and the final victory. Here the will for the unconditioned approaches the paradoxical. The ultimate truth of the series is this: he who thinks extinction, he who thinks of extinction, he who thinks "extinction is mine" and who rejoices in extinction—this man does not know extinction, does not know the path, is not to be counted among the "noble disciples."[53] Even in this region to feel desire and attachment—it may be a sublimated one—means not to realize the place and signification of real liberation.

At the instant of understanding this one apprehends and intuits supermundane safety and the end of anguish. One who thinks no longer either of existence or of nonexistence and thus who is not attached to anything beyond, now trembles no more but reaches the supermundane and supreme "security of calm."[54] He does not tremble and so does not crave—"not trembling, why should he crave?"[55] This summit must be apprehended by the "noble son," it must be his purpose. The strength and sureness of those who know no more anguish or fear is described as something that has a vertiginous and fearful effect on others, both human and superhuman; when they are faced by those who have conquered, and when they hear their truth, they become aware of their own unsuspected contingency, and the primordial anguish bursts forth unchecked. They see the abyss.

50. *Dhammapada*, 383–85.
51. *Majjh.*, 49.
52. Ibid., 22.
53. Ibid., 1; 102.
54. Ibid., 140.
55. Ibid.

When a man is capable of experiencing all these meanings, then his vocation is proved, he is on the road of personal revolution, he can attempt to follow the path that was rediscovered by Prince Siddhattha. But in this connection there must be no illusion, particularly in modern man. This point must be quite clear: development in accordance with the Doctrine of Awakening implies something akin to a rupture or a halt. The symbolism we have discussed should be remembered: as long as one "goes" it is impossible to reach the point where "the world ends." One must stop oneself dead. In some way an extra-saṁsāric element, called in Buddhism *paññā* (Skt.: *prajñā*), the opposite to *avijjā*, must manifest itself. This element, with its presence, arrests the "current," in the same way as the element *avijjā*, unawareness, the state of mania and of "intoxication," confirmed it. At this point already there occurs a partial or virtual suspension of all the elements influenced by *avijjā;* it is not only a matter of a suspension, but also of an inversion of the current: the flux or vortex that had generated the common man starts to generate a superior being, *uttamapurisa: paññā* becomes the central element that transforms and purifies all the constituent forces of the personality, removing and destroying in them the element *avijjā* and the influence of the *āsava*.[56] For this reason, the texts speak also of a special strength beyond knowledge, of a "superior and powerful energy" *(viriya),* which differs from the normal human energies and which alone works the miracle of "liberation of the will by means of the will";[57] it provides the strength for endurance and allows of advance toward supreme liberation.[58]

One of the aspects of Mahāyāna Buddhism that represents a decline from the original is the supposition that this element *paññā (prajñā)* is present in everyone; it considers each individual as a potential *bodhisatta* (Skt.: *bodhisattva*), that is, as a being capable of becoming a Buddha. Whatever from the standpoint of the doctrine may be said about it, this view cannot in practice be said to be at all "in conformity with reality" *(yathā-bhūtam).* The manifestation of this knowledge and of this strength, particularly in modern Western man, can rightly be called a kind of a "grace," in view of its marked discontinuity when compared to all faculties and forms of consciousness, not only in normal individuals but even in the most gifted of our contemporaries. The example of Prince Siddhattha—that is to say, the fact that he had no need of masters, transmitted doctrines, or initiations, to open the way to liberation, since the direct reaction of a noble spirit confronted with the spectacle of the contingency and burning of the world was enough for the purpose—this example should lead no one to repeat the adventure of Baron Münchhausen when he attempted to raise himself in the air by pulling himself upwards by his hair. In one way or another

---

56. Cf. Stcherbatsky, *Central Conception*, pp. 50, 73–74.
57. *Saṁyutt.*, vol. 5, p. 272 (Pāli Text Society edn.).
58. *Mahāparinirv.*, 16.

something must happen: a kind of profound crisis or break, or the receiving "grace," such as to provide a positive opportunity and a base for a "new life." It cannot be repeated often enough that the man of today, constitutionally, is profoundly different from the man of the ancient Aryan civilizations of the East. Views, such as that of Mahāyāna Buddhism already mentioned, are better ignored if we do not wish to deceive ourselves or others.

In Buddhism, the importance of the moment is stressed in every way. "Knowledge," in a text, is likened to a flash of lightning. One is exhorted to "rise and awaken" when one perceives one's own passiveness, one's own indolence, "without letting the moment pass"—if the right moment is allowed to pass, that moment when one would have been able to overcome the force to which both men and gods are subject, the demon of death will reassert his power.[59] "Battle must be joined to-day—to-morrow we may be no more. There is no truce for us with the great army of death. Only one who lives thus, struggling untiringly day and night, achieves beatitude and is called a blessed sage."[60] The following simile is used to illustrate this state of mind: what would a king do, to whom it was announced that the mountains were crumbling and moving and overthrowing all before them, closing in on his kingdom from the east, from the west, from the south, and from the north, and who knew clearly how difficult it is to achieve the human state of existence?[61]

To conclude this section, we shall refer again to the attitude of the Doctrine of Awakening toward the form of ascesis that is unilaterally connected with practices of mortification and penance.

Buddhism opposes all forms of painful ascesis. Having considered the "many kinds of intensive, painful bodily disciplines," Buddhism maintains that those who practice them, "at the dissolution of the body after death, go down by evil paths to suffering and perdition," since this is a "mode of living which brings present ill and future ill."[62] The methods of "painful self-mortification," according to the doctrine of the Buddha, are useless, not only for the purpose of "extinction," but also for one who aspires to achieve some form of "celestial" existence.[63] There are striking sketches of types of ascetics and of monks not unlike those who are found in Western asceticism and monasticism: "Shrivelled, arid, ugly, pallid, emaciated [men], who present no attractions to the eye that sees them." They are afflicted by the "disease of constraint," since they lead this life, in point of fact, against their will, through a

---

59. *Suttanipāta*, 2.10.1–3.
60. *Majjh.*, 131.
61. *Saṁyutt.*, 3.3.
62. *Majjh.*, 45.
63. Ibid., 71.

false vocation, lacking the support of a higher consciousness.[64] Fasting, mortification, sacrifices, prayers, and oblations, none of these purifies a mortal who has not conquered doubt and who has not overcome desire.[65] Two extremes are avoided by those who detach themselves from the world: "the pleasure of desire, low, vulgar, unworthy of the nature of the Ariya, harmful; self-mortification, painful, unworthy of the nature of the Ariya, harmful. Avoiding these two extremes, the middle way has been discovered by the Accomplished One, the way which gives insight, which gives wisdom, which leads to calm, to supernormal consciousness, to illumination, to extinction."[66] In distinguishing what is praiseworthy from what is worthy of reproof, even in cases where saintly knowledge has been attained, the fact of having attained it by means of self-torment is declared to be reprehensible.[67]

The texts often give some account of the life led by Prince Siddhattha before his perfect awakening. He too, "before the perfect awakening, as yet imperfectly awakened, still only striving towards awakening," had had the thought: "Pleasure cannot be conquered by pleasure: pleasure can be conquered by pain."[68] And thus, having abandoned his home against the wishes of his family, still "radiant, with black hair, in the flush of joyous youth, in the flower of manhood," unsatisfied by the truths taught by the various teachers of asceticism to whom he had in the first instance turned (these appear to have been followers of Sāṃkhya), he devoted himself to extreme forms of painful mortification. Having bent his will in all ways, "as a strong man, seizing another weaker man by the head or by the shoulders, compels him, crushes him, throws him down," he began with the body and practiced suspension of the breath until he came near to suffocation.[69] Finding that this led nowhere, he practiced fasting, until he grew so thin that his arms and legs resembled dry sticks, his spine a string of beads, with the vertebrae sticking out: his hair fell off, his eyes sank in, and his pupils shrank almost away, "like reflections in a deep well." He thus arrived at this thought: "All that ascetics or priests in the past have ever experienced in the way of painful, burning, bitter sensations, or that they may be experiencing in the present or that they will experience in the future is no more than this: further one cannot go. And yet with all this bitter ascesis of pain I have not attained the supermundane, the blessed riches of wisdom." There arose in him the conviction: There must be another path to awakening. And it was a memory that allowed him to find it: the memory of a day when, still in the midst of his people, seated in the cool

---

64. Ibid., 89.
65. *Suttanipāta*, 2.2.11; *Dhammapada*, 141.
66. *Mahāvagga (Vin.)* 1.6.17; *Saṃyutt.*, 42.12; *Majjh.*, 139.
67. *Saṃyutt.*, 52.12.
68. *Majjh.*, 85.
69. We must note that here is meant obviously forms of breath retention employed purely as ascetic practices, not of those special *haṭha-yoga* practices, with initiatory aims, of which we have spoken in our book, *The Yoga of Power* (Rochester, Vt., 1992).

shade of a rose-apple tree, he had felt himself in a state of calm, clarity, balance, peace, far from desire, far from disturbing things. Then there arose in him "consciousness in conformity with knowledge: 'This is the way.'"[70]

This manner of the Buddha's ascesis is significant: it clearly shows the features of an ascesis that is Aryan, "classical," clear, balanced, free from "sin" complexes and from "bad conscience," free from spiritualized and sanctified masochism. In this connection it is worth noting that one of the maxims of Buddhism is that one who, being without imperfection does not recognize, in conformity with truth: "In me there is no imperfection," is far worse than one who, on the other hand, knows: "In me there is no imperfection." And a simile follows: a polished and shining bronze vessel that is not used or cleaned would, after a time become dirty and stained; similarly, one who is not aware of his own uprightness is much more exposed to confusions and deviations of every kind than one who is so aware.[71] There is no question, here, in any way, of pride and self-conceit; it is a question of a process of purification through a just and dignified consciousness. This attitude should put in their place those who, through feeling themselves to be hermits, penitents, poor, clothed in rags or through observing the most elementary forms of morality, exalt themselves and believe that they are entitled to despise others.[72] The Ariyan ascesis is as void of vanity and stupid pride (which, as *uddhacca,* is considered as a bond), as it is permeated with dignity and calm self-knowledge.

This does not mean, however, that we should be under any illusion and believe that exceptional inward energies are unnecessary in Buddhism and that the most severe self-discipline should not be imposed. He who realized that the way of painful asceticism was not the right one, was yet capable of satisfying himself that he was able to follow it to its extreme limit. Thus, at the moment in which the vocation is determined and one has the sensation of the emergence of the element *paññā,* one must also have the strength to make an absolute and inflexible resolution. In the forest of Gosinga, on a clear moonlit night, when the trees were in full blossom and gave the impression that celestial scents were being wafted around, various disciples of the Buddha asked each other what type of ascetic could adorn such a forest, and discussed this or that discipline and this or that power achieved. When the Buddha was asked, he said: "An ascetic who, after the meal, seats himself with his legs crossed, his body erect and resolves: 'I will not rise from here until my mind is without attachment and free from any mania.' Such a monk can adorn the forest of Gosinga."[73] In the canonical texts something similar to a "vow" is often mentioned in these terms: "In the confident disciple, who energetically trains himself in the order

70. Cf., e.g., *Majjh.,* 12, 36.
71. Ibid., 5.
72. Ibid., 113.
73. Ibid., 32.

91

of the Master, there arises this notion: 'Willingly may there remain of my body only skin and tendons and bones, and let my flesh and my blood dry up: but until that which can be obtained with human vigour, human strength, human valour has been obtained, I shall continue to strive.'[74] Yet another text speaks of the desperate strength with which a man would struggle against a current, knowing that otherwise he would be carried into waters full of whirlpools and voracious creatures.[75] Struggle, effort, absolute action, iron determination, all these are essential—but in a special "style." It is—let us again repeat—the style of one who maintains his self-knowledge, who exerts his strength where it should be exerted, with clear knowledge of cause and effect, paralyzing the irrational movements of the mind, his fears and hopes and who never loses the calm and composed consciousness of his nobility and of his superiority. It is in such terms that the Doctrine of Awakening is offered and recommended to those who "still remain steadfast."

74. *Saṁyutt.*, 12.22; *Angutt.*, 8.13; *Majjh.*, 70.
75. *Itivuttaka*, 109.

PART II

Practice

8

The Qualities of
the Combatant and the "Departure"

The training or development *(bhāvanā)* presents in the Buddhist doctrine two stages. In the first place, there are the kinds of discipline that, not being carried beyond a certain point, serve only for this life; they are distinguished from those that are considered as "wisdom" and that relate to a more than human experience *(uttari-manussa-dhamma)*.[1] More important and more general, however, is the division of the whole ascesis into three sections: the preparatory section of "right conduct" *(sīla)*; the section of spiritual concentration and contemplation *(samādhi)*; and finally, the section of "wisdom" or transcendental knowledge and spiritual illumination *(paññā)*; (Skt.: *prajñā*).[2]

In what follows we propose to arrange the disciplines referred to in the texts into one or other of these three sections in the manner most satisfactory for the reader. Our aim is not purely informative; we hope to provide also, for anyone who may be interested, some practical guidance. The exposition, then, will be accompanied, where necessary, by an interpretation based on what can be considered as "constant" in a careful comparison of the various traditions.

Before we discuss the instruments of the ascesis we must make some general observations on the preliminary conditions required of the individual, apart from what has already been said about the determination of the vocations.

The first point is that in order to aspire to awakening one must be a human being. The possibility of achieving absolute liberation is offered primarily, according to Buddhism, only to one who is born a man. Not only those who are in lower conditions of existence than the human, but also those who are in higher conditions, such as the *devā*, the celestial or "angelical" beings, do not have this opportunity. While, on the one hand, the human condition is considered to be one of fundamental

1. *Majjh.*, 53; *Saṁyutt.*, 41.9.
2. Cf. *Dīgha*, 10, passim.

contingency and infirmity, on the other it is thought of as a privileged state, obtainable only with great difficulty—"it is a hard thing to be born a man."[3] The supermundane destiny of beings is decided upon earth: the theory of the *bodhisattva* even considers the possibility of "descents" to earth of beings who have already achieved very high, "divine" states of consciousness, in order to complete the work. As we shall see, liberation can occur also in posthumous states: but even in these cases it is thought of as the consequence or development of a realization or of a "knowledge" already achieved on earth. Man's privilege, as conceived by Buddhism along such lines, would seem to be one that is connected with a fundamental liberty. From this point of view man is potentially an *atideva,* he is of a higher nature than the "gods," for the same reason as is found in the hermetic tradition;[4] that is, since he contains in himself, not only divine nature to which angels and gods are tied, but also mortal nature, not only existence but also nonexistence: whence he has the opportunity of arriving at the supertheistic summit that we have discussed, and which is in fact the "great liberation."

Those who desired to enter the order created by Prince Siddhattha were specifically asked: Are you really a man?[5] It is taken as a premise in this case that not all those who appear to be human are really "men." The views, widespread in ancient India as elsewhere, that in some men animal beings were reincarnated—or vice versa: that some men would be "reborn" in this or that "animal womb"—may be understood symbolically:[6] they refer, that is, to human existences whose central element is guided entirely by one of those elemental forces that externally manifest themselves in the normal way in one or other animal species. We have, moreover, already spoken of the limitations arising out of the various "races of the spirit."

A third point is that an original condition imposed by the canon for admission into the order was that of being of male sex. Eunuchs, hermaphrodites, and women were not accepted.[7] The Ariyan road of awakening was considered as substantially and essentially manly. "It is impossible, it cannot be"—says a canonical text[8]—"that a woman should arrive at the full enlightenment of a Buddha, or become a universal sovereign *[cakkavatti]*"; likewise it is impossible for her to "conquer heaven, nature, and the universe," to "dominate celestial spirits."[9] The Buddha considered women insatiable in respect of two things: sex and motherhood; so insatiable that they can-

---

3. *Dhammapada,* 182.
4. Cf. *Corpus Hermeticum,* 9.4; 10.24–25.
5. *Mahāvagga (Vin.),* 1.76.1.
6. Cf. *Bardo Thödol,* p. 54.
7. *Mahāvagga (Vin.),* 1.76.1; 2.22.4. It may be observed that the same limitations are considered for the ordination of Catholic priests.
8. *Majjh.,* 115.
9. Ibid.; *Angutt.,* 1.20.

not free themselves from these cravings before death.[10] He repeatedly opposed the entry of women into the order: when he finally admitted them he declared that, as a flourishing field of rice prospers no longer when a parasitical grass invades and spreads in the field, so the saintly life in an order does not prosper if it allows women to renounce the world—and he tried to limit the danger by promulgating opportune rules.[11] Later, however, less intransigent views became widespread: even in the canonical texts—in spite of these words of the Buddha—there figure women who have entered into the current of awakening and who expound the doctrine of the Ariya, until in the texts of the *prajñāpāramitā*, instead of the simple mode of address "noble sons," there appears, without further ceremony, "noble sons and noble daughters"— a sign, among others, of the easing of the spiritual tension of original Buddhism.

We have now to discuss what are known as the five qualities of the combatant that are required in the disciple;[12] these involve both internal and external conditions. The first is the strength conferred by confidence *(saddhābala)*: confidence, if we refer to historical Buddhism, in the fact that its founder was perfectly awakened and in the truth of its doctrine; or, more generally, that there are beings who "have reached the summit, the perfection; that they themselves, with their supramundane power, have apprehended both this world and the other and are capable of promulgating their knowledge."[13] In a simile of an "unconquerable frontier citadel," this confidence of the noble son is likened to the central tower of the stronghold that, with its deep foundations, gives protection against enemies and strangers.[14]

Besides confidence, the "combatant" must be endowed with that "knowledge" and wisdom of the Ariya that "perceives rise and fall." Of this we have already spoken at length. Let us remember that, in an entirely general sense, by *bodhisatta* is meant one who, by means of this very knowledge, is already inwardly transformed, whose core is already composed of *bodhi* or *paññā* instead of saṁsāric forces.

Third, one must be genuine, not false, and one must be able to make oneself known according to truth for what one is to the Master or to one's intelligent codisciples. To have a pure heart, a free ductile mind—to be, symbolically, like a perfectly white cloth that can easily be dyed the desired color without showing blemishes or imperfections.[15]

10. *Angutt.*, 2.6.10.
11. Ibid., 8.51; *Cullavagga (Vin.)*, 10.1. Other Buddhist expressions about women: "seducers and astute, they destroy the noble life" (*Jātaka*, 263). "They are sensual, bad, common, base. . . . Women are continually in the power of the senses. Saturated with an impure and inexorable burning, they resemble fire which consumes all" (*Jātaka*, 61). And again: "The country dominated by a woman is to be despised. And so to be despised is the being who becomes dominated by the power of a woman" (*Jātaka*, 13). The original doctrine of the Ariya was firmly antigynaecocratic.
12. *Majjh.*, 90.
13. Cf. *Saṁyutt.*, 42.13.
14. *Angutt.*, 7.63.
15. *Majjh.*, 7; 56, etc.

Fourth we have *viriya-bala,* or virile energy (the root of *viriya* is the same as that of the Latin term *vir,* man in the particular sense, as opposed to *homo*), a strength of will, which here shows itself as the power of repelling unhealthy tendencies and states and of promoting the appearance of healthy ones. Above all, one must rely on this strength to replace delight in craving *(kāma-sukham)* by delight in heroism *(vīra-sukham);*[16] a substitution that is a basic point of the whole ascetic development: one must fundamentally change one's attitude in such a way that the heroic pleasure becomes the highest and most intense pleasure that the mind enjoys. Buddhism teaches: "Each man is master of himself—there is no other master; by ruling yourself you will find a rare and precious master,"[17] and again: "Not by others can one be purified";[18] "alone you are in the world, and without help."[19] Here again the *viriya-bala* provides the strength for standing firm in face of all this. In Buddhism, there are no masters in the true sense of the word *guru:* there are only those who can point out the road that has to be followed entirely by one's own efforts: "It is for you yourselves to carry out the work: the Buddhas (only) instruct."[20]

The fifth quality of the Ariyan combatant: he "is firm, vigorous, well set up, neither depressed nor exalted, balanced, fit to win the battle." The presence of blindness, deafness, or any incurable disease was, in the canon, a reason for nonadmission to the order.[21] To be old, ill, or needy are "unfavourable conditions for the battle."[22] "Manias to overcome by avoidance" is the heading given to those unfavorable states that arise in one who does not look after his own health and who does not take necessary measures to avoid physical disturbances and troubles caused by surroundings.[23] The loss of one's strength through excessive abstinence is considered as one of the possible causes—to be avoided—of the loss of tranquillity of spirit, and of eventually falling a victim in one of the many pastures sown with bait by the Malign One.[24] We have already spoken of the negative attitude of Buddhism toward the path of "mortification": training in privation and pain is salutary, but only up to a certain point; in the same way, a craftsman heats an arrow between two fires in order to make it flexible and straight, but he ceases when his purpose has been achieved.[25] Both excessive tension and excessive slackness must be avoided: "the strings must be neither too

16. Cf. ibid., 139.
17. *Dhammapada,* 160.
18. Ibid., 165.
19. *Majjh.,* 82.
20. *Dhammapada,* 276.
21. *Mahāvagga (Vin.),* 1.76.1.
22. *Angutt.,* 5.54.
23. *Majjh.,* 2.
24. Ibid., 25.
25. Ibid., 101.

slack nor too taut." One's energies must be balanced.[26] The mania of self-exalta-
tion must be overcome, just as the mania of self-humiliation, of self-vilification,
must be overcome.[27] Even-minded, fully conscious, one must consider oneself as
neither equal, inferior, nor superior to others, one must not place oneself among
the middle people, nor among the lower people, nor among the higher people.[28]

In speaking of the point of departure, therefore, we can talk of a state of "inward
neutrality": "Do not let your own imperturbable mind be troubled by pain, and do not
reject a just pleasure, persist in it without attachment."[29] "Craving does ill and aversion does ill; and there is a middle way by which to avoid craving and by which to
avoid aversion: a way which gives sight and vision, which conduces to calm, which
leads to clear vision."[30] We often meet with the term *satisam-pajañña,* which refers
to the state of one who maintains perfect awareness by the strength of his clear
vision. Let us remember what has been said on the recurrent theme: "to see in conformity with reality, with perfect wisdom."

Already in connection with the elementary stages the destruction of vain
imaginings, past or future, is taught. "What is before you put to one side. Behind you
leave nothing. To what lies in between do not become attached. And in this calm you
will progress."[31] One who would tread the path of awakening must cultivate such a
simplicity in his mind. An end must be made to the whole world of psychological
complications, of "subjectivity," of hopes and of remorse—in the same way as the
demon of dialectics is silenced. Become used to interior concentration: "the insight
which is varied and is based on variety, this one renounces; the insight which is
single and based on unity, wherein every attachment to worldly enticements is completely vanished, this insight one cultivates."[32] Here are some expressions that occur
in the canonical texts and that deal with what the symbolism of the alchemists would
call the "process of fire"—that is, the manner or rhythm of the interior effort: "To
persevere steadfastly without wavering, the mind clear and unbewildered, the senses
tranquil and undisturbed, consciousness concentrated and unified." "With tireless
and unremitting energy, with knowledge present and unshakable, with serene, untroubled body, with consciousness concentrated and unified."[33] "To persist alone,
detached, tireless, strenuous, with fervid, intimate earnestness"—this is the general
formula used in the texts for the discipline of those who, having understood the

26. *Angutt.,* 6.55.
27. Ibid., 4.106.
28. Cf., e.g., ibid., 6.49; *Suttanipāta,* 4.10.8; 4.15.20.
29. *Majjh.,* 101.
30. Ibid., 3.
31. Cf. ibid., 106; *Dhammapada,* 385.
32. *Majjh.,* 54.
33. *Majjh.,* 4; *Angutt.,* 3.40; *Majjh.,* 19.

doctrine, go on to achieve its supreme end. We are dealing here with predispositions, with qualities and at the same time with achievements—we shall see that among these qualities there are some which, in their turn, are the aim of particular ascetic practices to achieve.

As we have discussed the quality of objective vision, we should also mention—in passing—the style in which many of the oldest Buddhist texts are set out, a style that has been called "quite intolerable" because of its continued repetitions. What is the purpose of these repetitions? The usual interpretation of the Orientalists, that they are a mnemonic aid, is the most superficial. There are other reasons. In the first place, some ideas have been given a particular rhythm so that they are not arrested at the level of simple discursive intellect, but can reach a deeper and more subtle zone of the human being and there stir corresponding impulses. This agrees with the more general aim, explicitly stated in the texts, of permeating the entire body with certain states of consciousness, so as to cause certain forms of knowledge or certain visions to be experienced "bodily." Rhythm—both mental and, more important, that connected with breathing—is one of the most effective methods of achieving this. The modern intellectual, only interested in grasping an idea or a "theory" as quickly as possible in the form of a schematic and cerebral concept will entirely miss the point of the repetitions of the Buddhist texts—and it is natural for him to judge this as "the most intolerable of all styles."

But the repetitions—at least a certain class of them, particularly those in the *Majjhima-nikāya*—have also another aim: that of encouraging a certain degree of objective, impersonal, and strictly realistic thought. It is, in fact, easy to see that the repetitions form connected series in which the reality or fact, the thought that is formulated in grasping it, or the thought that is aroused from hearing them, the verbal expression of this thought or the exposition of the fact, are found in exact logical sequence. This is how the structure of the repetitions is built up: first of all the text describes the fact (objective phase); next, there appears the person who takes note of it and who comments on it, using the same words as those in which it was given in the first place by the text (subjective phase); thirdly, the person may refer the fact to others, in the same words once again, as a pure reflection of a thought conforming to reality. It may also happen that a second person—normally, the Buddha himself—asks others if the fact referred to is true, and we meet the same words for the fourth time. Stylistically, this is an absurdly tedious process. Spiritually, it is a rhythm of *Sachbezogenheit*, as one would say in German: it is the pure transparent passage of the same element from reality to thought, from objectivity to subjectivity, and from one subjectivity to another without any alterations. We must understand the attitude and the purpose with which texts of this kind are read. A patient reading of them can be a discipline: they give an example of impersonality and of crystallinity of thought that may themselves work formatively on the spirit of the reader, giving him much more than simple "concepts."

The first major action on the ascetic path is indicated by the term *pabbajjā*, meaning literally "departure." According to the scheme of the texts, one who hears the doctrine and discovers its deeper significance, and who thus arrives at "confidence," acquires a conviction expressed by this formula: "Home is a prison, a dusty place. The life of a hermit is in the open. One cannot, by remaining at home, fulfil point by point the completely purified, completely illumined ascesis." Comprehending this, the "noble son" after short time shakes off attachment to things and persons, leaves home and devotes himself to the life of a wandering ascetic.

We have translated the term *bhikkhu*, which designated the followers of the Buddha by "wandering ascetic," although it literally means a "mendicant," one who begs. Originally the *bhikkhus* were a kind of wandering and begging monks: the semiconventual nature of the Buddhist organizations only appeared at a later period. The term we have used possibly allows of fewer misunderstandings. For example, when we speak of "begging" it must be borne in mind that the circumstances included a society in which the acceptance—by an ascetic or a Brāhman—of something from an ordinary man was not a humiliation but a kind of grace. It was thought that an ascetic—by acting as a point of contact between the visible and the invisible—fulfilled a supremely useful, if intangible, function, a benefit even to those taking part in normal life. Giving—*dāna*—in these circumstances was conceived as an action that would produce benefits of the same kind as "right conduct" and contemplative development.[34] Thus—a thing that seems paradoxical today—as a sign of contempt or as a penalty, Buddhist assemblies in solemn conclave would indicate families or individuals from which the *bhikkhu* should refuse to accept anything, by symbolically reversing the receptacle or bowl he carried with him.[35]

These details apart, the *bhikkhus* originally were a kind of free order with a head, rather like an ascetic equivalent of the Western medieval orders consisting of the "knights-errant" and, later, the Rosicrucians with their "imperator." The Buddha recommended that two disciples should not take the same road.[36] The essential point, in any case, was the absence of bonds and of the desire for company, a liking for solitude, a freedom—also physical where possible—like that of the air, of the open sky. "Flee society as a heavy burden, seek solitude above all."[37] Having much to do, being busy with many things, avoiding solitude, living with people at home and in worldly

---

34. Cf. *Angutt.*, 8.30. As a reference *Suttanipāta*, 3.5.15: "Those who go through the world with themselves as their light, attached to nothing, entirely liberated—to those, in due time, men may offer alms."
35. *Angutt.*, 7.87.
36. *Mahāvagga (Vin.)*, 1.11.1.
37. *Majjh.*, 3.

surroundings—these are so many more "unfavorable conditions for the battle."[38] One who is not free from the bond of family—it is said in particular—may certainly go to heaven, but will not achieve awakening.[39] "Let the ascetic be alone: it is enough that he has to fight with himself."[40] "Only of an ascetic who dwells alone, without company, is it to be expected that he will possess pleasure in renunciation, pleasure in solitude, pleasure in clam, pleasure in awakening, that he will possess this pleasure easily, without difficulty, without pain."[41] And again: "He who enjoys society cannot find joy in solitary detachment. If joy is not found in solitary detachment, one cannot concentrate firmly on the things of the spirit; if this power of concentration is lacking, one cannot perfectly achieve right knowledge"—or the things that proceed from it.[42] The detachment and the solitude implicit in *pabbajjā*, the "departure," are naturally to be understood both under the physical and under the spiritual aspect: detachment from the world and detachment, above all, from thoughts of the world.[43] Therefore, do not let people's talk affect you, do not pay too much attention to words.[44] Do not dispute with the world, but judge it for what it is, that is to say, impermanent.[45] The texts speak of "being to oneself an island, of seeking refuge in oneself and in the law, and in nothing else.[46] If a man cannot find a wise, upright, and constant companion with whom he may advance in step, "he walks alone, as one who has renounced his kingdom, as a proud animal in the forest, calm, doing ill to none."[47] Here are some other illustrative expressions: "Strenuous in his determination to achieve the supreme goal, his mind free from attachment, fleeing idleness, firm, endowed with bodily and mental strength, let [the ascetic] go alone like a rhinoceros. Like a lion which does not tremble at any noise, like wind which is held by no net, like a lotus leaf untouched by water, let him go alone like a rhinoceros."[48] And again: a true ascetic is "he who proceeds alone and contemplative, on whom neither blame nor praise have effect, who, like a lion, feels no fear at the noises [of the world], who, like a lotus leaf, is not touched by water, who guides others, but whom others know not how to guide."[49]

Anyone who considers the problem of the adaptability of the ascesis of the Ariya to modern times, will ask himself to what extent the precept of "departure" as a real

38. *Angutt.*, 5.90.
39. *Majjh.*, 71.
40. *Mahāparinirv.*, 6–8.
41. *Majjh.*, 122.
42. *Angutt.*, 6.68.
43. Ibid., 4.132.
44. *Majjh.*, 139.
45. *Mahāparinirv.*, 2.1.
46. *Samyutt.*, 22.43.
47. *Majjh.*, 128; *Dhammapada*, 328, 329.
48. *Suttanipāta*, 1.3.34, 37.
49. Ibid., 1.12.7.

abandonment of home and of the world, and as the isolation of a hermit, must be taken literally. The texts sometimes consider a triple detachment, one physical, another mental, and the third both physical and mental.[50] If the last naturally represents the most perfect form—at least so long as the struggle lasts—it is the second that should claim the particular attention of most people today and that, moreover, was given greater emphasis in Mahāyāna developments, including Zen Buddhism. Besides, even the canonical texts mention the possibility of an interpretation of the concept of "departure" that is mainly symbolical; thus "home" is considered, for example, to be equivalent to the elements that make up common personality—and similar interpretations are given for wandering and for property.[51] A variation of a text we have quoted, says that "solitary life is well achieved in all respects when what is past is put aside, what is future abandoned, and when will and passion, in the present, are entirely under control";[52] elsewhere it is said that a man wanders like a *bhikkhu* justly through the world, when he has subjugated past and future time and possesses a pure understanding,[53] when he "has left behind him both the pleasant and the unpleasant, clinging to nothing, in all ways independent and without attachments" and so on. Similar expressions recur throughout; they largely refer, moreover, to the principal tasks of ascetic preparation and purification.[54]

Once detachment, *viveka,* is interpreted mainly in this internal sense, it appears perhaps easier to achieve it today than in a more normal and traditional civilization. One who is still an "Aryan" spirit in a large European or American city, with its skyscrapers and asphalt, with its politics and sport, with its crowds who dance and shout, with its exponents of secular culture and of soulless science and so on—among all this he may feel himself more alone and detached and nomad than he would have done in the time of the Buddha, in conditions of physical isolation and of actual wandering. The greatest difficulty, in this respect, lies in giving this sense of internal isolation, which today may occur to many almost spontaneously, a positive, full, simple, and transparent character, with elimination of all traces of aridity, melancholy, discord, or anxiety. Solitude should not be a burden, something that is suffered, that is borne involuntarily, or in which refuge is taken by force of circumstances, but rather, a natural, simple, and free disposition. In a text we read: "Solitude is called wisdom *[ekattaṁ monam akkhātaṁ]* he who is alone will find that he is happy";[55] it is an accentuated version of *"beata solitudo, sola beatitudo."*

From the external and social aspect also, it is interior liberty that counts: this,

---

50. *Angutt.,* 4.132.
51. E.g., *Saṁyutt.,* 22.3.
52. Ibid., 21.10.
53. *Suttanipāta,* 2.13.15.
54. Ibid., 2.13.5–6; cf. 3.6.28.
55. *Suttanipāta,* 3.11.40.

however, must lead no one to deceive himself. Thus, in the matter of bonds, the man of today must beware more of little attachments than of great ones—that is, of attachments connected with conventional and "normal" life, of habits, inclinations, and sentimental supports that, by making their own often unconscious excuses, are judged as being too irrelevant to be confronted. In this connection, there is a striking simile in the texts, that of the quail. It is addressed particularly to those who say: "What can come of this insignificant matter!" and who do not notice that in this way they establish "a strong bond, a firm bond, a bond without weakness, a heavy fetter." If a quail, caught in a noose of weak thread, thereby goes to perdition, captivity, or death, only a fool would then say: "That noose of weak thread in which the quail is caught and whereby it goes to perdition, captivity, or death, is not a strong bond for it, but a weak bond, a frail bond, an insignificant bond." The opposite case is that of a royal elephant "with large tusks, trained to attack, trained for the battle, tied with strong ropes and bonds" that, however, "by moving the body only a little snaps and breaks those bonds and goes where he will." Here again, only a fool would say: "Those strong ropes and bonds which tie the large-tusked royal elephant, trained to attack, trained for the battle, those bonds which he, by moving the body only a little, snaps and breaks and goes where he will, are a strong bond for him, a firm bond, a tough bond, a bond without weakness, a heavy fetter."[56] This simile well emphasizes the danger and the insidious character of many little ties—in connection with the modern world, we have cited those of a conventional and sentimental nature—whose apparent insignificance offer material for self-indulgence.

Detachment or interior freedom is further understood in the sense of a species of ductility—and we shall see that it is more and more developed in this very sense in course of the discipline. It is the opposite condition to that of the man who "clings with both hands and who is only removed with difficulty." We again remember the frequent simile of the perfectly trained thoroughbred that immediately takes the desired direction.

The detached life, thought of as free as air compared with "home" life, is thus connected with a feeling of being "satisfied with knowledge and experience." This spirit is open to everything, to every impression—and is, for this very reason, elusive. Here is the inward equivalent of the state of mind that the texts liken to a bird that "wherever it flies, flies only with the weight of its feathers"; an image that refers to the purified contentedness of the ascetic who is satisfied with the simplicity of his life and needs. It is once again evident that right at the beginning there must be present something that, in its ideal and absolute form, is represented at the final state: the sense of *suñña* or *suññatā*, the "void," which in

---

56. Majjh., 66.

Mahāyāna literature ends by being synonymous with the state of *nirvāṇa* itself, can already be seen in the various similarities between the earlier state of the spirit and the later.

The disciplines that, in the path of awakening, are considered as preparatory and that consist of the two sections of *samādhi* and of *sīla,* can be outlined as follows. On the one hand we have instructions that are of an entirely technical nature and refer to actions that the mind has to perform on the mind, in the form of concentration and meditation without special conditions or intermediaries. On the other hand, we have rules of conduct that could be called "ethical" but which, in reality—considering what "ethical" normally means today—are not, since their value lies entirely in their instrumental usefulness. Although the instructions of the first type can be carried out by themselves, for the purpose of the "neutral ascesis" we have mentioned, nevertheless the states of mind produced by *sīla*, by "right conduct," furnish more favorable conditions for this purpose. Both these forms of disciplines in the Buddhist path of awakening are animated by "insight," *vipassanā,* and are designed with liberation in view: "As the ocean is pervaded by a single taste, that of salt, so this law and this discipline are pervaded by a single taste, that of liberation."[57]

From the technical point of view, the tasks of ascetic action can be described thus. We have said that the stirring and eventual determining of the "heroic vocation" in the individual is already evidence of the awakening also of an extrasaṁsāric element, *paññā* or *bodhi.* A world of defense must be undertaken immediately: the most common mental processes must be mastered so that the new growth is not stifled or uprooted. Then the central element must be separated from any adulteration by the contents of experience, internal or external, so that the various processes of "combustion" through contact, thirst, and attachment are suspended; this should also fortify the extrasaṁsāric—or, let us say, "sidereal"—principle, so as to make it independent and capable of proceeding freely, if it wishes, in the "ascending" direction, toward more and more unconditioned states, and the region where the *nidāna* of the transcendental, preconceptional, and prenatal series act.

The initial phase could be compared to what in the symbolism of alchemy is called the work of "dissociation of the mixtures," of the isolation of the "grain of incombustible sulphur" and of the "extraction and fixation of mercury"[58]—"mercury," that shining, evasive, and elusive substance, being the mind, the "mixtures" being the experience with which the "incombustible grain of sulphur," the sidereal, extrasaṁsāric principle is mixed. This naturally suggests a cathartic

---

57. *Angutt.*, 8.19.
58. Cf. J. Evola, *The Hermetic Tradition* (Rochester, Vt., 1995).

action of gradual elimination of the power of the "intoxicants" and of the ma-nias—of the *āsava*—that can be defined as follows: do not be held back by, attached to, inebriated by enjoyment (in a general sense, therefore also in rela-tion to neutral states), so that in the "five groups of attachment" thirst does not become established, much less embittered;[59] "completely banish, extinguish that which in the desires is clinging to desire, snare of desire, vertigo of desire, thirst of desire, fever of desire,"[60] and this concerns both the direct evidence of con-sciousness and the unconscious tendencies, the *upadhi* and the *sankhāra*. The more external forms of this catharsis are connected with "right conduct" *(sīla);* the more internal ones, dealing with the potentialities, the roots, and the groups of saṁsāric being, are operated through special ascetic and contemplative exer-cises, the *jhāna.* This cathartic development of consolidation and, in a manner of speaking, of "siderealization" of one's own energies leads to the limit of indi-vidual consciousness, a limit that includes also the virtual possibility of self-identification with being, that is, with the theistically conceived divinity. If this identification is rejected, one passes into the realm of *paññā* (the third step) in which the liberated and dehumanized energy is gradually taken beyond "pure forms" *(rūpa-loka)* to the unconditioned, to the nonincluded *(apariyāpannam)* where mania is extinct and "ignorance" is removed, not only in the case of the being who was once a man but also of any other form of manifestation.

---

59. *Majjh.,* 149.
60. Ibid., 36.

9

❧❀❧

Defense and Consolidation

By way of immediate action, a stand must first be made against thought, against mental processes. "I do not know"—it is said[1]—"anything which, when unbridled, uncontrolled, unwatched, untamed, brings such ruin as thought—and I do not know anything which, when bridled, controlled, watched, tamed, brings such benefits as thought." Thought, which everyone lightly says is "mine," is, in reality, only to a very small degree in our power. In the majority of cases, instead of "to think" it would be correct to say "we are thought" or "thought takes place in me." In the normal way, the characteristic of thought is its instability. "Incorporeal"— it is said[2]—"it walks by itself": it "runs hither and thither like an untamed bull."[3] Hard to check, unstable, it runs where it pleases.[4] In general, it is said that, while this body may persist one year, two years, three years or even up to a hundred years and more in its present form, "what we call thought, what we call mind, what we call consciousness arises in one manner, ceases in another; incessantly, night and day"; "it is like a monkey who goes through the forest, and who progresses by seizing one branch, letting go of it, taking hold of another, and so on."[5] The task is to "arrest" thought: to master it and to strengthen the attention;[6] to be able then to say: "Once this thought wandered at its fancy, at its pleasure, as it liked: I today shall hold it completely bridled, as a mahout holds a rut-elephant with his goad."[7] "As a fletcher straightens his arrow, so a wise man straightens his flickering and unstable thought, which is difficult to guard, difficult to hold."[8] In the

1. *Angutt.*, 1.4.
2. *Dhammapada*, 37.
3. *Angutt.*, 1.20.
4. *Dhammapada*, 35.
5. *Saṁyutt.*, 12.61.
6. *Suttanipāta*, 3.1.20.
7. *Dhammapada*, 326.
8. Ibid., 33.

same text two considerations are of importance; first, the Upaniṣadic teaching is recalled in which the seat of true thought is not the brain but is hidden in the "cavern of the heart";[9] secondly, this simile is used: "As a fish taken from his world of water and thrown on dry land, so our thought flutters at the instant of escaping the dominion of Māra."[10] In point of fact it is a matter of reversing the relationship: in recognizing the fragility of the body, which yet shows itself much more stable than thought, thought itself is made firm as a fortress.[11]

A few explanations. If one day normal conditions were to return, few civilizations would seem as odd as the present one, in which every form of power and dominion over material things is sought, while mastery over one's own mind, one's own emotions and psychic life in general is entirely overlooked. For this reason, many of our contemporaries—particularly our so-called "men of action"—really resemble those crustaceans that are as hard-shelled outside with scabrous incrustations as they are soft and spineless within. It is true that many achievements of modern civilization have been made possible by methodically applied and rigorously controlled thought. This, however, does not alter the fact that most of the "private" mental life of every average and more-than-average man develops today in that passive manner of thought that, as the Buddhist text we have just quoted strikingly puts it, "walks by itself," while, half-unconscious, we look on. Anyone can convince himself of this by trying to observe what goes on in his mind, for example, when leaving his house: he thinks of why he is going out but, at the door, his thoughts turn to the postman and thence to a certain friend from whom news is awaited, to the news itself, to the foreign country where his friend lives and which, in turn, makes him remember that he must do something about his own passport: but his eye notices a passing woman and starts a fresh train of thought, which again changes when he sees an advertisement, and these thoughts are replaced by the various feelings and associations that chase each other during a ride through the town. His thought has moved exactly like a monkey that jumps from branch to branch, without even keeping a fixed direction. Let us try, after a quarter of an hour, to remember what we have thought—or, rather, what has been thought in us—and we shall see how difficult it is. This means that in all these processes and disordered associations our consciousness has been dazed or "absent." Having seen this, let us undertake to follow, without disturbing them, the various mental associations. After only a minute or two we shall find ourselves distracted by a flood of thoughts that have invaded us and

---

9. Ibid., 37. It is worth noting that in Chinese translations of the Buddhist texts "thought" is rendered by the character *hsin,* which also means "heart." There is an analogy in the ancient Egyptian tradition. Also Dante (*Vita Nuova,* 1.2) speaks of the intellect which is situated in the "most secret chamber of the heart."

10. *Dhammapada,* 34.

11. Ibid., 40.

that are quite out of control. Thought does not like being watched, does not like being seen. Now this irrational and parasitical development of thought takes up a large part of our normal psychic life, and produces corresponding areas of reduced activity and of reduced self-presence. The state of passivity is accentuated when our thought is no longer merely "spontaneous" and when the mind is agitated by some emotion, some worry, hope, or fear. The degree of consciousness is certainly greater in these cases—but so, at the same time, is that of our passivity.

These considerations may throw some light on the task that is set when one "ceases to go"; one reacts, one aims at being the master in the world of one's own mind. It now seems quite incomprehensible that nearly all men have long since been accustomed to consider as normal and natural this state of irrationality and passivity, where thought goes where it will—instead of being an instrument that enters into action only when necessary and in the required direction, just as we can speak when we wish to, and with a purpose, and otherwise remain silent. In comprehending this "according to reality," we must each decide whether we will continue to put up with this state of affairs.

In its fluid, changeable, and inconsistent character, normal thought reflects, moreover, the general law of saṁsāric consciousness. This is why mental control is considered as the first urgent measure to be taken by one who opposes the "current." In undertaking this task, however, we must not be under any illusions. The *dynamis,* the subtle force that determines and carries our trains of thought, works from the subconscious. For this reason, to attempt to dominate the thought completely by means of the will, which is bound to thought itself, would almost be like trying to cut air with a sword or to drown an echo by raising the voice. The doctrine, which declares that thought is located in the "cavern of the heart," refers, among other things, to thought considered "organically" and not to its mental and psychological offshoots. Mastery of thought cannot, therefore, be merely the object of a form of mental gymnastics: rather, one must, simultaneously, proceed to an act of conversion of the will and of the spirit; interior calm must be created, and one must be pervaded by intimate, sincere earnestness.

The "fluttering" of thought mentioned in our text is more than a mere simile: it is related to the primordial anguish, to the dark substratum of saṁsāric life that comes out and reacts since, as soon as it feels that it is *seen,* it becomes aware of the danger; the condition of passivity and unconsciousness is essential for the development of saṁsāric being and for the establishment of its existence. This simile illustrates an experience that, in one form or another, is even encountered on the ascetic path.

The discipline of constant control of the thought, with the elimination of its automatic forms, gradually achieves what in the texts is called *appamāda,* a term variously translated as "attention," "earnestness," "vigilance," "diligence," or "reflection." It is, in point of fact, the opposite state to that of "letting oneself think," it is the first form of entry into oneself, of an earnestness and of a fervid, austere concentration. When it is understood in this sense, as Max Müller has said,[12] *appamāda* constitutes the base of every virtue—*ye keci kusalā dhammā sabbe te appamādamūlakā*. It is also said: "This intensive earnestness is the path that leads toward the deathless, in the same way that unreflective thought leads, instead, to death. He who possesses that earnestness does not die, while those who have unstable thought are as if already dead."[13] An ascetic "who delights in *appamāda*—in this austere concentration—and who guards against mental laxity, will advance like a fire, burning every bond, both great and small."[14] He "cannot err." And when, thanks to this energy, all negligence is gone and he is calm, from his heights of wisdom he will look down on vain and agitated beings, as one who lives on a mountaintop looks down on those who live in the plains.[15]

The struggle now begins. The symbolism connected with the Khattiya, the warriors, is again used. The texts speak first of a fourfold, just striving *(cattāro sammappadhāna)* to be won by bringing to bear *viriya-bala,* the heroic force of will,[16] which has already been considered as a requisite for the Ariyan disciple or combatant. Once the previously deserted center of the being has been reoccupied, and thought has been put under control, action must be taken against the tendencies that spring up. This is done in a fourfold manner: "Summon the will, arm the spirit, bravely struggle, fight, do battle" (1) to "prevent bad, not good things, yet unarisen, from arising"; (2) to repel them if they have arisen; (3) to encourage the arising of good things as yet unarisen; (4) to make them endure, increase, unfold, develop, and become perfect when they have arisen.[17] Understood in their fullness, these battles also concern further special phases and disciplines that will be discussed later—for example, the first and the second are related to the "watch over the senses" (cf. p. 139–40); the third is related to the "seven awakenings" (cf. p. 142); the fourth to the four contemplations.[18] But, at this stage, we are dealing with a general form of action, in connection with which the texts offer a series of instruments. An image or a simile is normally associated with each one of them. The reader should pay particular attention to these similes— as indeed to most of those with which every ancient Buddhist text is liberally sprinkled. Their value is not simply poetic ornament or an aid to understanding; they often have besides a magic value. By this, we mean that when they are considered in the right state of mind they can act on something

12. Max Müller in the edition of the *Dhammapada* found in the *Sacred Books of the East,* vol. 10, p. 9.
13. *Dhammapada,* 21.
14. Ibid., 31.
15. Ibid., 26–29.
16. *Angutt.,* 5.15.
17. Ibid., 4.13–14; *Majjh.,* 78.
18. *Angutt.,* 4.14.

deeper than the mere intelligence and can produce a certain interior realization.

The first instrument is substitution. When, in conceiving a particular idea, "there arise harmful and unworthy thoughts images of craving, of aversion, of blindness" (these are—let us remember—the three principal modes of manifestation of the *āsava*), then we must make this idea give place to another, beneficial idea. And in giving place to this beneficial idea it is possible that those deliberations and images will dissolve and that by this victory "the intimate spirit will be fortified, will become calm, united, and strong." Here is the simile: "Even as a skilled builder with a thin wedge is able to extract, raise up, expel a thicker one," just so, the immediate substitution of one image by another has the power of dispersing and dissolving the tendencies and the mental associations that the first was in course of determining or of arousing. What is "unworthy," in one text, is defined like this: "That, whereby fresh mania of desire sprouts and the old mania is reinforced; fresh mania of existence sprouts and the old mania is reinforced; fresh mania of error sprouts and the old mania is reinforced."[19] We are not dealing with moralistic aspects but with what may be described as ontological or existential references. It is a matter of overcoming and obstructing saṁsāric nature, of neutralizing the possibilities of fresh "combustions" in oneself. Particular aid is given by the idea of the harmfulness of certain thoughts: upon the appearance of a "thought of ill will or cruelty," one must summon "wisdom conforming to reality" and then formulate this thought: "There is now arisen in me this thought of ill will or cruelty; it leads to my own harm, it leads to others' harm, it leads to the harm of both, it uproots wisdom, it brings vexation, it does not lead to extinction, it leads to self-limitation." If this thought is formulated and apprehended with sufficient intensity and sincerity, the bad thought dissolves.[20]

This leads us immediately to the second instrument: expulsion through horror or contempt. If, in the effort of passing from one image to another as the first method prescribes, unworthy thoughts, images of craving, aversion, or blindness still arise, then the unworthiness, the irrationality, and the misery they represent must be brought to mind. This is the simile: "Just as a woman or a man, young, flourishing and charming, round whose neck were tied the carcass of a snake, or the carcass of a dog, or a human carcass, would be filled with fear, horror, and loathing," so, the perception of the unworthy character of those images or thoughts should produce an immediate and instinctive act of expulsion, from which their dispersion or neutralization would follow. Whenever an affective chord is touched, then by making an effort one must be able to feel contempt, shame, and disgust for the enjoyment or dislike that has arisen.[21]

In order to employ this ascetic instrument of defense to its best advantage we

19. *Majjh.*, 2.
20. Ibid., 19.
21. Ibid., 152.

have to presuppose in the individual an acute form of interior sensibility and a capacity for immediately projecting the qualities that arouse instinctive repulsion onto the image of what is to be eliminated or neutralized. Hindus have the myth of Śiva, the great ascetic of the mountaintops, who with one glance of his frontal eye—the eye of knowledge—reduced Kāma, the demon of desire, to ashes when he tried to disturb his mind. In reality, we must take account of the existence of "serpentine" processes of interior seduction—serpentine, because they develop in the subconscious and the semiconscious, trusting entirely *that no one is looking,* and that a particular "contact," which will eventually produce the thought in the mind, is not noticed. To be able to turn round immediately and see will paralyze these processes. But seeing implies detachment, an instinctive and ready reaction that causes immediate withdrawal as soon as the contact and the infiltration are noticed. Other illustrations are given in the texts: as the man who inadvertently touches burning coals with his hand or with his foot immediately recoils;[22] or as when two or three drops of water land on a white hot iron vessel: those drops fall slowly, but they vanish very rapidly. If this reaction is to be effective, one's experience of the intrusion of undesired inclinations and emotional formations must proceed in a similar manner.[23]

To discuss "cravings": when training this sensibility and instinct we must not forget the "wisdom" that measures the significance of "cravings" from the point of view of the unconditioned, of the extrasaṁsāric. The fundamental theme here is that "the cravings are insatiable" precisely because each satisfaction only goes to inflame the cravings and to charge the individual with a fresh potentiality for desire. The texts provide detailed similes: cravings are like dry bones, without flesh and only with a smear of blood, and however much a dog may gnaw them they well never drive away his hunger and fatigue; they are like a flaming torch of straw carried by a man against the wind, and if he does not immediately throw it away, it will burn his hand, his arm, his body; they are like alluring dream visions that vanish when the sleeper awakes; they are like joy over a treasure amassed from things borrowed from other people who, sooner or later, will come and reclaim them; they are like the points of lances or the blades of swords that cut into and wound the inner being; and there are many more such similes.[24] According to the degree to which this steady and lived knowledge, conforming to reality, truly pervades the mind of the man who trains himself, so the possibilities of this second instrument, and also of the others, will multiply and the defense will increase in strength.

The third instrument is dissociation. When undesired images and thoughts arise, they must remain meaningless and be ignored. The simile is: as a man with good sight,

22. Ibid., 48.
23. Ibid., 152; 66; *Saṁyutt.,* 35.203.
24. *Majjh.,* 14; 22; 54.

who does not wish to observe what comes into his field of view at a particular moment can close his eyes or look elsewhere. When attention is resolutely withheld, the images or the tendencies are again restrained. The simile we have just quoted brings out clearly what we have said about the state of passivity in which man finds himself during most of his mental and emotive life: has he, indeed, this power of looking or of withdrawing his sight at will? Images, psychoaffective aggregates of fear, desire, hope, despair, and so on, fascinate or hypnotize his mind, subtly tying it, they "manipulate" it by their influence and feed on its energies like vampires. It is essential that this ascetic instrument not be confused with the common and simple process of "chasing away" a thought, a practice that often has the opposite effect, that is, of forcing it back, strengthened, into the subconscious, according to the psychological law of "converse effort." It is rather a matter of destroying by not seeing, by neutralizing the disposition and by leaving the image alone. The preceding instrument, also, should be regarded in this light: it is not repulsion by one who is struggling, but a reaction arising from a superior state of awareness and from an earnestly lived sense of the "indignity" and irrationality of the images and inclinations that appear.

The fourth instrument is gradual dismemberment. Make the thoughts vanish one after another successively. The relevant simile gives the idea of the technique very clearly: "Just as a man walking in haste might think: 'Why am I walking in haste? let me go more slowly' and, walking more slowly, might think: 'But why am I walking at all? I wish to stand still' and, standing still, might think: 'For what reason am I standing up? I will sit down' and, sitting down, might think: 'Why must I only sit? I wish to lie down' and might lie down; just so if harmful and unworthy thoughts, images of craving, of aversion and of blindness, again arise in an ascetic in spite of his contempt and rejection of them, he must make these thoughts successively vanish one after another." This method of making the infatuation disappear by separating its constituent parts one by one in a gradual series and considering them with a calm and objective eye one after another, provides, in the preparatory stage of the ascesis, an example of the very method of the whole process. And image corresponds to image. The state of one who achieves extinction is, in fact, likened to that of the man who runs parched and feverish under the scorching sun and who finally finds an alpine lake with fresh water in which he can bathe, and shade where he can relax and rest.[25] Another simile is given by the texts, still in connection with the method of dismemberment. It speaks of the pain that a man would feel in seeing a woman he favored flirt with others. He arrives, however, at this thought: "What if I were to abandon this favoring?"—in the same spirit as he might say: "Why do I run? what if I were to walk calmly instead?" and then were to walk calmly. Having thus

25. *Saṁyutt.*, 12.68; *Majjh.*, 40.

banished his inclination, that man can now witness the sight that pained him before with calm and indifference.[26] The texts also speak of the conditioned nature of desire: desire is formed only because of a preoccupation of the mind that, in turn, is established only "if there is present something which we may call an obsession, a possession [papañca-saññā]."[27] This is the theoretical basis of the method of neutralization by means of gradual dismemberment.

It is possible, however, that the mind in its irrationality may not be subdued even by this method. In that case one must pass to direct action, that is, one must come to grips with oneself. Whence, the last instrument: if, while making the thoughts gradually disappear one after another, irrational impulses and unworthy images continue to arise, then, "with clenched teeth and tongue pressed hard against the palate, with the will you must crush, compel, beat down the mind." The simile is: "as a strong man, seizing another weaker man by the head or by the shoulders, compels him, crushes him, throws him down." Again, for real success in this direct form of struggle one must be able to call upon the illumination, the energy, and the superiority that proceed from what is outside the simple "current." Only then is there no danger that the victory will be merely exterior and apparent, and that the enemy, instead of being destroyed, has disengaged and entrenched himself in the subconscious.[28]

In order to clarify the various stages of this subtle war, an author has adopted the following simile. It is not possible to avoid the appearance of images and inclinations in the mind: this occurs spontaneously and automatically until what is called voidness, suñña, is reached. To the disciple, to the fighting ascetic, some of these images are like strange and indifferent people whom we meet on the road and who pass by without attracting our attention. Others are like people we meet who wish to stop us; but since we see no point in it, we ourselves withdraw attention and pass on. Other images, however, are like people we meet and with whom we ourselves wish to walk, in the face of all reason. In this case we have to react and assert ourselves: the tendency of our will must be opposed from the start.

In the Buddhist text to which we referred above, the result of this work of defense by means of dissolving the irrational deliberations and images that reawaken the threefold intoxicating force of the āsava is invariably expressed thus: "the mind becomes inwardly firm, becomes calm, becomes united and concentrated." This is the path—it is said—along which an ascetic becomes "master of his thoughts": "Whatever thought he desires, that thought will he think, whatever thought he does not desire, that thought will he not think. He has extinguished thirst, he has shaken off the bonds."[29] These disciplines, however, can also be used in an ascesis in a general

---

26. *Majjh.*, 101.
27. *Dīgha*, 21.2.
28. All this is in *Majjh.*, 20.
29. Ibid.

sense, that is, independently of a supermundane end. To use them in this manner an easy adaptation of details is enough.

In terms of "fighting," one is naturally advised to take the initiative in attacking what one intends to overcome. The expression is: "renounce a tendency or a thought, drive it away, root it out, suffocate it before it grows."[30] There is also the simile of the herdsman who takes good care to destroy the eggs or the young of insects and parasites that might harm the animals entrusted to him.[31] In these circumstances, the methods of the wedge and of repulsion, as if some filthy thing had been hung round one's neck, can be particularly effective.

All this naturally demands the degree of mastery of the *logos* in us that enables our discriminating exactly between our thoughts.[32] Those that can be organized and used in the required direction should be consolidated and established, working on the principle that the mind inclines toward what has been considered and pondered for a long time.[33] In this respect, however, nothing can equal the benefits that come from a sense of innate dignity, as of a special race of spirit: then a reliable instinct will act and very little uncertainty will be felt in the task of "renouncing the low impulses of the mind."[34] When this sense is weak, consolidation may be effected through reaction by means of what is known as the "justification" method, which consists of awakening the sense of one's own dignity by calmly contrasting one's conduct with that of others. There is a whole series of formulae dealing with this, of which we have chosen the following: "Others may lie, we shall not"; "Others may be egotists, we shall not"; "Others may be malicious, we shall not"; "Others may be yield, we shall persist"; "The mind of others may become clouded, our mind will remain serene"; "Others may waver, but we shall be sure of our purpose"; "Others may be provoked, but we shall not be provoked"; "Others may concern themselves only with what is before their eyes, they may grasp it with both hands, they may become detached from it with difficulty, but we shall not concern ourselves only with what is before our eyes, we may not grasp it with both hands, we shall easily become detached from it," etc. What Islam calls *nyya*, the decision of the mind, is important and should be strengthened by the use of these formulae and of this style of thought.[35] These instruments can naturally also be used as supports in the building up of *sīla*, that is, of "rightness."

The overcoming of fear in all its forms deserves a special word. It is achieved by firmly maintaining the feeling of one's own rightness and detachment in face of all denials by one's imagination. There is nothing to hope, there is nothing to fear. The

30. Ibid., 2.
31. *Angutt.*, 11.18.
32. *Majjh.*, 19.
33. Ibid.
34. Ibid., 21.
35. Ibid., 8.

heart must no longer tremble, either through fear or through hope. There is no god or demon who can instill fear in the man who is internally detached both from this world and from the other. Whence it is said: "Whatever fears may arise, they arise in the foolish man, not in the wise; whatever [sense of] danger may arise, it arises in the foolish man, not in the wise": only the former offers material in which the fire can start and spread.[36] One text speaks of a discipline against fear. The Buddha himself recalls how, after well establishing the feeling of his rightness—in Latin it would be called *innocentia* and *vacare culpa*—he chose remote and wild places where fear might come at any moment, and how he awaited these moments in order to challenge and destroy any feeling of fear. This is the method: if one is walking, continue to walk, if one is standing, continue to stand, if one is sitting down, continue to sit down, if one is lying down, continue to lie down until the mind has overcome and banished the fear.[37] These disciplines must not be dismissed with the idea that fear only arises in children or in timid women. There are profound, organic forms of fear, forms that may almost be called transcendental since they are not confined to simple psychological states of an individual but which come from certain abysmal contacts. To be incapable of feeling fear in these cases may even be a sign of deadness or of spiritual flatness. It is said that when Prince Siddhattha was sitting under the "tree of illumination," resolved not to move until he had reached transcendental knowledge, he underwent an attack by the demoniacal forces of Māra, who was determined to move him from there, in the form of flames, whirlwinds, tempests, and fearful apparitions. But Prince Siddhattha remained unshakable and all these apparitions finally vanished.[38] Here we can see a variant of an idea that is found, even with the same symbols (e.g., the tree), in several other traditions—but we can also see something more, something beyond a mythical and legendary revival. Anyone who is familiar with ancient literature of the mysteries will recall similar experiences that appear as so many tests for the man who wishes to reach the light. In whatever form they may appear, they still deal with the emergence of profound forces of the being rather than of simply individual or even human ones— and "destruction of fear" is possibly the best term to describe positive victory over them. When a "*Yakkha* spirit" makes himself "felt" by the Buddha and asks if he has fear, the reply is: "I have no fear: I merely feel you contaminating contact"—and later in the same text these words are put into the Buddha's mouth: "I do not see, O friend, either in this world together with the world of angels, of bad and good spirits, or amongst the ranks of ascetics and priests, of gods and men, anyone who can scatter my thoughts or break my mind."[39] The attainment of such unshakability calls, however, for more

36. Ibid., 115; *Angutt.*, 3.1.
37. *Majjh.*, 4.
38. *Lalitavistara*, 19–21.
39. *Suttanipāta*, 2.5, passim.

extreme states of interior discipline than those we have assumed for the present discussion about fear. In this last respect a few words of emphasis may not be out of place. Where a text states that these two are not frightened at a sudden flash of lightning: one being he who has overcome mania and the other, the noble "elephant,"[40] the commentary warns us that these are two quite different cases: fear gains no access in the first case because there does not exist an "I," in the second case because the "I" is extremely strong. This should eliminate any "titanic" interpretation of the discipline in question. We are not dealing with the development of almost animal strength and courage, but with elusiveness. The bond by which anguish might have arisen has been destroyed. There is nothing so rigid that it cannot be broken: but water cannot be compressed.

By striving with the "fourfold, just endeavor" and by using these instruments of defense, the personality—the extrasaṁsāric element appearing in the personality—is gradually integrated by a fourfold strength, to which corresponds, in the texts, the technical term *cattāro iddhipādā*. We have, in the first place, the power that confirms the renunciation in its aspect of detachment from every form of desire, with the pure element of "will" giving support. In the second place we have the power of inflexibility, of perseverance in training, of paying no attention to defeats, of being able to start again with renewed energy. In the third place there is the power of supporting the mind, of recollecting it, of unifying it, of defending it both from states of exaltation and from states of depression, states that, on a path like this, could be entirely avoided only with the greatest difficulty. Finally there is the power of "perception," to be understood as a kind of intellectual integration of the preceding one such that it becomes impossible for the mind to accept false or vain theories. This fourfold power is to some extent summed up by a text we have already quoted: "and he [the ascetic] reaches the admirable path discovered by the intensity, the constancy and the concentration of the will, by the intensity, the constancy and the concentration of the energy, by the intensity, the constancy and the concentration of the mind, by the intensity, the constancy and the concentration of investigation—with a heroic spirit as the fifth."[41] The term *iddhi* (Skt.: *siddhi*) normally refers to powers of a supernormal character. Here it must be understood especially in relation to energies that are associated with warlike discipline—*hatthisippādīni*—without forgetting, however, that, on the path of awakening at least, we are dealing at the same time with forces on which the *bodhi* or *paññā* element confers a quality that is not only human and that is not comparable to any that *saṁsāra* can offer, since it contains something of the "incomparable sureness" (*anuttarassa yogakkhemassa*).

---

40. *Angutt.*, 2.6.6.
41. *Majjh.*, 16.

10

Rightness

We must now deal with *sīla,* that is to say, with "right conduct," which is complementary to the disciplines we have discussed, insofar as they lead to consolidation of the spirit. We are translating the term *sammā,* which figures as the general attribute of the virtues included in the so-called eightfold path of the Ariya *(ariya atthangika magga)* by "upright" or "right" because of the intrinsic evocative power of this word: upright is the position of things that stand, as opposed to that of things that have been knocked over or have fallen. In primordial symbolism the upright position, represented by the vertical I, belongs to virility and fire, while the horizontal position, —, corresponds to the feminine element and to the "waters." Thus, by "rightness" we must understand more than an accepted morality: it is rather an internal mode, a capacity for standing fast at all times without deviating or wavering, by eliminating every trace of tortuousness. The only point of reference here is, fundamentally, oneself: the "virtues" are essentially so many duties to oneself that the reawakened interior sensibility brings to light; but once they have been put into practice, they encourage, strengthen, and establish a state of calm, of transparency of mind and of spirit, of balance and of "justice" by which every other discipline or technique is made easier.

We have already said that there is a complete absence of any moralistic mythology in Buddhism, since it is a creation of the pure Aryan spirit. Moralistic and moralizing obsession is another of the signs of the low level of the modern world. It is even thought now that religions only exist in order to support moral precepts; precepts that, incidentally, only tend to chain the human animal socially. This attitude is indeed an aberration. The fact is, and we must state it categorically, that every moral system, in itself, is completely void of any spiritual value. In the traditional world, each ethical system drew its true justification from a supramundane purpose (which must not be unthinkingly considered as being a kind of *do ut des*, or as being inspired by the idea of sanctions or rewards that await the soul after death) and from the objective and impersonal fact that to follow or not to follow a particular line of conduct produces corresponding modifications in the essential nature of the individual. Morality, as it is thought of today, is only secularized religion and, as such, purely contingent; this is so much the case, that we are almost always forced to refer, in order to justify it, to the factual conditions of a particular historical society. But even on this level the words of one Buddhist text that discusses the order of *bhikkhus* are still valid: that when beings deteriorate and the true doctrine decays then there are more rules and fewer men live steadfastly.[1]

In Buddhism then, as in every truly traditional teaching, ethics have a purely instrumental value and are therefore conditioned. They are not imposed on anyone: they are advocated purely from the point of view of knowledge. It is a question of knowing objectively what effect on the human being will result from following or not following certain principles and, having discovered this, of behaving accordingly. There is a context that clearly states the matter: "The fire has never thought, 'I wish to destroy the foolish man'—but the foolish man who wishes to embrace the burning fire destroys himself."[2] We must speak, then, of stupidity or foolishness, and not of "sin"; of knowledge, and not of "good" and "evil." We have already quoted the Buddhist simile of the raft: as a man once he has crossed a river, will leave behind the raft that was built for that purpose, so we must leave behind the reference points of "good and evil" that served to encourage right conduct, once this conduct has been achieved. That the world of true spirituality has nothing to do with "good and evil" was also, moreover, a basic concept in the preceding Indo-Aryan tradition.

Having made this clear, let us now consider the various parts of *sīla. Sīla* is divided into three grades. The lowest, *cūla-sīla*, prescribes a mode of conduct that is expressed by this fixed canonical formula:

> (1) [The ascetic] has ceased from killing, he keeps himself far from killing. Without a staff, without a sword, tender-hearted, full of sympathy, he inculcates love and compassion for all living beings. (2) He has ceased taking what is not given, he keeps himself far from taking what is not given. He does not take what is not given him, he accepts only what is given, without thought of theft, with a heart become pure. (3) He has ceased from lust, he lives chaste, faithful to his renunciation, far from the vulgar habit of copulation. (4) He has ceased from lying, he

---

1. *Majjh.*, 65.
2. Ibid., 50.

keeps himself far from falsehood. He tells the truth, he is devoted to the truth, upright, trustworthy, neither hypocrite nor flatterer of the world. (5) He has ceased from malicious speaking, he holds himself far from malicious speaking. What he has heard here he does not repeat there, and what he has heard there he does not repeat here, and thus divide one person from another. He joins the divided, he rejoices in agreement, his words unite. (6) He has ceased from rough words, he holds himself far from rough words. Words that are without offense, cordial and urbane that delight many, that encourage many: such words he speaks. (7) He has ceased from idle words. He speaks in due time, according to fact, careful of his meaning, with a discourse full of content, adorned on occasion with similes, clear and pertinent, adequate for its purpose.[3]

In connection with not taking what is not given, another text adds: "not even a blade of grass" and gives this simile: "as a leaf plucked from a branch cannot again become green, so a disciple who takes what is not given is not an ascetic and is not a follower of the son of the Śākya."[4] Elsewhere, a characteristic example is cited: that of a man who sees a gold coin on the ground and who neither picks it up nor pays any attention to it. Referring to sexual abstinence, this other simile is given: "As a man whose head has been cut off cannot continue to live amongst others with only his trunk, so one who does not practise sexual abstinence is not an ascetic and is not a follower of the son of the Śākya."[5] Finally, one who intentionally takes the life of another is likened to a block that has been split in half and cannot be put together again.[6]

All this constitutes the "lower *sīla*." The precepts of *majjhima-sīla* or the "middle *sīla*" deal with a kind of spartanization of life: reduction of needs, cutting away of the bond formed by a life of comfort, with particular reference to eating, sleeping, and drowsing. There are also precepts that come under the heading of a "departure," of a physical or literal leaving of the world: for example, avoidance of business or undertakings, nonacceptance of gifts, abandonment of possessions and refusal to assume fresh ones, and so on. Included in this part of "right conduct" is abstention from dilectical discussions and speculation—this takes us back to the neutralization of the demon of intellectualism (cf. p. 38).

The last part of right discipline, *mahā-sīla*, concerns not only abstention from practicing divination, astrology, or mere magic, but also from abandoning oneself to

---

3. *Dīgha*, 1.1.8 ff.
4. *Mahāvagga (Vin.)*, 1.78.3.
5. Ibid., 1.78.2.
6. Ibid., 1.78.4.

the cult of some divinity or other. One can therefore speak in some measure of sur-mounting the bond of religion in the sense of a bond that makes one lead the saintly life with the notion: "By means of these rites, vows, mortifications, or renunciations I wish to become a god or a divine being." But it is evident that this includes some elements that are supposed to have been already removed in the determination of the vocations.[7]

In any case, it will be as well to discuss the elements of "right conduct" as a whole, so that we may see them in perspective. It is clear that some refer exclusively to an absolute form of "departure," that is to say, of a material as well as a purely interior or spiritual detachment from the world; that is to say, to the asceticism of the monk or anchorite. The degree to which they are strictly to be observed today de-pends, then, on what each individual may decide is necessary. A good number of the elements of the middle and higher *sīla* can, however, be applied with simple adapta-tion to an asceticism that is practicable to some extent in the "world": thus, the pre-cepts dealing with astrology, divination, and the like, could easily refer to the mod-ern debased practices of like nature in the form of "occultism," spiritualism, and so on. Measured with the ideal of awakening all this has thus the character of a danger-ous straying.[8]

Of greater importance are the precepts of "right conduct" that belong to the lower *sīla*. They are widely applicable, independent of particular historical condi-tions. And that some of them clearly correspond to the principles of Ariyan morality, to the morality of a well-born man, is plain enough. The following may be taken as a general maxim of *sīla:* "Though I be hurled head down into the infernal regions, I will do nothing that is ignoble."[9] Such is the case, in the first place, with the precept of not taking what is not given—"not even a blade of grass"—of wholly eliminating all intention to steal. Among the ancient Aryan peoples theft was considered a much graver offense than it is today, since they had in mind the inward rather than the material and "social" aspect of the matter. For this reason there is no question of degree: as regards taking what is not given, it is just as dishonorable to do so by taking a cigarette from a companion—to refer to modern times—or a paper from one's office, as it is to stage a full-scale bank robbery and carry off a large sum of money.

In the second place, the rule of speaking the truth, the absolute inability to lie, is specifically Aryan. Nothing, among the Aryan people, was considered so ignomini-ous and degrading as falsehood, especially from the point of one's own relations with oneself and of the duties that one owes first and foremost to one's self and to

7. *Dīgha*, 1.1.8 ff.
8. Cf. J. Evola, *Maschera e volto dello spiritualismo contemporaneo*, 2nd edn. (Bari, 1949).
9. *Jātaka*, 40.

one's own interior dignity. "In one who has no shame in conscious falsehood, no evil thing is impossible"—so runs a text—whence the firm determination of the ascetic: "Not even for a joke will I lie"; this is the exact equivalent of the saying attributed by Western Aryan antiquity to the figure of Epaminondas: *ne joco quidem mentiebatur.* In this text there is also a simile: only when a man has made up his mind can he be said to be committed definitely, just as when it is seen that a royal elephant that has been trained for battle is using his trunk one can say: "This royal elephant has renounced his life: nothing is now impossible for the royal elephant."[10] Another text: "I would not tell a falsehood even if the mountains were moved by the wind, even if the moon and sun were to fall to earth and the rivers were to run backward."[11] This, in fact, is an essential point in all practice of rightness, it is essential for the man who would be upright and integral, not tortuous, not oblique, not masked. In an Aryo-Persian text it is even said that killing is not as serious as lying.

Avoidance of malicious speaking needs no special comment. Whether we give vent to rough words or not obviously depends on the degree to which we allow other people to put us in a temper, to reach our spirit and wound it as if it can be wounded. It is, then, essentially a problem of interior mastery and of awareness. Besides, only an individual who is not carried away by anger or irritated by insults can succeed in putting a presumptuous man in his place. Buddhism, indeed, would agree with the ancient Roman maxim that it is better to suffer an injustice than to commit one, that one should not react to evil by producing more evil in one's turn. These precepts are essentially designed to overcome the bond of the personality, and we shall return shortly to a discussion of their interpretation when we come to deal with the precept against killing. They are valid, naturally, for the practice of asceticism and not for life in the world.

Control of the tongue is emphasized and the absolute elimination of all useless, disordered, hasty, inconclusive, indefinite, illogical, or empty speech. There is something of the classical style here in speech that is suited to the subject, sober, clear and determined, timely, free from effusions and uncontrolled expansiveness; something of the style of Tacitus. It is with silence that Prince Siddhattha often replies. Little streams of water—it is said[12]—make a noise between their steep and narrow banks: the vast ocean, instead, is silent. "He who is insufficient makes a noise; he who is complete in himself is calm." We shall see that an Accomplished One maintains a similar style in his gestures and behavior.

One of the aims of *sīla* is to create a state of harmony and equilibrium both with oneself and with the outside world. This is how we must interpret the precepts of

10. *Majjh.*, 61.
11. *Jātaka.*
12. *Suttanipāta*, 3.11.42–3.

cordiality, of abstention from malicious speaking, of not contributing to the creation of discords, of contributing instead to the uniting of those who are disunited. This leads to the precept of not killing intentionally, a precept that, in the later forms of Buddhism, became much exaggerated—the respect for life was extended to even worms and insects. Originally, however, it referred particularly to the killing of human beings. However, even with this limitation, some people wish to interpret this precept as a kind of humanitarianism, little in harmony with the spirit of the Aryan Khattiya, or warrior tradition; a tradition to which Prince Siddhattha had belonged, and which, in the *Bhagavadgītā* produced an entirely metaphysical justification for the heroism that spares neither one's own life nor the life of others in a just war. The fact is that this precept of not killing must be understood as having a particular interior and ascetic aim; and therefore, like all the others, it has only a conditioned value. Already on the plane of *sīla* a certain impersonalization and universalization of the "I" is to be aimed at. When one has to do with other people one must try to anticipate the state of consciousness in which another person is felt as being oneself, not in the Christian, humanitarian, or democratic sense, however, but with reference to a superindividual consciousness. Seen from this height it becomes evident that "I" is one of the many forms that, in certain conditions, may variously clothe the extrasaṁsāric principle; a principle that may appear in the person of this or that being and there become manifest. We are dealing, then, with something very different from the respect of one "creature" for another "creature." The other "creature" is considered, instead, from a higher point of view, from the point of view of a "totality." This being so, it would obviously be abnormal to act or react against a part unless one felt oneself to be only a part. For this reason, the precept of not killing and of not causing others to kill is associated, in a text[13] with the formula of identification: "As I am, so are they, as they are, so am I" and we have already quoted the simile of the split block for one who kills. Again, we are simply dealing with a discipline that may produce an orientation of pragmatic value and subordinate to the higher aim. This same significance will be found again both in the "fourfold irradiant contemplation," which also includes love, and also when we come to discuss *pubbe-nivāsa-ñāṇa*, that is to say, superindividual insight that penetrates multiple existences.

The last of the precepts of the *cūla-sīla*, that which relates to chastity, leads us to a short discussion of the sexual problem. Its solutions vary according to the degree of absoluteness to which ascetic practice is to be carried. Originally in Buddhism, for those who were not, properly speaking, *bhikkhus* but only "followers," only adultery was forbidden. Regarding adultery we must not forget that in the Aryan East every man belonging to a higher caste had several women at his disposal, but whose status

---

13. *Suttanipāta*, 3.11.27.

was really more that of objects of use than "wives" in the Western sense, especially with those "ladies" or "life companions" who nevertheless allow themselves today to take the initiative and gain emancipation or divorce. In this state of affairs adultery simply came under the heading of taking what was not given and as such was considered to be dishonest.

More generally, as regards relations between the two sexes, it is evident that one who wishes to achieve the basic condition for awakening, that is to say, calm detachment and interior sufficiency, must train himself in such a manner that he will continually feel less need of a woman. The physical need, to some extent, is still allowable, like that of eating or of other animal functions. It is the "spiritual" need that must be eliminated at an early stage, since this affects a much deeper element that has nothing to do with the body and since it testifies to deficiency and to inconsistency of spirit. The danger that a woman represents, particularly today, is not so much her female aspect as the fact that she encourages the need for support, for reliance upon someone else who may be a weak soul unable to find in himself a meaning for his life. A story is told of the men who were searching for a fleeing woman and who were asked by the Buddha: "What think you, O youths, which is better for you, that you seek a woman or your selves?" The reply is: "For us, Lord, it is better that we go in search of our selves." And the Buddha says: "If that is so, O youths, seat yourselves, and I will expound the doctrine for you."[14] The same Indo-Aryan tradition records a saying attributed to a *yogin,* an ascetic: "What need have I of an external woman? I have an internal woman within me"—meaning that he had within himself the element of self-completion, of fulfillment, an element that the common man confusedly seeks, instead, in woman.[15] In this respect too we find ourselves today in completely abnormal conditions. Modern men mostly little know what spiritual virility and internal sufficiency mean; through "soul" and "sentiment" they descend to the level of women who, often enough today, and without appearing to be so, are the directors of man's life.

The precept of chastity must be considered on a higher level of the discipline. In Buddhism, as in all really traditional teaching, it has a purely technical justification. Only religions noticeably affected by the Semitic spirit have carnal ethics; this is now so much the case that sexual matters have almost become the measure of sin and virtue. And Buddhist texts opportunely censure incomplete, impure, and murky forms of chastity, including that followed by those who aim at a celestial world.[16] The precept of chastity for those who follow the path of awakening with *all* their energies has nothing to do with such an order of things; it has the transcendental

14. *Mahāvagga (Vin.),* 1.14.2–3.
15. Cf. our work *The Yoga of Power.*
16. *Angutt.,* 7.47.

justification, which takes us beyond the field of *sīla*, of "right conduct" pure and simple. The fact is that, in a being subject to "craving," sexual energy is, in some ways, the radical energy. Through it one enters saṁsāric life and through it the life-spark of one being is lit by another. The ancient esoteric teachings therefore considered that the suspension and change of polarity of this force was a fundamental condition for effectually "stopping the current" and "reversing it." In fact, there even existed a precise and direct technique for acting on the force that normally appears as sexual energy and sexual desire, and for diverting it to another state where it could serve as the basis for a birth, not in time, but in what is beyond time.[17] There is no mention—at least in original Buddhism—of such direct methods that have a connection and with Dionysism and sexual magic. It can be said, however, that the whole Buddhist ascesis is a process that will itself act in this way on the sexual energy, now no longer dissipated thanks to the discipline of chastity.

In speaking of sexual abstinence we must not, however, forget the Buddhist precept of the gradualness of each aspect of discipline, nor the simile of the serpent that twists round and bites if it is not grasped in the correct manner. Christian mysticism provides good examples of the lethal effects that are produced by a unilateral and unenlightened suppression of every sex impulse. These are the energies that, when they are simply repressed—*verdrängt*, to use the classical term of the psychoanalysts—pass, reinforced, into the subconscious and produce all sorts of upsets, hysteria, and anxieties. We must never act "dictatorially" in dealing with such matters, but always by degrees, so that every achievement is of an organic nature, gradually increasing. Equally, we must beware of unconscious "transpositions" of the sexual impulses, of the system of compensations and supercompensations to which they may give rise, thereby fooling the conscious mind that wrongly believed it had gained mastery through a mere veto. This last observation will also serve to put us on our guard against the exclusively psychoanalytical and Freudian interpretation that, in dealing with sexual impulses and, in general, the libido, admits of no other action than either "repression" *(Verdrängung)* that creates hysteria and neuroses, or alternatively "transposition" and "sublimation." A high ascesis is neither one nor the other, and we must be very careful that during development we maintain a just balance and that the central force, spiritually virile and awakened and strengthened by the various disciplines, gradually absorbs the whole of the energies that call for expression once the road to animal generation is barred. Only one who feels that the interior process is developing in this manner can keep without danger the precept of complete sexual abstinence. Otherwise it is far better to wait than to force the pace—

---

17. This is, for example, the sense of the so-called *kuṇḍalinī-yoga* and of the Tantric *pañcatattva* with Tantric *maithuna*, on which cf. *The Yoga of Power*.

always provided that we are not being misled by pretexts provided for the conscious personality by the entity of craving. How important it is to divert the basic energy of life from subjection to the saṁsāric law of craving and thirst, which is clearly dominant in the field of sex, is clearly illustrated, moreover, by the Buddhist simile that states that one who does not keep this precept of *sīla* is like a man who would try to go on living among others with his head cut off.

A particular rule of *sīla*, of which we have not yet spoken, is abstention from "strong" or intoxicating substances, especially from alcoholic drinks.[18] This precept, too, has a technical origin. Such substances produce a state of inebriation that, in the case of ancient man rather than in the man of today, might even produce a favorable condition when the accompanying "exaltation" *(pīti)* was made to act in the right way. This would, however, be a "conditioned" exaltation that would harm the "I": where one's own energy ought to have acted an exterior force has intervened, so that the corresponding state is infected, fundamentally and from the outset, by renunciation of initiative and passivity. Somehow or another, a "debt" has been created and we find ourselves bound by an obscure "pact"—this is a thing that happens, though to a greater extent in all forms of what is known as ceremonial magic. Both in India, in the case of Tantrism, and in the West, among the pre-Orphic Dionysians, the possibility was considered of mingling activity and passivity in a state of exaltation (not unrelated to the sexual energies), and this was carried to a point where, by means of ecstasy, the antecedents became of no further account.[19] Such methods, however, would not befit the path of clear and "Olympian" ascesis that the teaching of original Buddhism represents.

As we are examining these elements whose power *sīla*, as a whole, should diminish, we will take this opportunity of referring to the theory of the five bonds that plays an important part in the Buddhist teaching, particularly as regards the various degrees of achievement and their consequences. These bonds, which bind the "ignorant common man, insensible to what is Ariya, remote from the doctrine of the Ariya, inaccessible by the doctrine of the Ariya," are: firstly, attachment to the "I," the illusion of individualism *(attandiṭṭhi* or *sakkāyadiṭṭhi);*[20] secondly, doubt *(vicikicchā),* doubt regarding the doctrine and the Master, and also, more generally, about the past or the future;[21] it is also doubt about the vocation existing in oneself, the road that one is following and what may result from the states of aridity, depression, and

---

18. Cf., e.g., *Mahāvagga (Vin.),* 1.56.
19. We have also spoken of these rituals in our book, *The Yoga of Power.* They were used in that form of Tantric Buddhism known as *vajra-yāna,* "the road of the diamond and of the lightning."
20. The term *sakkāya* may possibly derive from *sat-kāya,* which deals with the illusion of a man who believes that the person insofar as it consists of the body is a reality *(sat).*
21. *Dhamma-saṅgani,* 1004.

nostalgia, which are inevitable in the early phases of a life of detachment; thirdly, belief in the efficacy of simple conformity, of rites and ceremonies *(sīlabbata-parāmāsa)*;[22] fourthly, sexual desire and all bodily pleasure and craving *(kāma* or *rāga)*; finally, there is ill will, aversion *(paṭigha)*. If they are not neutralized, if they are strengthened through conduct dominated by "ignorance," these bonds "lead downward" toward the lowest and darkest forms of saṁsāric existence.[23] As we have said, at this stage it is a matter of limiting the power of these negative inclinations in their more external and immediate forms. Their complete annihilation occurs in more advanced stages of the ascesis, where the "five bonds" appear related to the so-called "five impurities of the spirit" (cf. p. 141).

As for the positive side of the general work of consolidation and its developments, we have the well-known and rather stereotyped formula of the eightfold path of the Ariya *(ariya atthangika magga)*. This deals with eight virtues, to each of which is applied the term *sammā*, "right," a term to be understood mainly in the sense we have already indicated, that is to say, as the attribute of one who "stands," who holds himself erect, as opposed to the oblique or horizontal direction of those who "are driven." First: right vision, which consists of keeping in sight the "four truths," of being aware both of the contingency of existence and of the way in which, by following a particular method, it can be overcome. Second: right intention (in Pāli, *sammāsankappo)*, which refers to active determination, volition, or desire, and is, therefore, the determination of one who opposes the "flux" and who proceeds on the upward path. Third: right speech, which is inflexible sincerity, open speech, abstention from malicious words and gossip, as has already been stated. Fourth: right conduct, which is conduct conforming to the aforesaid precepts of not taking what is not given, of not killing intentionally, of abstinence from lust. Fifth: right life, which is a life supported by blameless means, is sober and avoids pampering, extravagance, and luxury. Sixth: right effort, which is interpreted essentially as the "four just endeavours" (cf. p. 110). Seventh: right meditation, of which we shall speak later as it deals essentially with what is known as "perpetual clear consciousness" (cf. p. 131–32). The term used here is *sammāsati. Sati* literally means "memory," that is to say, continual practice of mindfulness of oneself; and of self-awareness. Eighth: right contemplation, which brings us to the *"samādhi"* section with which we shall deal later (p. 146), since it is essentially concerned with the four *jhāna*, by which the catharsis leads to the limit of conditioned consciousness.[24]

---

22. Ibid., 1005 specifies thus: "It is the theory, held by ascetics and priests foreign to our doctrine, which claims that purification is achieved by precepts of conduct, or by rites, or by precepts of conduct and rites."

23. *Majjh.*, 64.

24. Cf., e.g., *Dīgha*, 22.21.

It can be seen that this formula serves as a schematic representation. Returning to *sīla*, we see that it aims at further consolidation: it eliminates much material that might rekindle and reestablish the saṃsāric flame. The "virtues" of *sīla* are said to be "praised by the Ariya, inflexible, integral, immaculate, unsullied, conferring liberty, appreciated by the intelligent; virtues that are inaccessible [by craving and delusion], that lead to concentration of the mind."[25] The fixed formula that, in the canonical texts, accompanies the exposition of *sīla* is: "With the accomplishment of these noble precepts of virtue [the ascetic] feels an intimate, immaculate joy." When this feeling arises it must be mastered, fixed and established, as it is a precious foundation for further progress. This is naturally not possible without a precise effort. But, in this respect, Buddhism has further instruments of defense by prevention.

The texts speak, for example, of the conditions for achieving power over the body and over the mind. The principle is that pleasant feeling that arises in the body binds the mind through the impotence of the body; painful feeling, however, binds the mind through the impotence of the mind itself. Experiencing a pleasant feeling, "the ignorant common man craves for pleasure, falls a prey to craving for pleasure"—and it is here that one must intervene and bar the way leading from the body, not in the sense of excluding the pleasant feeling, but of preventing it from binding one and carrying one away. Thus the impotence of the body is remedied. When painful feeling arises, such a man "becomes sad and overwhelmed, he laments and falls a prey to despair." Here one must act directly on the mind, for it is now the mind that shows itself to be impotent. In this way one begins to gain power over both the body and the mind, and interior balance is strengthened.

This form of effort is more successful when aided by the necessary discipline. A particular experience may provoke pleasant feeling, unpleasant feeling, or feeling that is neither unpleasant nor pleasant. This is how one must then train oneself: "Let me, during what is unpleasant, remain with a pleasant perception," or: "Let me, during what is pleasant, remain with an unpleasant perception," or lastly: "Pleasant and unpleasant, avoiding the one and the other, let me remain indifferent, collected, present to myself."[26] A variation of the same discipline concerns the repugnant and the attractive. From time to time one should consider the attractive as repugnant, in order to lessen desire or inclination (for places, foods, person, etc.); and the repugnant as attractive (in order to allay feelings of repulsion, irritation, or intolerance); and what is neither repugnant nor attractive as either repugnant or attractive; and, finally, one should be able to maintain a balanced, watchful mind, aware of oneself above states of either kind.[27] Any real progress in such disciplines naturally depends

25. *Angutt.*, 3.70; *Saṃyutt.*, 40.10.
26. *Majjh.*, 36; 152.
27. *Saṃyutt.*, 54.8.

upon all aspects as a whole and, above all, upon exercises aiming directly at nonidentification, which we shall now consider.

In a commentary on the *Anguttara-nikāya*[28] we read: "When confidence is tied to vision and vision to confidence, when the will is joined to concentration and concentration to the will, the balance of the forces can be considered as achieved. Self-awareness *[sati]* is, however, essential always. It must always be energetically cultivated." The discipline called *satipaṭṭhāna* aims at this in particular.

---

28. *Angutt.*, 6.55. Also on p. 86 of the edition of *Die Reden des Buddhas* by Nyānatiloka (Munich, 1922–23).

11

✺

Sidereal Awareness: The Wounds Close

The term *satipaṭṭhāna* is made up of the word *sati,* which we have already explained as memory, or self-awareness, and *paṭṭhāna,* which means "to construct," "set up," "establish." In English this term is normally translated by "setting-up of mindfulness" (Rhys Davids), and in German by *Pfeiler der Geistesklarheit*—whence the expression used by de Lorenzo: *pilastri del sapere* (pillars of knowledge—in the sense of self-knowledge). The whole formula of the text is: *parimukhaṁ satiṁ upaṭṭhapeti,*[1] which could be rendered thus: "to place the memory of oneself before oneself." The aim of the discipline with which we shall now deal is, in fact, to begin to disengage the central principle of one's own being by means of an objective and detached consideration, both of what makes up one's own personality and also of the general content of one's own experience. The very fact of standing apart from all this, as if it were something external or foreign, purifies and stimulates the consciousness, brings one back to oneself and further develops impassive calm. In this sense the four principal groups of objects that are considered in this discipline serve as so many supports for "knowledge"; they represent something solid for a reaction leading to an unfettering of oneself, to a return to oneself. The four groups of the *satipaṭṭhāna* refer to the body *(kāya),* to the emotions or feelings *(vedanā),* to the mind (*citta*), and lastly to the *dhammā,* a general term that here includes phenomena and states brought about by the ascetic discipline itself in its higher stages.

1. *Contemplation of the body.* To quote the canonical formula, the ascetic, after overcoming the cares and desires of the world, devotes himself in the first place "with a mind clear and fully conscious" to contemplation of the body. This procedure is carried out in various stages.

(a) To begin with, the ascetic practices conscious breathing or self-awareness

---

1. *Dīgha,* 22.2.

130

while breathing *(ānāpāna-sati);* this is said to be one of the most rapid methods of attaining unshakable calm.[2] The ascetic must choose a quiet and secluded place and there practice consciousness of breathing in and out. He breathes in deeply and knows: "I am breathing in deeply," he breathes out deeply and knows: "I am breathing out deeply"; he does the same with short breaths. He then practices thus: "I wish to breathe in feeling the whole body," "I wish to breathe out feeling the whole body," "I wish to breathe in calming this bodily combination," " I wish to breathe out calming this bodily combination." And so on. A simile that shows what a perfect awareness is required in this exercise states: just as an expert and careful turner, when turning quickly, knows: "I am turning quickly," and, when turning slowly, knows: "I am turning slowly."[3]

Exercises of this kind are particularly important since, according to the Indo-Aryan teaching, breathing is connected with the subtle force of life—*prāṇa*—that forms a substratum to all the psychophysical functions of a man. The whole organism is animated and pervaded by subtle currents—*nāḍī* (a term usually translated rather primitively by "winds")—whose source is located in *prāṇa* and in the breath. Thus an Upaniṣad says: "As the spokes of a wheel rest on the nave, so all [in the organism] rests on the *prāṇa*."[4] These teachings derive from knowledge of the breath that is not understood by modern man and that he can only revive through a special effort. When, however, the breath or respiration comes to be felt as *prāṇa*, it can then be made to serve as a "way through": when the breath has been made conscious, when clear consciousness has been grafted onto the breathing, one is able to discover the "life of one's own life" and to control the organism and the mind in many ways that are quite impossible for the ordinary consciousness and will. Furthermore, by taking the rhythm of the breath as a "vehicle," it is possible to render certain states of consciousness "corporeal" and "organic," to make them, that is to say, act upon the life-forces of the saṁsāric entity in such a way as on the one hand to stabilize and consolidate them, and on the other to modify the saṁsāric stuff accordingly. Further developments of the discipline of breathing are dealt with by Buddhism. From purely bodily mastery, we pass to psychic mastery, and formulae like these are used: "I wish to breathe in feeling joy, I wish to breathe out feeling joy"; "I wish to breathe in feeling the mind, I wish to breathe out feeling the mind"; "I wish to breathe in gladdening the mind, I wish to breathe out gladdening the mind"; "I wish to breathe in concentrating the mind, I wish to breathe out concentrating the mind"; and the same for relaxing. Finally, conscious breathing is practiced with other contemplations and states; it confers a rhythm on them and is itself a channel through which they become

2. *Angutt.,* 5.96.
3. *Dīgha,* 22.2.
4. *Chāndogya Upaniṣad,* 7.15.1.

united with the subtle counterpart of the human make-up. It is said that when the breathing is thus watched and practiced, "even the last breaths cease mindfully, not unmindfully."[5] In the Upaniṣad it had already been said: "Truly these beings arrive in the wake of the breath, depart in the wake of the breath."[6]

At this stage, however, the aim of the practice is only contemplative. It is a matter of making the breath unautomatic at certain moments, of making it conscious, of placing oneself before one's breathing and one's breathing before oneself, by experiencing the breath essentially as *prāṇa*, as the life-force of the body.

(b) In the second place, we have contemplation of the body and of all its parts, with the coolness and the precision of a surgeon at an autopsy. The canonical formula is: "Behold, this body bears a scalp of hair, it has body-hair, nails, teeth, skin, flesh, tendons, bones, marrow, kidneys, heart, liver, diaphragm, spleen, lungs, stomach, intestines, membranes, feces, bile, phlegm, pus, blood, sweat, lymph, tears, grease, saliva, mucus, articular fluid, urine." And the following simile is given in order to show how to perform the operation: as though a man with good eyesight having a sack full of mixed grain might untie the sack and carefully examining the contents might say: "This is rice, these are beans, this is sesamum." Naturally, the best thing that can be done by anyone wishing to follow these disciplines is to go to a morgue or to be present at an autopsy: he will thus obtain particular vivid and effective images as a basis for such meditations. The purpose is always the same: to disidentify oneself, to create a gap: "This am I, this is my body, it is made thus and thus, composed of these parts, of these elements."[7] There are some texts that prescribe, as an additional fortifying exercise, contemplation of the various diseases to which the body is exposed.[8]

(c) For the third exercise, the body is considered to be a function of the four "great elements" that are present in it. Whether he is moving or still, the ascetic must consider the body that he bears as a function of these elements: "This body consists of the earth element, of the water element, of the fire element, of the air elements."[9] This kind of meditation had a somewhat different significance for ancient man from what it may have today. Ancient man, in fact, regarded the "great element," *mahābhūtā*, not merely as "states of material," but rather as manifestations of cosmic forces such as the elements that were taught by the ancient and medieval Western traditions. In any case, the aim of the meditation is to comprehend the body as a function of the impersonal forces of the world that follow their laws with complete

---

5. *Majjh.*, 62; 118; *Angutt.*, 10.60.
6. *Chāndogya Upaniṣad*, 7.15.1.
7. *Dīgha*, 22.5.
8. *Angutt.*, 10.60.
9. *Dīgha*, 22.6.

indifference to our person. In the second place, we have to understand that these "great elements" also are subject to the laws of change and dissolution. Thus some texts advocate the practice of calling vividly to mind the periods both of power and of decline and dissolution of the cosmic manifestations of the four elements, so that we come to this conclusion: if change and cessation befall even these powers of the world, why should they not also befall this body, "less than eight spans high, produced by thirst for existence"? Are "I," "mine," or "I am" its real attributes? In actual fact, "It has nothing."[10] According to a simile for this third operation: in recognizing in the body this or that element one must proceed in the same manner as a man who, butchering a cow, separates the various parts and considers them well, takes them to the market and then sits down—that is to say, one must return to oneself, one must finally become aware of oneself. By arousing the knowledge that the organism, though still alive and "ours," follows the objective and elementary laws of the great elementary forces, quite independent of the world of the "I"; by awakening this sense, the body once again provides the basis for a reaction, for a detached and free realization of the extrasaṁsāric factor in man.

(d) *Maraṇānussati, contemplatio mortis.* Here one has to imagine a corpse in all the phases of its decomposition: stiff, then swollen up and rotting, then stripped of flesh with only the tendons left, then without either flesh or tendons, then as scattered bone, as bones heaped up and mixed with others, and finally as bones rotting away and as bones crumbled to dust. With this, one has to comprehend: "My body, too, has a like nature, so will it become, it cannot avoid coming this fate."[11] These similes should awaken particularly vivid feelings without, however, arousing Hamlet-like reflections nor those of the Semitic minstrel with his *vanitas vanitatum.* The decay of the body, in all its crudity, is here considered as helpful to progress because, rather than depress the mind, it should awaken a detached consciousness capable of imagining with perfect calm and dispassion the fate of one's own body after death. It is, once again, a matter of consolidating the sidereal, extrasaṁsāric element. Should these meditations result in a feeling of pessimistic depression, of desolation, of Leopardian shipwreck, then they have been quite wrongly carried out. They are performed correctly when they result in a state of mind where one can consider a disaster overtaking one's body, and even physical death itself, as though another's body were concerned. This state may even transform itself into a force capable, in certain circumstances, of acting positively on the organism. Thus the texts speak of a sick ascetic who recovered his strength and overcame his disease at the moment of understanding and apprehending the teaching about the perfect meditation on the

---

10. Cf. *Majjh.*, 28; 140.
11. *Dīgha*, 22.7–10.

body.[12] It is said: "If the body is ill, the mind shall not be ill—thus have you to train yourselves. The Ariya are not obsessed by the idea: 'I am materiality, materiality is mine, materiality is my self,' and for this reason they do not change when the material body changes and grows old" or when the same fate overtakes the other constituents that make up the personality.[13]

This is the fourfold form of the Buddhist contemplation of the body, which constitutes the first support. Its importance in regard to the goal, which we have already discussed, is confirmed by the statement that this contemplation, well practiced, well exercised, gives a foretaste of *amata* (Skt.: *amṛta*), that is to say, of the deathless.[14]

2. *Contemplation of the feelings.* After the body, the feelings *(vedanā)* form the basis for the sidereal awareness of oneself. The canonical formula is: "Among the feelings within, the ascetic watches over the feelings; among the feelings without, he watches over the feelings; among the feelings within and without, he watches over the feelings. He sees how the feelings arise, how the feelings pass away, how the feelings arise and pass away. 'This is feeling'—such knowledge becomes his support because it leads to wisdom, it leads to reflection."[15] Such exercises can be correlated with what is called the control of the six internal-external sensory realms, although this latter is normally included in the fourth section, namely, that concerning the *dhammā*. Here we are dealing with the sphere of the senses, including the mental organ. The formula is: "The ascetic understands the eye, he understands visual forms and he understands that all combinations resulting from both are bonds. He knows when these combinations occur, he knows when the combination that has occurred ceases and he knows when the combination that has occurred will no longer appear in the future." The same formula is repeated for the ear and sounds, for the tongue and tastes, for the touch and contacts, for the mind and mental objects.[16] To begin with we may not understand the action that is to be performed: how do we obtain this separate knowing of the sensible faculties and of their objects, as if we were complete strangers to both, and what is the purpose of tracing their combinations in the same spirit as a chemist follows the process of the combining of two substances? We should understand the meaning of the discipline in this way: that we must make ourselves aware of the nature of common experience, and of how it exhausts itself in the "flux." What we have already said about a passive way of thinking is mainly true in the case of the various senses. In reality, to say "I see," "I taste," "I hear" is, in saṁsāric existence, rather a euphemism. Indeed there exists

12. *Angutt.*, 10.60.
13. *Saṁyutt.*, 22.1.8.
14. *Angutt.*, 1.21.47; *Milinadapañha*, 336; *Majjh.*, 119.
15. *Majjh.*, 10.
16. *Dīgha*, 22.15.

here only the fact of vision, the fact of hearing, the fact of taste and so on, which arise from the promiscuous contact of object and subject, and which proceed from the elementary self-identification of consciousness with its experience in processes of "combustion." The discipline we are discussing aims at dissociating this irrational mixture until one can truly say: *"I* see," *"I* taste," *"I* hear," *"I* touch," *"I* smell," *"I* think"—with the same clarity and self-awareness as one who grasps an object in his hand or lets it fall and who knows: "I am grasping this object, I am letting it fall." When we consider the domains of the senses and of the mind itself, we must seek to cultivate a real feeling that they are actual organs that are consciously used, but always at a certain "distance": I am here, the thing seen or felt or tasted is there, and the result is the experience, and the "combination" of the two as an elementary fact or "bond," is also just as clearly before me. The texts provide a simile: "As from the contact of two pieces of wood when they are rubbed together heat is born and fire springs up, and as the heat formerly produced by them ceases, becomes extinguished when they are separated": just so, must we clearly come to understand that "This feeling is arisen," "this feeling is extinguished." The texts add, with particular reference to the general aim of these contemplations: "There remains only passiveness which is pure, clear, ductile, flexible, resplendent."[17] As an example of this contemplation, on an everyday level, let us take the case of a meal: the mouthful is put into the mouth, it is consciously circulated in the mouth so that none remains unmasticated and so that none remains in the mouth when it is swallowed; when it has been swallowed, the next mouthful is taken; "the ascetic feels the taste whilst he takes the food, but he does not derive pleasure from it":[18] one must taste with awareness and yet remain detached. A considerable inward effort is necessary to extend this kind of control beyond occasional moments of practice: it is, in fact, a case, not only of substituting one habit for another, but of coming to grips with the blind force of identification that acts in the former habit. The natural development of this contemplation is what is known as the "watch over the senses" or the "curing of the wounds" of which we shall say more below (p. 139).

3. *Contemplation of the mind.* The term *vedanā* can mean not only feeling, but also emotion or sentiment, and we can pass naturally from the sphere of the second contemplation to that of the third, which aims at awakening "knowledge" in the presence of all states and changes of one's mind. The canonical formula is: "An ascetic knows the craving mind as craving and the non-craving mind as non-craving; the hateful mind as hateful and the non-hateful mind as non-hateful; the deluded mind as deluded and the undeluded mind as undeluded; the concentrated mind as concentrated

17. *Majjh.*, 140.
18. Ibid., 91.

and the distracted mind as distracted; the upward-tending mind as upward tending and the mind of low feeling as of low feeling; the noble mind as noble and the common mind as common; the tranquil mind as tranquil and the anxious mind as anxious—he knows the liberated mind as liberated and the bound mind as bound."[19] This means that, in the first place, one must cultivate an attitude of absolute, inflexible sincerity and objectivity with regard to one's interior, psychological, and emotive life. In the second place, we are again concerned with the energy that is aroused by the disidentifying "insight." The sign that progress has been achieved on this road is one's ability to regard one's own emotions, feelings, states of mind, and passions as if they were another's—as though, naturally, they were taking place in someone about whom one were quite indifferent and who served merely as an object of observation. Once again, the aim is an active form of depersonalization. A text reads: "As the clouds arise, pass, become transformed and dissolve in the open sky, so also is it with the passions in the mind of the wise man." In its liberty and intangibility, the mind of the wise man is thus likened to the sky. As its clarity is unaltered by the changing vicissitudes of the clouds, so his mind is unchanged by the passions and emotions that form, transform, and pass away there according to their laws. As the *Bhagavadgītā*[20] speaks of one who "does not desire desire, into whom, instead, all desires flow as the waters flow into the sea which, [continually] refilled, [yet] remains unchanged," so in Buddhism the ideal state is likened to the "depths of the ocean, where no waves arise, but where calm reigns."[21] We shall find other cosmic and elemental images of liberty and intangibility when we discuss the "irradiant contemplations." Here, this serves but as a signpost to point out the way of contemplation.

4. *Contemplation of the dhammā.* The term *dhammā* has a wide meaning, as we have said, and this section includes contemplation not only of phenomena and states of consciousness of various kinds, but also of the ascetic processes themselves. Thus it is said that awareness is to be practiced in regard to the "five hindrances," that is to say: craving, aversion, slothful laziness, pride and impatience, doubtful uncertainty.[22] And it must be practical as well in regard to the estimation of their absence, or of their development, or of their disappearance at the moment of intervention by the dissolving action of which we shall treat below. The same awareness is practiced in order to observe the manifestation and the cessation of attachment in each of the five groups of personality in turn—we are dealing, in other words, with variations of the contemplation of states of the mind. Further disciplines take as their object higher states of ascetic consciousness, such as the "seven spiritual awakenings" or

19. *Dīgha*, 22.12.
20. *Bhagavadgītā*, 2.70.
21. *Suttanipāta*, 4.14.6.
22. *Dīgha*, 22.13.

bojjhanga,[23] and the direct supermundane apprehension of the "four truths."[24] In this further region recurs the necessity for maintaining a perfect, detached state of consciousness even in the development of the higher ascesis, as well as the necessity for avoiding identification even with supersensible experiences and for emphasizing at all times the absolute sidereal and extrasaṁsāric element in such experiences. Loss of control and "agitations" must never take place, a calm and steady light must shine on every experience and on every action. At the very limit of the supreme realization, the pure and detached element of consciousness—*sati*—must constitute, in a manner of speaking, a higher "dimension" than the content of *any* ordinary experience.

This is the fourfold form of *satipaṭṭhāna.* As we have said, what is realized in individual exercises should be developed into the form of a *habitus* of clear consciousness maintained at all moments of daily life. This, in fact, is considered in the texts as a development of the first contemplation, and is expressed in this formula: "The ascetic knows when he is walking, 'I am walking,' he knows when he is standing, 'I am standing,' he knows when he is in this or that position that he is in this or that position." In a word, he ends by literally bearing his own body. In a commentary on the texts, in this connection, the characteristic question is asked: "Who is walking?" The answer being: "It is not the 'I' that is walking"; "Whose walking is it?" "It is not of an 'I'"; "Who determines the walking?" "An act of the mind, transmitted and assumed by the breath *(prāṇa)* which pervades the body and moves it."[25] The texts further specify: the ascetic is clearly conscious in coming and in going, in looking and in detaching his gaze, in bending and in raising himself, in wearing his robe, in eating and in drinking, in masticating and tasting, in defecating and urinating, in walking and standing and sitting, in falling asleep and waking, in speaking and in keeping silent.[26] As in a mirror, he "looks at himself again and again before performing an action; he looks at himself again and again before saying a word; he looks at himself again and again before harboring a thought."[27] It can easily be seen that by following such a path a man naturally transforms himself into a kind of living statue made up of awareness, into a figure pervaded by composedness, decorum, and dignity, a figure that inevitably calls to mind not only the whole style of the ancient Aryan aristocracy but also that made famous by the ancient Roman tradition in the original type of the *senator,* the *pater familias,* and the *maiores nostri.* In reality, there is a natural relationship between these effects of the discipline of

---

23. Ibid., 22.16.
24. Ibid., 22.17.
25. On *Dīgha* (W. 357).
26. *Dīgha,* 22.3–4.
27. *Majjh.,* 61.

self-awareness and the traits that, together with the "thirty-two signs of the superior man," tradition has bestowed on the enlightened Ariya in the following terms: "As an Accomplished One speaks, so does he act and as he acts so does he speak";[28] he goes neither too fast nor too slowly; the lower part of his body, while he walks, neither swings nor moves through the effort of the body. In seeing, he looks in one direction: straight ahead, not upwards nor downwards, nor does he walk glancing here and there. He always sits composedly, not lolling his body, nor making useless movements with his hands, nor crossing his legs, nor resting his chin on his hand. He remains calm, "girded with isolation."[29] Calm, sidereal self-awareness cannot help but result in stylization since it acts on the irrational, oblique, and hidden part of the human being, rather in the way that the calm and severe glance of the schoolmaster is enough to quell the prankishnesss of the pupil who thought himself unobserved. So we can say that the substitution of energies that is the essential aim of the whole ascesis of the Ariya has already begun to have its effect externally. Whereas, before, every movement and every action of the individual was motivated by an irrational vital force or saṁsāric element, now this element is replaced by pure awareness, which cannot but bring about—as we have said—an increase of simplicity, composedness, and dignity in the manner and the outward appearance of one who seriously follows this path. One might even discern a certain aspect of racial catharsis, too, in these disciplines, since, as we have just said, these elements of a style of life existed naturally, *ab origine,* among people of a higher racial type, whose characteristics various factors, above all crossbreeding, have successively altered and encroached upon.[30]

Let us see where we have arrived in our exposition. When defenses against the most immediate forms of mental disturbance have been raised, the assimilation of the principles of "right conduct" arouses in the mind an "intimate, unalloyed joy" joined with the stability and sureness of one who feels himself in a state of "justice." For which we are given the simile of a lawfully crowned king who knows that his enemies are routed and that there is no threat of any kind to his sovereignty.[31] We have also acquired the strengthened "neutrality" or "sidereality" of the mind that, thanks to the fourfold contemplation, has further freed itself and is now at the center of all its experience, both internal and external. At this point we undertake the really cathartic action whose aim is to neutralize, by degrees, any possibility of "combustion" and of self-abandonment to the multiple variety of "contacts." Contacts wound;

---

28. *Angutt.,* 4.125.
29. *Majjh.,* 140. It is said of the assembly of the fathers of the order: "it does not gossip, it does not speak, it consists of essentiality, it is the blessed seat for the world" (ibid., 118).
30. Cf. our *Sintesi di dottrina della razza* (Milan, 1941).
31. *Dīgha,* 2.63.

contacts consume by exciting the fire that burns the body and the mind, which nourishes the saṁsāric stem and prostrates the higher principle. "The fool, struck by force, perishes; the wise man, when struck, does not tremble," he remains intact, remains unshakable, remains elusive;[32] we must become like the wise man. It is a question, then, of dealing a blow at the transcendental "desire" that lurks in the visual and other senses, in the *khandha* (the groups of the personality), in the elements, and which is corruption, disease, suppuration.[33] All this must naturally take place, not on the psychological or moral plane, but on the existential and metaphysical one. The beginning of the process of alteration lies in the senses, which are likened to so many "wounds."[34] They present us with forms or sounds or tastes or smells or tactile sensations, "desired, loved, delightful, pleasant, associated with craving, alluring," whence, "in the five cords of desire, in one or other seat of the senses, may arise inclination of the mind" or assent.[35] We have used this word to translate the term *anunayo,* which Woodward renders as "lurking tendency"[36] and which can actually be likened to the attitude of someone who spies, who waits ready to identify himself, in this case, with pleasure, if there is a pleasant feeling, or with pain, if instead the feeling is painful, or with opaque indifference (with "ignorance"), if the feeling is neither pleasant nor painful.[37] And here, naturally, the reference is also to the primordial anguish that lies at the base of saṁsāric existence and that produces attachment. In this way there arise formations or combinations that attach themselves to one or other of the five groups of the personality, that is to say, to the groups of materiality, of feeling, of perception, of the formations, of individuated consciousness. This being so, in order to "bandage the wounds" and neutralize the infection provoked by contacts, we must ensure that "the internal sight, the internal smelling, the internal hearing, the internal tasting, the internal touching, the internal thinking are not distracted," that is to say, that we are present in the sixfold seat of the senses in such a way that we can immediately prevent any self-relaxation, self-attachment, self-intoxication, any luring of ourselves by enjoyment. There will be, then, no further building of combinations, at first in the fundamental stem of the will, and then in the five stems of the personality.[38] This is the essence of the new work of catharsis.

This work is based on what is known as the "watch over the doors of the senses," for which the canonical formula is: "Upon perceiving a form with the eye, the ascetic

---

32. *Majjh.,* 82; cf. *Itivuttaka,* 28; *Angutt.,* 6.55.
33. *Saṁyutt.,* 27.1–10; 35.90.
34. *Majjh.,* 33; 105.
35. Ibid., 122.
36. [In English in the original.—Trans.]
37. *Saṁyutt.,* 36.3.
38. *Majjh.,* 28; 149.

conceives no inclination, no interest. Since craving and aversion and damaging and harmful thoughts soon overcome the man who lives with the eye unguarded, he remains vigilant, he guards the eye, he remains vigilant over the eye." Upon hearing a sound with the ear, upon smelling an odor with the nose, upon tasting a flavor with the tongue, upon touching a contact with the body, upon representing to himself a mental state with the mind, he conceives no inclination, he conceives no interest. Since craving and aversion and damaging and harmful thoughts soon overcome the man who lives with his mind unguarded, he remains vigilant, he guards the mind, he remains vigilant over the mind."[39] To fail in this vigilance at some point is to suffer the fate of the tortoise: when the tortoise unthinkingly put out one of its limbs a jackal seized it by that limb and carried it off to its ruin.[40] In this matter then, we have to come to grips with the saṁsāric entity with which we are associated and that constitutes our double, composed of thirst. A continually tightening circle closes round it. It is effectively likened to an enemy who, knowing that he cannot openly defeat his adversary, gets himself employed by him as a servant and gains his confidence so that he may then defeat him by treachery: this—it is said—is the part that the illusory "I," created by identification, plays in us until the time of initiation into the doctrine of the Ariya.[41] That the discipline of the watch over the senses or binding the wounds leads to a higher liberation is shown by the simile of the man who has at a crossroads a thoroughbred team and can guide them wherever he pleases.[42] The man who does not know or who forgets this practice is dominated by forms, sounds, smells, tastes, contacts, and thoughts, instead of being their master.[43]

In another way this discipline can also be summed up by the word *silentium:* "to gird oneself with silence," silence in the technical and initiatory sense, in the sense of the Eleusinian σιωπή. Impressions are arrested at the periphery, at the limit of the senses. Between them and the "I" there is now a distance, a zone of "silence." We thus become endowed with that form of silence that consists of not pronouncing either the exterior word or the interior word, and this in turn implies not hearing, not seeing, not imagining. This theme has also been expressed in a popular form. It is, in fact, the deeper, hidden significance of the well-known statuette of the three sacred monkeys of Benares, one with the ears closed, one with the mouth closed, and one with the eyes closed: speak not, hear not, see not. And we may here also recall the curious hermetical formula: "Who has ears, let him open them [in the sense of a close watch on every impression], who has a mouth, let him

39. *Dīgha,* 2.64.
40. *Saṁyutt.,* 35.199; cf. 202.
41. Ibid., 22.85.
42. Ibid., 35.198.
43. Ibid., 35.202.

keep it shut [in the sense of the aforesaid silence, of calm, intangible 'neutrality'].''

It is thus that the conditions for further liberation and then for awakening the extrasaṁsāric principle are consolidated. We shall see that development in this sense is directly continued in the four *jhānas.*

As the natural counterpart of the watch on the doors of the senses, a world of disintoxication is carried out within the zone that is now isolated, in order to eliminate or reduce those internal smoldering embers of agitation and self-identification that may be made to burst into life by external contacts. This is what is known as the removal of the five *nīvaraṇa,* a term that means a "dross," a "hindrance," or an "impediment." The five *nīvaraṇa* are: desire *(kāmacchanda);* hate or anger *(vyāpāda);* slothful idleness *(thīna-middha);* pride and impatience *(uddhacca-kukkucca);* doubtful uncertainty *(vicikicchā).* The action of these five hindrances is clearly indicated by the following similes: it is like trying to look at one's reflection in water wherein all kinds of colors are mixed (desire), or in boiling water (hate and anger), or in water full of mud and moss (slothful idleness), or in water agitated by the wind (pride and impatience), or finally, in dark and murky water (doubt).[44] Removal is effected by direct action of the mind on the mind, together with accurate and calm self-examination. The discipline is described in the texts in the following manner. The ascetic finds a solitary place and begins to meditate. A well-known yoga position is counseled: sit with legs crossed and body straight upright. This traditional Indo-Aryan position is, however, only suitable if one is so accustomed to it that it is quite natural and requires no special effort and does not produce fatigue. In general, the position recommended for this, as for other contemplations, must be one of equilibrium, which does not have to be changed; it must have a kind of symbolical meaning of self-awareness and it must not demand efforts that would distract the mind. This is the formula for the meditation: "The ascetic has given up worldly craving and now rests with his mind free from craving, he purifies his mind of craving. He has given up hate and now rests with his mind free from hate, he purifies his mind of hate. He has given up inertia and accidie; lover of the light, clearly conscious, he purifies his mind of inertia and accidie. He has given up pride and restlessness, with his mind inwardly tranquil he purifies his mind of pride and restlessness. He has given up wavering, he has crossed over from doubtful uncertainty; he has no doubts about what is bene-ficial, he purifies his mind of wavering."[45] It is fundamentally a more advanced development of the states already induced by *sīla* or "right conduct." The aim here is obviously to bring us to a deeper zone by means of the strengthened power of internal vision that we have gained through the preceding disciplines. It is a matter of attacking, to some degree, the *sankhāra,* that is to say, the innate and

---

44. *Angutt.,* 5.193.
45. *Dīgha,* 2.68–74; *Angutt.,* 1.2.

congenital tendencies that come, in part, from the extra-individual heredity that we have assumed.

Here, too, the purity achieved at certain moments comes to be developed until it has almost attained a state of permanency. This is how we must understand what is known as the "threefold watch": "by day, walking and sitting, turn the mind away from disturbing things; in the first watch of the night, walking and sitting, turn the mind away from disturbing things; in the middle watch of the night, lie down on the right side, like the lion, one foot on the other, bringing to mind the hour of waking; in the last watch of the night, after arising, walking or sitting, turn the mind away from disturbing things."[46] This is a kind of continuous examination of consciousness. The *yāma*, the watches of the night that are recognized in this discipline consist, according to the Buddhist tradition, of four hours each; the first runs from six until ten in the evening, the second from ten until two in the morning, the third from two to six in the morning. Thus, strictly speaking, the period of true sleep or of the state that in the common man would correspond to sleep (cf. p. 181) is restricted to four hours only, from ten in the evening until two in the morning. In this we must not see an "ascetic" discipline in the Western sense of mortification: on the contrary, it is natural that in advancing along the road of illumination the need for sleep is considerably reduced, and this reduction produces no ill effect. Here, too, a unilateral "authoritarian" intervention would only serve to create states of fatigue and inattention unfavorable for spiritual life by day.

With attentive care of the "wounds" and with action taken against the hindrances or impediments, the zone of "silence" is strengthened, and a gradual interior increase of the extrasaṁsāric quality takes place therein; this increase should be aided by illuminated effort and it is related to the aforesaid "seven awakenings"—*bojjhanga*. These "awakenings" are the positive counterpart of the cathartic or prophylactic action, that is to say, they are a "defence against intoxication produced by action." The canonical formula is: "[The ascetic] rightly causes the awakening of mindfulness derived from detachment, derived from dispassion, derived from cessation [of the flux], ending in renunciation, he causes the awakening of investigation—of inflexible energy—of enthusiasm—of calm—of concentration—of equanimity, of these awakenings derived from detachment, derived from dispassion, derived from cessation, ending in renunciation."[47] Various interpretations of the place of these awakenings in the whole development are, nevertheless, possible. Their sense as a whole, indeed, reflects that of the four *jhānas*, of the contemplation that is to be performed in complete detachment from external experience. Here, however, we may under-

46. *Majjh.*, 53; *Saṁyutt.*, 35.120.
47. *Majjh.*, 77.

stand them on a more relative plane, as a kind of transfiguration and liberation of faculties that are already pervaded by the element of *bodhi,* whence the expression *bojjhanga.* It must be realized that we are not dealing with a simple schematic enumeration, but rather with a series in which the meditation whereby they are apprehended should pursue an intimate causal linking of the single terms so that we are naturally led on from one to the next, and so that in the one we see the integration and resolution of its predecessors. Thus, we must first achieve nondistracted meditation; then we must awaken the state of "mindfulness," fix it in the mind, develop it, master it, and see how this state leads to the second awakening and passes into "investigation," which may find support in some element of the doctrine; this investigation, when developed, fixed, extended, and mastered must lead on to the awakening of "inflexible energy," whose perfect conquest should herald a state of special, purified "enthusiasm," of purified joy. By further developing the meditation, we should realize that this enthusiasm, this joy, awakened and perfectly developed in a body that is becoming calm, in a mind that is becoming calm, will become resolved and liberated in the next awakening, which is that of "calm." When calm has been developed, extended, fixed, and mastered, "concentration" awakens; this, in its turn, when completely developed, becomes established and shines forth in the "equanimity" that is the seventh awakening.[48] These form a series of landmarks in meditation that is concerned with realization and they are connected by an inherent continuity. Through these, one is led in another way to the confirmation of what was already becoming established in the *satipaṭṭhāna,* the fourfold contemplation of detachment, that is to say, one is led to that impassibility that is qualified as "pure, clear, ductile, flexible, resplendent," but which has nothing to do—it should be noted—with the indifference of a blunt mind, with the indifference "of a fool, of an ignorant man, of an inexpert common man."[49] For our part, we think it opportune to add that the state in question must on no account be confused with apathy or atony, and that it develops together with a feeling of purified intellectualized and heroic joy, although this may at first seem difficult to understand. The *Bhagavadgītā* says: "When the mind, tamed by ascesis, becomes quiet; when [the ascetic], seeing the self in the self, rejoices in himself, knows that boundless joy which, transcending the senses, can only be apprehended by the intellect and, when fixed in it, does not stir from the truth . . . he knows that this detachment from union with pain is called yoga."[50] At the same time, Buddhism speaks of a pleasure that is "like dung" when compared to that based on detachment, calm, and illumination.[51] Furthermore, such sequences as these are

---

48. Ibid., 118.
49. Ibid., 137.
50. *Bhagavadgītā,* 6.20–23.

frequent: "In the ascetic joy arises; this joy makes him blissful; being blissful, his body becomes calm; with the body calmed, serenity arises; in this serenity the mind comes to rest, becomes concentrated"; this is a preparation for the four *jhāna*.[52] This is another sequence that has the character of a connected series, developing in an upward sense, not unlike that which, through the twelve *nidāna,* led us downward to saṁsāric existence (cf. p. 57). The point of departure of this new series is, in fact, the state of suffering, of agitation, of contingency, which corresponds to the last *nidāna* of the descending path. Beyond it, there is the state of confidence; this leads to purified joy—*pāmujja;* then follows serenity, which gives place to bliss, passing on to equanimity—the term used here literally means also to vanish, to cease being in a place: it is a question of detached equilibrium, and for this reason *pāmujja* also sometimes figures as the antecedent of extinction.[53] In this text the supreme realization has behind it a linked series in which special states of liberated joy play a particular part: a kind of joy that Plato contrasted with all mixed and conditioned forms of joy or of pleasure. Let us quote another text that represents the state at which we may reckon to have arrived at this point of our exposition: "Concentration which knows neither increase nor decrease, which is not based on wearisome subjugation, which, because of its detached nature is constant, because of its constancy is full of bliss, because of its bliss cannot be destroyed—such concentration has supreme wisdom as its result."[54]

This should destroy the idea that the path of awakening is arid and desolate, that it kills all joy, that it offers only renunciation and destruction. That everyone whose furthest horizon is still within the effective, saṁsārically conditioned world should have this idea is quite natural but is of very little account. A text reminds us that only an Awakened One can comprehend the Awakened One. An expressive simile demonstrates this: two companions leave a city together and reach a rock that one of them climbs. He says to the other: "I see from up here a wonderful view of gardens, woods, fields, and lakes," but the other retorts: "It is impossible, it is inadmissible, friend, that from up there you can see all that." Then the companion standing on the

---

51. *Angutt.,* 8.86; cf. 2.7.1–5, where two kinds of joy are considered and contrasted, the one bound to life in the world, to mania, to enjoyment, the other to ascesis or to ultramundane states of detachment and of freedom from mania; and it is said that the second is the higher joy. "Extinction—it is sad (*Majjh.,* 75)— is the greatest joy." With reference to the state of the first *jhāna* (cf. p. 148–49), it is said that, were the idea of lust to arise in the ascetic, he would feel it "as sickness (*ābādha),* as suffering like pain which torments a healthy man" (*Angutt.,* 4.114). It is in order to possess a higher joy that those who find pleasure in the burning of desire are not envied (*Majjh.,* 75); it is through finding that a joy beyond theirs—"heroic joy"—is better, that craving and aversion are abandoned (*Majjh.,* 14). Joy, in many Buddhist sequences, comes, in fact, after "energy."

52. *Dīgha,* 2.75.

53. *Saṁyutt.,* 12.23.

54. *Angutt.,* 9.37.

rock comes down, takes the other by the arm, makes him climb up on the rock and, after he has recovered his breath, asks him: "What do you then see, friend, standing on the rock?" The other replies: "I see a wonderful view of gardens, woods, fields, and lakes." "And your previous opinion?" "While I was obstructed by this great rock, I could not see what is now visible." It concludes: it is impossible that what is knowable, discernible, capable of achievement, capable of realization through detachment, can be known, discerned, achieved, realized by one who lives among desires and who is consumed by desires.[55] Quite apart from the higher "sidereal" principle, the Buddhist also knows the kind of joy that is contentedness, rejoicing, jubilation, enthusiasm, exultation, transport of the spirit and that, among others, is considered as "a factor of the great awakening"—*pīti-sambojjhango.*[56]

55. *Majjh.*, 125.
56. *Dhamma-sangani,* 285. Countering those who believe that the Buddhist road is one of desolation and aridity, L. de la Vallée-Poussin (*Nirvāṇa* [Paris, 1925], p. 62) most opportunely writes: "We must, rather, recognize that India is difficult when it comes to being and bliss; that as she puts being beyond existence, so she puts bliss beyond sensation."

12

The Four Jhāna:
The "Irradiant Contemplations"

We have so far dealt with the two sections of the whole system of disciplines called *sīla* and *samādhi*. This last term has, in original Buddhism, a different meaning from that which it has in the general Indo-Aryan tradition, where it usually designates actual states of enlightening contemplation; in Buddhism *samādhi* refers, instead, to the cultivation of consolidation, catharsis, and preliminary liberation, all of which are integrated by the results of "right conduct," of *sīla*. There are, however, some texts in which the four *jhāna*, the contemplations of which we are about to speak, are included in the *"samādhi"* section.[1] The fact is that these contemplations can be apprehended and performed with varying intensity and in a varying spirit. On a lower level they continue the action of purification. When they are carried out with greater vehemence they lead to supersensible states, to the limit of individual consciousness, since they are equivalent in their results to the four "irradiant contemplations" that determine the possibility of a state of union with the theistic god.

In any case, by passing into the realm of the *jhāna*, as we shall now do, we find that ascetic realization removes those horizons that limit the Stoical doctrines as well as all "superman" theories. Let us briefly discuss this point. The limit of Stoical ascesis is *apatheia*, the destruction of any possibility of disturbance of the spirit through passions or outside contingencies. A well-known symbol is the rock that remains firm and still while stormy waves break against it.[2] To this is added tranquility of mind based on consciousness of one's own rectitude and a certain *amor fati*, that is to say, a confidence in cosmic order. From this standpoint, the irrelevancy of all that is

---

1. Cf., e.g., *Dīgha*, 10.2.1–20.
2. This simile is found in Marcus Aurelius, 4.49, and it is entirely similar to that of *Angutt.*, 6.6.55 (*Dhammapada*, 81), which speaks of a mountain rock, uncracked, all of one piece, which does not shake nor tremble nor move as a result of the storms and tempests that strike it from all directions.

purely individual and terrestrial is considered and experienced. As for the doctrines of the "superman," they are based on the reinforcement of the vital energies and of the "I" such as will produce invincibility and superiority to all tragedy, to all misfortune, to all human weakness, a pure force that, though it may be bent, cannot be broken, a will to power that defies men and gods.

In the sphere of the Buddhist *jhāna*, both of these forms of ascesis are surpassed since the human condition in general tends to disappear. Only if the discipline of the Ariya were to stop at *sīla* and *samādhi* could its achievements be likened to that of the most enlightened Stoicism. But Buddhism—like all initiations—has higher and freer realizations, and so, instead of the rock against which stormy waves uselessly break, the simile of air that one may try in vain to capture in a net or cut with a sword is far more appropriate. Imperturbability and calm fixedness *(samatha)* equivalent to the Stoical *apatheia,* along the path of awakening is, in fact, considered at a certain point as a bond from which one frees oneself in order to approach the domain of "nonexistence."[3] At the same time, the "sidereal" element here encourages such detachment as will induce Olympian quality in all higher states of consciousness and destroys in that detachment any residue of *hybris,* of pride or of will for power attached to the "person." To "life"—even at its summits—Buddhism opposes that which is "more than life." The term superman—*uttamapurisa*—also figures in Buddhism as an epithet of the Ariya ascetics.[4] But this ideal is here transfigured, it is carried effectively onto a supersensible plane in which the dark tragedy that is always hidden in the "titan" and the "superman" is completely resolved. We shall see almost at once that in order to achieve such an ideal a special enlightened use of sentiments such as love and compassion is even employed: a technique that carries us far beyond the plane of the contradictions against which fought without hope, for example, the soul of Nietzsche and Dostoyevsky. We mentioned this in dealing with the two ways of overcoming fear (cf. p. 116).

The term *jhāna* is translated by some as "deepening self-examination" *(Selbstvertiefung),* a rendering that should be remembered: indeed, in the disciplines of which we shall speak, we shall be dealing with a descent through successive purifications and simplifications into the deeper layers of one's own being, where, in the common man, we find the kingdom of the subconscious. We then tread the very same path that is marked by the hermetic and alchemic maxim: *Visita interiora terrae, rectificando invienies occultum lapidem, veram medicinam.*[5] Less happy,

---

3. *Majjh.,* 105. Cf. *Majjh.,* 106, where it is said that by loving and esteeming indifference, by letting consciousness rest there and become attached to it, the supreme aim of the ascesis is not achieved.
4. Cf., e.g., *Saṁyutt.,* 22.57; *Dhammapada,* 97.
5. Cf. our work, *The Hermetic Tradition.*

however, is the translation of *jhāna* as *Versenkungen* ("sinking below") and still worse as "trances" or "raptures" since the normal meaning of these terms is just the opposite of what we are dealing with here. The term, "trance," makes us think at once of the state of a "medium,"[6] a passive state of subconsciousness, of subpersonality and of obsession, whereas the Aryan ascesis is hallmarked by superconsciousness, by full activity and self-awareness. Equally, the term "rapture" implies an idea of ecstatic passivity and has a mystico-religious flavor, neither of which has much to do with the states in question. It is, therefore, preferable to retain the Pāli term *jhāna* (Skt.: *dhyāna*) after we have become quite certain of its connotations. States of "trance," of confused thinking or of "possession" can only occur in one who has been unable to resist the challenge offered by such experiences.

It happens that in the texts the *jhāna* are given immediately after the four contemplations which are designed to create self-awareness and the girdle of isolation from internal and external experience.[7] This being so, their meaning can be explained as follows. With the disciplines we have already discussed, contained in the *samādhi* section, one isolates oneself, one cuts oneself off, one detaches oneself. Even the "seven awakenings" refer to the appearance, after this, of a positive force from within, which is related to the states achieved in the *jhāna*. These states radiate from the now isolated center and proceed to reoccupy, in a manner of speaking, the abandoned zones, so that contingent elements are there reduced and these areas are reclaimed from the dominion of *saṁsāra*. It is, in fact, prescribed that these states, after they have been perfectly achieved by the mind, should be transmitted to the whole of one's being, even to the bodily structure itself. For this reason, it is said that "death" finds access to one who does not practice the *jhāna* and penetrates him as a heavy stone ball thrown on a mass of moist clay; "death" finds the way barred, on the other hand, by one who has achieved the *jhāna*, and his attempts are likened to a light clew of thread hurled at a planed block of hard wood.[8]

The first *jhāna* is defined by this fixed formula: "The ascetic, far from desires, far from any disturbing state of mind, maintaining feeling and thought, in a state of serenity born of detachment and pervaded with fervor and bliss, reaches the first contemplation *(jhāna)*." This has the same significance as: "to dwell in the body watching the body, without thinking any thought connected with the body; to dwell in the feelings watching the feelings, without thinking any thought connected with the feelings; to dwell in the mind watching the mind, without thinking any thought connected with the mind; to dwell in the mental states *(dhammā)* watching the mental

---

6. [These terms in English in the original.—Trans.]
7. *Majjh.*, 119.
8. Ibid.

states, without thinking any thought connected with the mental states."[9] This, in a manner of speaking, is a summary of all that has been achieved in the preceding phases. All the waves are calmed. Serenity pervades the entire being and unifies it, while there is clarity, detachment, and silence in every sensation that may arise or image that may present itself. In the first *jhāna* consciousness is still resting on feeling and thinking, on perception and representation—*vitakka* and *vicāra*.

These two elements have to disappear in the next *jhāna,* either in a single simplification process or else in two phases: in the second case sensory impressions are first silenced and then representations or mental images. (Under these circumstances, there are sometimes considered to be five rather than four *jhāna,* with the one we are now discussing counted as two.) The fixed canonical formula is: "After having achieved feeling and thinking, the ascetic attains serene inward calm, intellectual simplicity arises which is free from perceptions and images, born of concentration, pervaded with fervour and bliss, he reaches the second contemplation." By "having achieved feeling and thinking," we must understand a state of perfect equilibrium of these faculties so that they can, in a manner of speaking, be left to themselves and can eventually be overcome and abandoned. The term we have given as "intellectual simplicity" is *ekodibhāva.* Some have translated it by: "the mind emerges alone and simple," others "the mind grows calm and sure, dwelling on high," whose corresponding state is said to be "self-evolved"; yet others use the expression "single-mindedness" or "one-pointedness";[10] finally, some authorities speak of spiritual unity—*Einheit des Geistes.* It seems to us that our expression "intellectual simplicity" is nearest to the sense of the state in question; at the same time, it recalls equivalent terms figuring in ancient Western asceticism, particularly in Plotinus, Iamblichus, Proclus, and in the hermetic texts. It is a manifestation of the mind as a unique and simple essence no longer dependent upon psychical functions, sensations, or formed images and thoughts. This achievement results from the power and intensity of self-concentration that has been developed to a point where, as in the episode referred to by a text, not even the noise produced by a large number of wagons is in any way noticed.[11] It is, in fact, much more a kind of "growing" of awakening than any form of direct "emptying" action that in many cases, to use two similes of Zen Buddhism, is like trying to drown an echo by raising the voice or trying to chase away one's shadow by running after it: we can thus see the error of certain modern theosophical trends with their ideas of "making a vacuum" in a purely mental sense. Furthermore, we must emphasize that to be able to dismiss the

9. Ibid., 125.
10. [The second, fourth, and fifth phrases are in English in the original.—Trans.]
11. According to Buddhaghosa's commentary, the concentration of the second *jhāna* is identical with that *citt' ekaggatā,* which produces the arrest of the mental flux and with the collection of the mind in a single point, which is dealt with in yoga (quoted by T. W. Rhys Davids, *The Yogavacara's Manual,* p. xxvii).

supports of consciousness, namely, sensations and representations *(vitakka* and *vicāra),* without passing into the subconscious or into sleep, and by participating, instead, in the miracle of the separation and manifestation of the pure intellectual substance, comes only as the result of a very special inward strength. Unity of the mind—unity that is almost organically felt—is necessary, as well as effort nourished by *sīla,* by "right conduct." Therefore, it is said that, just as it is not possible to gain mastery over the sphere of transcendental knowledge *(paññā)* without having first mastered the sphere of concentration, so it is not possible to master the sphere of concentration without having first gained mastery over the sphere of right life *(sīla),* without which right concentration has no foundation.[12] One must possess power—simply a "mental" power—of self-mastery and of calm practiced in detachment, confirmed by inward simplification and consolidated by the disidentifying contemplations, in order to furnish within oneself a support for consciousness and self-awareness when the "silence" is absolute and sensations or images no longer present themselves. Thus the term *ekodibhāva* has not unjustly been compared with "simplicity of the *will* without thoughts." The "intellectual simplicity" that is the center of the second *jhāna* is not a simple mental state, but rather the point in which a pure will power concentrates and frees itself, an inwardly directed willpower having itself both as its object and as its base.

In the third *jhāna:* "The ascetic, dwelling even-minded, clearly conscious, controlled, having eliminated fervor and bliss, feels arising in his body the felicity of which the Ariya say: 'The even-minded wise one lives in felicity.' Thus he reaches the third contemplation." As in the second *jhāna* feeling and thought having been brought to a state of perfect transparency and equilibrium by the first *jhāna,* were left behind, so here we leave behind the element of "fervor and bliss," which in the second *jhāna* comes to be felt as an impurity, as a disturbance, as something "compounded" and conditioned. It is not a contradiction that as a result of this further simplification there yet arises something that might almost seem to be a feeling. We can take it that there occurs in the third *jhāna* the removal of the general bodily sensation and its substitution by the "intellectual felicity" of which we have spoken. This appears to be the transformation that takes place when the pure intellectual consciousness, aroused in the second *jhāna* and now still further purified, comes into contact, almost as a "reagent," with "coenesthesia," or the general sensitivity of the body. We can connect this state—at least in some measure—with the "perfect serenity which, when it ascends from this body and arrives at the supreme light, appears in its true aspect," with that light that exists within the body, a glimpse of which may be known to have been gained when, upon making contact with the body heat is

12. *Angutt.,* 5.22, 24.
13. *Chāndogya Upaniṣad,* 8.3.4; 3.13.7–8.

felt in it—a state referred to by the Upaniṣads.[13] Special strength is required for this realization too; in order to prevent what is to be absorbed and transfigured from itself absorbing and submerging the sidereal element, in which case the experience would resolve itself in organic sensations, and one would fall into a state of trance or sleep. It should, in fact, be maintained that the first three *jhāna* are developed in an internal zone that, in the life of an ordinary man, would correspond to periods of fantasy, reverie, or sleep. This is shown by the fact that in the following phase, the fourth *jhāna*, there may occur, according to the texts, the suspension not only of discursive thought (of "words"), feelings, images, and emotive states themselves, however purified they may be, but also of the rhythm of the vital force, that is to say, of the breath, whose movement is now become an impurity and a disturbance:[14] this is a state that outwardly resembles death. We shall have more to say on this subject since this and similar phenomena really appear on the scene in the later phase of the contemplations that are without form, and they only occur in the *jhāna* when these are realized and experienced with special intensity.

The fourth *jhāna:* "After detachment from pleasure and pain, after disappearance of previous joy and sorrow, the ascetic passes into a state beyond sorrow, beyond joy, into a state of equanimity, of purity and of illumination—into the fourth contemplation."[15] Here we have arrived at the extreme summit of individuated consciousness. The catharsis or simplification must be capable of removing even the sensation of pure transfigured intellectual joy so that a state of utter "neutrality" may be achieved, a supreme point of balance, which is without color, without form, completely free of any support whatsoever. This is the frontier between two worlds, the point beyond which consciousness, if it still has enough strength and the will for the absolute not to stop, to advance, to destroy all anguish, can no longer be the consciousness of an "I," that is to say, of a particular finite being bound by a particular physical form. It is, in fact, the threshold of transfiguration in a literal sense, that is to say, the point at which one goes beyond "form," beyond the "person." In the texts, in fact, the fourth *jhāna* represents the boundary that separates the contemplations bound to "form" from those that are *arūpa* or free from form, not "formal" but "essential."

A few considerations, both on the practice and on the "place" of these four *jhāna:* in order to develop them successively, it is of prime importance that the will for the unconditioned should completely occupy the mind. Only then will its advance not be obstructed. Only then, when each single *jhāna* has been wholly apprehended, can one be aware of what that *jhāna* still retains that is "compounded," that is

---

14. *Saṁyutt.*, 36.11.
15. On the four *jhāna* cf., e.g.: *Dīgha*, 2.75–82; *Saṁyutt.*, 28.1–9; *Angutt.*, 3.58.
16. *Majjh.*, 52.

"conditioned,"[16] and thus find a way that leads still further. When contemplating the phenomena proper to each *jhāna* in their appearance and development, the ascetic must confront them without inclination, without interest, without ties, without being attached, with his mind not limited by them, and he must apprehend "There is a higher liberty"; and by developing his experience he will, in fact, see: "There is."[17] The demon of identification and of satisfaction raises its head here also. It must be anticipated and conquered. Every feeling of enjoyment or of satisfaction that may arise upon the realization of each *jhāna* is immediately seen as a possible bond for the mind and is to be rejected.[18] One must apply here the general Buddhist principle that all enjoyment through attachment is lethal, be it either of the "heavens" or of *nibbāna* itself, since "a fire lighted with sandalwood burns no less fiercely than any other fire." The action must be neutral, absolutely purified and naked. As in the Carmelite symbolism of the ascent of the mountain, the path that does not become lost, which leads straight up to the summit, is that to which are attributed the words: *nada, nada, nada*—"nothing, nothing, nothing." The difference is that in the Ariyan path of awakening there is found no equivalent to the crisis that Saint John of the Cross called the "dark night of the soul." In the texts the impersonality of the action is evident also from the fact that the four *jhāna* are given as phases of a development from within, phases that occur normally as a result of the fundamental direction that one's own being has taken, without "volitional" intervention in a strict personal sense. In the four *jhāna*, as in the later experiences, one must never think: "It is *I* who am about to achieve this *jhāna*," or: "It is *I* who have now achieved this *jhāna*," or "It is *I* who am surmounting this *jhāna*." On the contrary, the mind, having rightly been set in motion, should lead from one to the other.[19] Any intervention by the normal personal consciousness would only arrest the process and lead back to the point of departure, in the same way as Narcissus, at the moment of gazing at his image, prepared his own end. The Mahāyāna saying, "there exist the road and the going, but not he who goes," seems not out of place here. We can also remember the Taoist maxim: "To achieve intentionally the absence of intentions."

Active intervention in the normal sense can only be allowed in the process of consolidating each of these states so that they may be summoned at will. This presupposes a special scrutiny of each one once they have severally manifested themselves. The texts record the following episode: by his supernormal power, the Buddha appeared to a disciple who, upon coming out of *jhāna*, found that the perceptions

17. Ibid., 111.
18. Ibid., 36; 138.
19. *Saṁyutt.*, 28.1–9; cf. *Angutt.*, 10.2, where the principle of graduality and of increase is expressed: "Thus, O disciples, from one phenomenon arises another, one leads to the taking place of another, so that these very states of the world finally lead to the goal beyond the world."

and states he had already overcome were reappearing and reestablishing themselves. The Buddha taught him how to carry the exercise further so that he might be able to get the better of all such residual states: every distraction must be eliminated and austere concentration reinforced; the mind must be composed, completely mastered, and concentrated in a single point—*ekodi-karohi*.[20]

This brings us to the "place" of the realizations that are represented by the *jhāna*. Their "place" depends on the degree of intensity of the realizations themselves and on the extent to which they are animate with "knowledge," *vipassanā*. In the extreme case, there can occur through them the complete destruction, without residue, of the "manias," of the *āsava*, and therefore liberation. In other cases, when the action remains more peripheral and only a part of the saṁsāric being is thereby neutralized, only some of the bonds are effectively broken, and liberation does not occur during life; indeed, upon the decease of the body, one may even rearise in states of existence that, although they may be more than human, are yet conditioned. We shall discuss these various possibilities in detail in a later chapter (p. 196–97ff.). The possibility also exists of developing the four *jhāna* in a "neutral" manner, on an essentially mental plane, not for the purpose of awakening, but rather as means of acquiring and of exercising certain extranormal faculties *(siddhi)*.[21]

While still on the subject of the "place" of the *jhāna* we must state generally that these realizations, like the others of which we shall speak later, are not to be understood as being on a purely "psychological" or abstractly spiritual basis—as simple spiritual states of the individual, but are to be regarded as having a kind of ontological or existential counterpart. The development must be regarded above all as carrying one beyond normal consciousness, into prenatal and preconceptional states that normally correspond to the unconscious that rules in the states of dreaming, sleep, and catalepsy. In the second place, the idea of "sphere" or of "realm" is frequently found in the texts in connection with the *jhāna;* that is to say, the *jhāna* introduce us to one of the "spheres" that are included in the objective hierarchy of the multiple states of being. There is even mention of "heavens": with the *jhāna* one is supposed to reach the "heavens of pure forms" or at least to prepare a way that leads to them.[22] There is also mention of spirits or gods or angels of one or other *jhāna* sphere,[23] and contacts that ascetics have had with them are discussed. Details are actually given. The *bodhisattva*, that is to say those who are advancing toward full illumination, are supposed, to begin with, to perceive a bright formless splendor; by purifying the "eye of knowledge" form also is

---

20. *Saṁyutt.*, 40.1ff.
21. In *Angutt.*, 6.29, the acquisition of such powers is directly connected with the development and frequent practice of the fourth *jhāna*.
22. *Dhamma-saṅgani*, 160ff.
23. *Angutt.*, 4.123; 3.114.

perceived; at a later stage actual contacts ("to converse together") may even take place and, furthermore, they may come to recognize the hierarchical place of these beings ("to which celestial world they belong").[24] A close study is also made of the causes that lead to the interruption of such experiences, to the "vanishing of the splendor and of the vision of the forms."[25] In the course of the development of Mahāyāna Buddhism there appear outright personifications of the *jhāna* as so many mythological Buddhas, and divinities of all kinds take the place of the various planes of contemplative and transcendental realizations. It is of importance, particularly in connection with this kind of literature, to understand clearly what is the right point of view: on the one hand the "psychologistic" interpretation must be avoided; when one is in the *jhāna* or in similar states, the center of one's own being, even if only for a time, is "elsewhere," in worlds different from that perceived by the usual waking consciousness and one is not undergoing a process that has a merely subjective value. On the other hand, when the presentation, particularly in later Buddhism, is objective and almost theological, with reference to divinities and cosmic or celestial hierarchies, then, stripping off the mythology, the matter must be understood in its essential form as a function of states of consciousness, of transcendental experiences. This holds good not only of doctrine but also in cases of genuine apparitions. Such possible apparitions are only "projections," that is to say, exteriorized forms of particular states that are experienced, and the personification takes place on the basis of images fixed in the mind or in the subconscious of the individual who is practicing. Thus Tibetan Buddhism goes as far as admitting that, in a particular phase of practice, the Buddhist can see the Buddha transformed into a Mahāyāna god, just as a Christian will see the Christ or a Muslim Muhammad. Everyone supplies the image that he has himself cultivated or that he has received from his saṁsāric tradition, as the mode—in the guise of a form, an image or an apparition—in which he experiences a particular state of ascetic or initiatory consciousness. In connection both with the *jhāna* and with other states of experience it is, therefore, important to achieve a point of view that is higher than the ontological-theological as well as the "psychologistic" or "spiritualistic" attitude. Only such a superior point of view can "conform to reality" and be suffused with true knowledge. Based on this knowledge, the Buddhist ascesis completely dismisses the whole ghostly world that is made up of "astral" or "mental" visions, phenomena, apparitions, and so on, and that plays such a great part in the deviations of Western theosophy and anthroposophy; even the substantialist aspect of strict theology is left behind. The references in the earliest texts to the gods and to the angels of the various "regions,"

---

24. Ibid., 8.64.

25. *Majjh.*, 128. Some of the "impurities of mind" that paralyze the vision are doubt, inattention, fear, exultation, excessive effort, relaxed effort, complacency, perception of diversity.

where they do not represent interpolations and infiltrations of popular beliefs, are entirely schematic. The Ariyan ascetic achieves the various states that are the substance of such "worlds" and goes beyond, without allowing his attention to be distracted by a phenomenology that is only made possible when "direct knowledge" wavers and when one is subject to the play of one's own unconsciously objectivizing imagination. The world of the original Buddhist contemplation is extremely clear, almost Doric. Such fantastic creations are entirely foreign to it—and it is for this reason that in some short-sighted people there has arisen the idea that we are here dealing with states that are merely "psychological" or, at the most, "mystical."

When intensely experienced, the *jhāna* transform not only consciousness but also particular faculties—speech, thought, and breath—"purify" them and take us well beyond the catharsis. We have seen that these faculties remain suspended during practice of the *jhāna;* and consequently they become quiet and mastered.[26] This suspension means, in fact, that consciousness has been taken beyond their source and that it continues to exist beyond them. Thus these faculties are brought into virtual subordination, by means of consciousness, which has now become the essential foundation of the faculties, and passes on to them the calm that it has achieved in itself. The catharsis of certain conditioned feelings is also considered,[27] and it is emphasized that the force, thus advancing, cuts off not only the bond represented by "evil thoughts" (which disappear in the first *jhāna*) but also the bond of "good thoughts" (which disappear in the second *jhāna*).[28]

On emerging from the *jhāna,* even the general form of experience is not the same as before. In this connection, three modes of "contact" are mentioned, given in some texts also as three "liberations": contact of the "void," contact of the "signless," contact of the "without tendency"—*suñña-, animitta-, appaṇi-hita-phassa.*[29] We can consider these as new "categories," new modes of experience, which appear, in general, at the moment when the ascetic, after going to the limit of conditioned consciousness, returns to normal existence. It will be as well, however, to discuss such forms of experience at a later point since they can only be considered in conjunction with the *jhāna* if we assume that these latter have been so intensely experienced as almost themselves to lead to liberation, while normally in the texts, after the *jhāna,* there are other transformations of the consciousness that come under the heading of *paññā,* or transcendental knowledge. There are, however, some texts that consider special forms of contemplation in which the *jhāna* use the "void," the "signless" and

26. *Saṁyutt.,* 36.11.
27. *Angutt.,* 4.200.
28. *Majjh.,* 78.
29. Ibid., 43.

the "without tendency" as a base from which to produce a higher degree of "purification," characterized, in fact, by those three elements: *suddhika-suññatam, suddhika-animittam, suddhika-appaṇihitam.*[30]

The perfection of the four *jhāna* implies their "embodiment," and this also signifies a transformation of the invisible structure of the human organism (with particular emphasis on the saṁsāric being which is its root), which is brought about by the pervasion of this structure by the states corresponding to the *jhāna*. The texts, in fact, speak of an actual "bodily reliving in oneself" of "those saintly liberations, which are high above all form, formless,"[31] and this is considered as a higher stage of achievement. Thus, there is a distinction between one who is "liberated on both sides"—*ubhatobhāga-vimutta*—and one who is only liberated "as to knowledge"—*paññā-vimutta*. The second is the case of the man who "has not bodily achieved those blissful liberations that are beyond form, formless" and in whom the intoxications, the "manias" or *āsava,* are for this reason only removed in part.[32]

To show this process of "embodiment" of the four *jhāna*, appropriate similes are given throughout; they are important since they also serve to throw further light on the essence of each of the practices in question.

Here is a simile that concerns the first *jhāna:* "As an expert bath attendant or bath attendant's apprentice puts soap powder in a bath, soaks it with water, mixes and dissolves it in such a manner that its foam is completely permeated, saturated within and without with moisture, leaving none over: just so the ascetic pervades and infuses, fills and saturates his body with the serenity born of detachment, perceptive and thoughtful, pervaded with fervor and beatitude, so that not the smallest part of his body is left unsaturated with this serenity born of detachment."

Second *jhāna:* "As a lake with a subterranean spring; and into this lake there flows no rivulet from east or from west, from north or from south, nor do the clouds pour their rain into it, but only the fresh spring at the bottom wells up and completely pervades it, infuses, fills, and saturates it, so that not the smallest part of the lake is left unsaturated with fresh water; just so the ascetic pervades and infuses his body with internal serene calm, born of self-recollection, pervaded with fervor and beatitude." We should note, here, the simile of the internal spring, the idea of something fresh that spreads out from the inside and from the "bottom"—from the detached "intellectual simplicity" which has been achieved—unsullied by any influx of outside currents; that is to say, with all vital saṁsāric nourishment neutralized.

Third *jhāna:* "As in a lake with lotus plants some lotus flowers are born in water,

30. *Dhamma-saṅgani,* 344–53; 505–27.
31. *Majjh.,* 6.
32. Ibid., 70.

develop in the water, remain below the surface of the water, and draw their nourishment from the depths of the water, and their blooms and their roots are pervaded, infused, filled, and saturated with fresh water, so that not the smallest part of any lotus flower is left unsaturated with fresh moisture: just so the ascetic persuades and infuses, fills and saturates his body with purified joy, so that not the smallest part of his body is left unsaturated with purified joy." While in the preceding phase we spoke only of a deep internal spring, here we have a further development, we have a state that now encloses, permeates, and nourishes the entire bodily structure, by transforming the general sensation that corresponds to it, just as we have already said.

Fourth *jhāna:* "As a man might cloak himself from head to foot in a white mantle, so that not the smallest part of his body was left uncovered by the white mantle: just so the ascetic sits, having covered his body with a state of extreme equanimity and purity and clarity, so that not the smallest part of his body is left uncovered by the state of extreme equanimity and purity and illumination." We are, then, at a third phase: the body is not only pervaded but also covered by the new force, it is enveloped in the force as if the body did not contain the force but the force contained the body. The ascetic dominates his body, covers his body.[33]

The similes we have just given are among those that, to a great extent, serve as "magic keys": they have a power of illumination for those who use them as a starting point when elaborating this phase of embodying the experience corresponding to the four *jhāna.*

The path leading through the *jhāna* is not the only one considered by the Buddhist teaching. The texts indicate a second path that, from its effects, would seem to be equivalent. It may be called "path of saintliness" or "wet path," as opposed to the other which is mainly in the nature of a "dry path." While the *jhāna* are necessarily achieved by way of an intellectual catharsis and spiritual concentration, in the other path, which we shall now briefly discuss, feeling plays a large part, although it is employed in conjunction with perfect awareness and is used purely instrumentally.

This second path consists of four awakenings that are called *brahmavihāra-bhāvana,* that is, "unfolding of the divine states," or *appamaññā,* "the limitless," the "infinite (states)." We shall use the term *irradiant contemplation.* The method aims at dissolving the bond of finite consciousness by means of the irradiation of an ever vaster, more disindividualized and more universal feeling, so developed that it ends by leading to the same state as the fourth *jhāna,* to a state of almost discarnate

---

33. *Dīgha,* 2.82. The white mantle of some western monastic orders that is provided with a hood covering the head also, in special rites, has a symbolical value that may be interpreted on these lines; a value that in the Church has been lost.

equanimity and mental clarity. This path entails the recognition that: "Before, this mind of mine was limited and obstructed. But now, it is limitless and unfolded, and no limited action can still exist in it or maintain itself in it."[34] Again we have a catharsis. The four *appamaññā* are conceived as containing, in fact, a "purification"; thus it is said that one who has realized them "has bathed with the inner bathing" and has no further need of external rites of purification.[35] They produce "the limitless redemption of mind."[36]

Here are the formulae that are given by the canon for the four irradiant contemplations: "The ascetic dwells with his spirit pervaded by love *(mettā)* and irradiates one direction, a second, a third, a fourth, so across and upward and downward: identifying himself in all things everywhere, he irradiates the whole world with spirit pervaded by love, with ample, profound, unlimited mind, free of hate and rancor." The formula is repeated three more times, unchanged except for the term, love, which is replaced in turn by compassion *(karuṇā)*, sympathetic joy *(muditā)*, and lastly equanimity, immutability, or stability *(upekkhā)*. After the irradiation of the feeling of love, follow compassion and sympathetic joy. Through love the ascetic feels himself in all beings, noble or common, happy and unhappy, both of this world and of every other world; he feels their destiny as though it were his own, he takes upon himself the contingency of their life, he feels with their feeling or suffering (compassion)—but he then irradiates joy, as if the darkness in each being had dissolved, as if the feeling he irradiates were beneficial to the beings and were sustaining, clarifying, and liberating them. Then follows the last irradiation, that of immutability or stability: the ascetic, still developing this universal consciousness, is as if he willed the "being" of each being. He aims at infusing in every creature that same calm, that same quality of stability and of equanimity that he has developed in himself, by projecting in them the quality of "being," that same unshakability or security that he has achieved by completing this process of universalization. In this connection, we may call to mind these words: "Peace I leave with you, my peace I give unto you: not as the world giveth, give I unto you. Let not your heart be troubled, neither let it be afraid."[37] The formula is repeated, changing only, for each contemplation, the quality of the basic feeling that is to be aroused first in oneself and then to be irradiated: "The ascetic dwells with compassionate—joyful—immutable mind and irradiates one direction, then the second, then the third, then the fourth, above, below, across: identifying himself everywhere in all things, he dwells irradiating the

34. *Angutt.*, 10.208.
35. *Majjh.*, 7.
36. Ibid., 43.
37. John 14:27; cf. *Mahāparinirv.*, 40: "The Awakened One is peace to himself and bears peace for the entire world."

whole world with compassionate—joyful—immutable spirit, with ample, profound, unlimited mind, free of hate and rancor."[38]

To set free one's heart by unfolding a love that turns to compassion, a compassion that turns to joy, a joy that turns to unchangeability, to impassible clarity and unshakable detachment, is the aim of this fourfold contemplation. To achieve it entirely, that is to say, to dissolve all trace of finite and unquiet subjectivity, is, according to Buddhism, to have achieved the condition necessary for a state of union with the theistic god, with Brahmā—*brahmā-sahayatā.* One text, in connection with the fourth irradiant contemplation, even states: "Thus, O disciples, an ascetic dwells as a god."[39] In any case, by this path that, as we have said, is comparable to the "way of saintliness," the *anāgāmi-phala* or the "fruit of no return" may be achieved: the individual in question, after the dissolution of the body, arises in the world of Brahmā, a world, as de Lorenzo has rightly pointed out,[40] of which Dante's whole paradise is but an allegorical representation; a world that for Buddhism, however, is only a stage to be passed, a world that, when compared with absolute liberation, appears as something inferior—*hīna*—as something yet conditioned.[41]

As in the *jhāna,* so also in these irradiant contemplations an interior and invincible force is set free and expands, once the preliminary ascesis has sufficiently barred the roads along which external contingencies might disturb the internal being. The states to be aroused and irradiated, including unchangeability, acquire the characteristics of absolute forces—rather than of feelings in the normal sense—which are such that they may even make themselves objectively felt at a distance,[42] of forces that derive from a cosmic consciousness that completely dominates feeling and overcomes all suffering and all reaction of the spirit to an extent almost inconceivable. The irradiant contemplations are in this way related to the power of *patientia,* to the capacity for unwavering endurance of all that can come from the world of men by engulfing it in the vastness of the liberated mind. Whether people behave with love or with hate, whether their words are kind or unkind, sincere or false, whether their action tends to produce joy or suffering, the heart of the ascetic who practices the *appamaññā* must remain undisturbed, no evil word must escape him; he must, instead, remain friendly and compassionate, his spirit must be loving and without secret malice. With a loving

---

38. *Majjh.,* 7.

39. *Angutt.,* 4.190.

40. G. de Lorenzo, *I discorsi di Gotamo Buddho* (Bari, 1916–27), footnote to *Majjh.,* 97.

41. Cf. *Majjh.,* 120, where it is said that he who aims at extinction goes beyond all the divine spheres, "he does not arise in any place, he does not arise at any point." Furthermore, the absolutely neutral state in the path of awakening stands higher than any beatitude, even celestial. When this state wanes, beatitude, formerly overcome, springs up again; ibid., 102.

42. According to *Saṁyutt.,* 42.8, the irradiated forces are perceived by all beings like the sound of a trumpet, blown without effort, in the four regions.

spirit the person who may have acted for good or ill is irradiated; starting from him, the ascetic will then irradiate the whole world with a loving spirit, with ample, profound, limitless spirit, free of impurities and rancor. And some cosmic similes are added: with spirit like the earth, like water, like the air, like fire.

"Like the earth"—says the Buddha—"practice ascesis. Just as upon the earth there is thrown the pure and the impure, excrement and urine, mucus and pus and blood, yet because of this the earth is not distressed nor saddened nor troubled: so also you, like the earth, must practice ascesis: for if you, like the earth, practice ascesis, your mind, touched by joy or suffering, will not be disturbed." And the same for water: as in water there is washed the pure and the impure, or as in the fire there is burned the pure and the impure, or as the wind blows on the pure and the impure, or as, lastly, space is not limited by anything, so must one practice ascesis, like water and fire, like wind and space: and the mind, touched by joy or suffering, will not be disturbed.[43]

There is a similar cycle of similes that again point out the cosmic nature of the feelings to be aroused and irradiated in such contemplations. It is said: "Should a man arrive with a hoe and a box and speak thus: 'I will clear away the earth' and should he hoe here and there, and remove the soil here and there, and throw it here and there and speak thus: 'You shall be without earth'—what think you now, disciples: Could this man clear away the earth?—Surely not, Lord," is the answer. "And why not?—The earth, Lord, is very deep and vast, and could certainly not be cleared away however much that man might toil and labor." And likewise in the case of the air: if a man should come with lac and other colors, and attempt to draw figures in the sky, he would never succeed, since "the sky is formless and invisible, and a figure could certainly not be drawn there however much that man might toil and labor." Finally, in the case of water: the fool who with a bundle of lighted straw were to try to dry up the Ganges would never achieve his aim. Thus, with a mind like the earth, like the air, like water, like fire, like space, with ample, profound, unlimited mind, free of hate and rancor, should one irradiate the whole world, never letting the heart be distressed, never allowing an unkind word to escape, remaining friendly and compassionate. The extreme example given is this: "Even if, O disciples, brigands and assassins with a two-handed saw were to sever your joints and limbs, one who for this reason were to become angry would not be carrying out my teaching. Therefore you must, O disciples, thoroughly train yourselves thus: 'Our mind must not be troubled, no evil word must escape our mouth, we shall remain friendly and compassionate, with loving mind, without hidden ill-will we shall irradiate that person; passing on from him we shall then irradiate the whole world with loving mind, with ample,

43. *Majjh.*, 62; *Angutt.*, 9.11.

profound, unlimited mind, free of hate and rancor.' Thus, O disciples, must you thoroughly train yourselves."[44] In the course of this text it is emphasized that the mind must be put to the test at the very moment in which we are faced by injustice: that is to say, we must neutralize and conquer our reaction also when it has most reason to exist. Naturally, we are in the field of pure ascesis, of pure discipline, and it would therefore be a great mistake to attempt to transfer this attitude to the plane of normal life. It should be further noted that there is no question at all of "forgiving"—and still less of "forgiving" that we may be "forgiven." At a certain point, the whole matter resolves itself into an objective inability to be touched or wounded. The attacker and the unjust find themselves in exactly the same condition as the man who seriously imagined he could remove the earth with his hoe or draw figures in the air. For this reason, the nonreaction of the ascetic must be understood—to use one of Kremmerz's similes[45]—as the measureless goodwill of a world boxing champion toward a spindly youth who arrogantly challenges him to a trial of strength and skill and who hits or kicks him to provoke him. The champion knows that he could lay out his assailant with no effort at all.

This leads us to a consideration of the part that love—*mettā*—plays in the Doctrine of Awakening. In the first place, it does not appear as an absolute value—as *charitas,* the theological attribute "God is love," but rather as an ascetic instrument that, at the fourth stage, gives way to impassibility, to a state of mind that is detached from all beatitude, that is "neutral" in a higher and sovereign sense. In the second place, it has nothing to do with a human "love for one's neighbor," but rather with the irradiant and almost objective power that proceeds, in a natural way, from an integrated and liberated mind. This is evident from the Buddhist view that of one who seeks his own health rather than that of others and the one who seeks the health of others rather than his own, the former is judged to be superior:[46] this takes us far indeed from "humanitarianism," but likewise from "egoism." The point is, that he who has not cannot give. Love, here, is not a matter of running after others with cures and solicitude and effusions, but is something that is based on "obtaining one's own health"—that is, one's own spiritual fulfillment—until it becomes "radiant," and like the light of the sun that shines equally, irresistibly, and impersonally upon the good as upon the evil, without any special "affection," without any particular intent.

In this connection, we recall the discrimination made by Christian theology in order to explain the possibility of loving even those for whom one harbors a natural aversion and repugnance so strong that one may have to restrain oneself physically

44. *Majjh.,* 21.
45. Cf. G. Kremmerz, *Dialoghi sull'ermetismo* (Spoleto, 1929), pp. 53–54.
46. *Angutt.,* 4.95.

from giving expression to it. Here the distinction is between natural and supernatural love, between love based on the senses and love based on will and liberty. The former is, in fact, conditioned by feeling and is not free, since it does not stir until confronted by an object corresponding to a tendency; for this reason, when the object changes or when the mind alters its outlook, the love decreases or gives place to another feeling. In this form of love the individual, in fact, only loves himself or, more correctly, it is the saṃsāric being in him that loves; and this is so not only with lustful love but also with sublimated forms of love and affection. This is all part of the world of *dukkha,* it is an alteration, a bond, a disturbance of the spirit. The Ariyan path of awakening does not recognize love in this sense, and regards it in all its forms as a limitation and an imperfection.

Different is *amor intellectualis,* which, though preserving the characteristics of an affective state *sui generis,* is based not on sensibility but, as we have said, on will and liberty. In Christian theology this is "loving all creatures in God"; which means that we here remember each individual's transcendental source, liking in him that which he is in the impersonal, metaphysical sense, and resolutely excluding any like or dislike proceeding from our particular nature. In this case liberty of spirit triumphs over the conditioned character of the senses, and love becomes the purer and the sign of higher liberty the less it depends upon particular satisfactions and attachment to single beings.[47]

Only if we think of love in these terms can we understand that its value is simply instrumental and cathartic: in the ladder of Buddhist realizations it takes its place simply as the equivalent of the earlier *jhāna,* that is to say, of the contemplative simplifications designed to remove the limitation of the individual and to neutralize the "five bonds." And we can then understand another thing, which is the magical power attributed by Buddhism, in certain circumstances, to love. There corresponds to this love, that is deeply experienced in the "intellectual" sense already described, a certain removal of the I-thou relationship, not as combination with or losing oneself in the loved one, but in the sense of establishing a concord between whole and part, between creator ("father") and created ("son"), between the limitless and the limited. In loving, one goes outside oneself, that is to say, beyond the state in which the other person may be "one like us," one creature facing another—one assumes, one makes one's own the being of the other person, who then finds himself facing a profundity that he himself cannot attain and consequently against which he is powerless.[48] He loves him, as it were, himself, not finitely, however, but infinitely; it is himself with an extra dimension that is created by the very act of love. In this man-

47. Cf. I. Le Masson, *Avis spirituels et méditations* (Tournai, 1911), p. 23ff.
48. Cf. J. Evola, *Fenomenologia dell'individuo assoluto* (Turin, 1930), p. 247ff.

ner, when love is developed into an objective intensity it may give rise to a magic
force that is able to paralyze all unfriendly acts of which the other person may be
capable. Thus it is said that one who practises and truly develops love, thereby freeing his mind, also develops a state such that fire, and poison, and weapons have no
longer power over him.[49] This same idea is expressed in various Buddhist legends.
By irradiating with unlimited mind, full of love and compassion, vast as the earth,
Prince Siddhattha is supposed to have halted the onrush of an elephant set upon him
by an enemy. On being told of the death of a disciple from snakebite, the Buddha
says that this would not have happened had the disciple irradiated the world of snakes
with loving mind; and here we have the confirmation of the very idea we have just
discussed: love creates a defense, paralyzes hostile beings, disarms them and makes
them retreat, because it arouses in them the feeling that their limited selves are
facing the limitless. Thus we read, in connection with the irradiant contemplation of
love: "Infinite is the Awakened One, infinite is the the doctrine—you, instead, are
finite beings. I have created my protection, I have sung my hymn of defense—let all
living beings retreat."[50] We can see from this how ignorant of Buddhism are those
who practically deny to it the dignity of a proper "religion" since they understand it
as a simple ethic of "love" and "compassion" in an adulterated, equalitarian, and
humanitarian sense.

Some texts advocate a combination of the irradiant contemplations with the
jhāna; in which case, it is in those states of abstraction and internal transparency
belonging to the *jhāna* that, at a later phase of the discipline, the awakenings of the
"four divine states" should be practised through the successive stages of irradiation
already described.[51] One kind of "purification" thus raises the other to a higher power;
and here we may pause to consider the possibility of the existence of beings who,
according to Buddhism, from their distant, unknown solitudes, irradiate the world
with influences far more efficacious and valuable than those that any visible human
action can provide.

As we have said, the four irradiant contemplations are equivalent, in practise, to
the four *jhāna.* They also lead us to the extreme limit of individuality, to the point
beyond which there are the regions "free from form"—*arūpa-loka*—or the
"supercelestial" regions, whichever one prefers. As long as one's horizons have not
been made to appear relative by the will for absolute liberation, these states of love
and of universalization, up to and including the purity of the fourth "limitless" contemplation, which correspond, one might say, to the mode of pure "being," may

49. *Angutt.*, 8.1.63.
50. *Cullavagga (Vin.)*, 5.6; cf. *Angutt.*, 4.67; *Jātaka*, 203.
51. *Angutt.*, 8.63; *Dhamma-saṅgani*, 251.

serve as a way to liberation from the self and from finite will, and bring one as far as the *unio mystica,* that is to say, the *brahmā-sahayatā* already mentioned. We know already, however, that this is "too little" for the Ariyan vocation. The Awakened One knows the path that leads to the state of unity, which may be realized in life or after death, with the theistic divinity: he even goes so far as to say (a thing that should be noted by certain Catholic apologetics when it pronounces every kind of foolish judgment upon Buddhism), that for him to point out such a path as this is as easy as for a man who is a native of a village to point out the road leading to that village.[52] The truth he proclaims is, however, that there exists "a higher liberty." The mania of "saintliness" is to be overcome, in the same way as those of desire and existence.[53]

Of the four *brahma-vihārā,* the irradiant contemplations, considered in themselves, we must say: "this does not lead to turning away, not to cessation, not to calm, not to wisdom, not to awakening, not to extinction—but only to ascension into a world of saintliness."[54]

52. *Majjh.,* 99.
53. *Angutt.,* 10.20.
54. *Majjh.,* 83.

13

⋐⋙⋩⋐⋙⋫

The States Free from Form
and the Extinction

The region of the later realizations of the Ariya, up till the great liberation, corresponds to the *arūpa* world. Having overcome sensible existence *(kāma-loka)* having overcome the possibility of rearising in the world of pure forms *(rūpa-loka)* one still must proceed, if one has the power, to the overcoming of existence free from form *(arūpa-loka)* and of the "desire" of which it may be the object *(arūpa-rāga).* By *arūpa-loka,* we must understand the sphere in which only that which is "essence" remains, only pure possibility of manifestation, or "meaning"; while the formal and manifested aspect, which may, among other ways, manifest itself through the phenomena of supersensory vision, entirely falls away. From the individual's point of view, this is the space that extends beyond the fourth *nidāna, nāma-rūpa,* that is to say, beyond individuation. Dissociation from the saṁsāric being occurs when we enter into this higher ascetic and transcendental region, in which we still have to remove the first three *nidāna* of the series: firstly, *viññāṇa,* understood as both the general possibility of a definite and dependent existence, and also the absolutely original *motus* that may lead to such an existence, in its double aspect of "nonwisdom" *(avijjā)* and of intoxicated energy, *sankhāra* and *āsava.*

In the same way that, after the phase of defense, consolidation and preliminary detachment, the ascetic was offered two nearly equivalent paths, namely, the four *jhāna* and the four irradiant contemplations, so, in this final development, a twofold path is again offered. The first of these is by way of completely abstract contemplations "without form" and is developed, in fact, in the same sense as the aforesaid *jhāna;* indeed, the term *arūpa-jhāna* is often used here. The other path, on the contrary, is made up of special illuminating visions—*abhiññā*—and is imbued much more with the spirit of the irradiant contemplations.

Before we deal with these paths, it will be profitable to take the opportunity of referring to certain initial techniques and instruments that are considered by Buddhism as auxiliary and preparatory means—*parikamma-nimitta*—both for the *jhāna* we have yet to speak of, and for those we have already discussed. The texts speak of eight "liberations" *(vimokkhā)*, five of which are the *āyatana,* that is, the contemplative states of the region "without form," while three are clearly contemplations preliminary to them. In the first of these latter contemplations one considers, in one's own being, the single element "form," and one completely concentrates one's mind upon it: this is not entirely unrelated to some methods known among ancient Mediterranean initiations and associated with the formula: "to go out (from the body, from individual consciousness) through the skin." To feel only the "form" of one's own organism is like feeling its surface, the "skin." According to those ancient mystic teachings, to isolate this sensation of the "form" and almost to lose oneself in it can, in certain cases, be a way of "going out."[1] And it is a method of Tibetan yoga firstly to identify one's body with that of a divinity and then to apprehend it as empty, as if it were made only of a shining and transparent skin.[2] The second "liberation" consists of forgetting one's own form, one's own body, and absorbing oneself instead in an outside form, which alone must engage the mind and the sensibility. This is connected with the technique of the *kasina* that we are just about to discuss. The third "liberation" is connected with "splendor" and "beauty"—there are even texts that consider that these two elements only are the supports in the passage to the formless.[3] There thus appears on the scene something that recalls the part played by aesthetic feeling in the Platonist and Neoplatonist mystiques, namely, a kind of enthusiasm or rapture that acts as a vehicle for the attaining of the supersensible. The difference is that here we are not dealing with the joy of the artist or of the lover of art, but rather with a quintessential and abstract feeling that is roused, not by an image or a living creature or an aspect of nature, but simply by a pure color, light, brilliance, or fire in a mind that has already been brought to the limit of purely individual and human consciousness as the result of the ascesis we have so far described. This refers to the *kasina* themselves.

The term *kasina* means, literally, "totality." It denotes a procedure that would be described today as "hypnotic," a procedure by means of which consciousness is led to become absorbed by identification in an object, until they form together a

---

1. Cf. G. Meyrink, *Golem,* chap. 18: "The key is found purely and simply in making oneself aware of the 'form of one's own I,' of one's own skin, I mean, sunk though one may be in sleep; in discovering the narrow crack through which consciousness finds its way between the state of wakefulness and that of the deepest sleep." It must be understood that, in the *kasina,* the power of concentration produces conditions analogous to those of sleep.
2. Texts in W. Y. Evans-Wentz, *Tibetan Yoga and Secret Doctrines* (London, 1935), pp. 173–75, 190.
3. *Dīgha,* 15.35; *Angutt.,* 8.66; *Majjh.,* 77.

"wholeness," one single thing. This process of identification produces isolation of the mind not only from physical impressions but also from one's own person; the "five hindrances" being overcome, the passage to the abstract contemplations is made easier or hastened.

As to technique: one may start with a disc of some perfectly pure color, dark blue, yellow, red, or white, which is placed in front of the person who is to perform the exercise. Alternatively, a round opening can be made, through which an area of bright sky may be seen, or the same can be done in a screen placed in front of a fire in such a manner that a disc of flame is visible. In one way or another, one must arrange to have before one a regular shape occupied by a pure and even color or luminosity. The mind should be detached from all longing or worry and should warm to the thought of the truth and of the awakening of the Ariyas. Thus the mind is prepared for concentration and is pervaded by the thought that the action about to be undertaken will facilitate the grace of the mind's own liberation. After this is done, one must gaze fixedly at the luminous disc, "with eyes neither too widely open nor half-closed, as one looks at oneself in a mirror," without interruption, without blinking, concentrating wholly on this perception, until there is created a false image (today we would say, an hallucinatory image) of the shape. One must then continue to concentrate on this image, with the eyes both open and closed, if necessary "a hundred or a thousand times," until the mental image is established in such a way that one continues to see it even involuntarily, with the eyes closed or open and with the gaze removed from the object. The first phase of the operation is complete when the "reflex," the mental counterpart of the physical image of the disc, called *uggaha-nimitta*, is equally visible with the eyes open or closed. One can then stop sitting in front of the disc and pass on to the second phase of the exercise.

In this further phase the "reflex" must, in its turn, serve as the basis for concentration that is now, in a manner of speaking, of the second degree. It is no longer the physical eye that fixes its gaze, but the eye that has been opened by the *7na—jhāna-cakkhu*. The procedure, however, is the same: one again has to identify oneself with the mental image, forgetting everything else, just as was done previously with the image provided by the senses. If this second concentration on the interior image is rightly carried out, there finally springs out from this image a new reflex of the second degree, something purely spiritual—*paṭibhāga-nimitta*—"without form, without color." This resembles the melting of a fog, or the shining of the morning star, or the appearance of the moon from behind clouds, or is like the flash of a mirror taken from its case, or of a perfectly polished gem. These terms are used to describe the appearance of the new image that "shatters" and annihilates the preceding "hallucinatory" image, and "rises, a hundred, a thousand times more clear." At the moment when this experience occurs, the obstacle formed by one's own individuality and by the "five bonds" is removed, the power of the *āsava* is neutralized, and the passage of the mind to the apprehension of the states free from form, or of pure forms, is made easier.[4]

The so-called light *kasina* is appreciably different; it is indicated in the texts thus: "The ascetic fixes his attention on perception of light, he fixes his mind on the perception of day: as by day so by night, as by night so by day. Thus he trains himself, with his mind aware, untroubled, in the contemplation of light." Correctly and constantly practiced, this exercise should ease the opening of the "eye of wisdom."[5]

Another process of "emptying" is more mental in character and is based on successive abstractions. Forgetting oneself and one's connection with common human existence, one allows only the image "forest," for example, to remain, as if it were the only thing in the world that existed, until the spirit is relaxed, made firm, and freed. This produces a feeling of "voidness," of "real, inviolable vacancy"— *suññatā*. One then drops the idea of forest, leaving as the only object for the mind the idea of "earth," putting aside, however, all its characteristics; "as the hide of a bull is well cleaned with a scraper, and its wrinkles smoothed out," there exists nothing but "earth" in the world. And one apprehends the same feeling of liberty, or voidness, in conceiving that only the idea "earth" persists as support of the mind. From "earth" one finally moves to the idea "infinite space"—with which one achieves the passage to the object of the first *arūpa* and meditation, that is to say, of the first of the meditations beyond form.[6]

Before going any further, we must forestall any misunderstandings that may arise regarding the implications of these forms of approach that are based on what is almost a hypnotic technique. It is quite possible that those idle people who go in search of "occult exercises," of short-cuts by which to reach the supersensible without effort, may believe that they have found something on these lines in the color and light *kasina*, they may then mistakenly believe that by practicing a form of hypnosis they can do without any renunciation, discipline, or spiritual effort. This would be a grave mistake. These material procedures mean very little in themselves: their only purpose is to neutralize peripheral sensitivity. It is then a question of seeing, firstly, *if* something of consciousness still remains, once the neutralization has been achieved; and secondly, if it does, what is the nature of any experience that may result. Everyone knows that procedures similar to those of the color and light *kasina* have been used both in the practice of magic and by visionaries, and in modern times, among forms of experimental hypnosis. The technique of the "magic mirror" will be familiar to some, a technique

4. *Visuddhi-magga*, 4 (W. 293 ff.); *Angutt.*, 1.20; cf. *Majjh.*, 77.

5. *Angutt.*, 4.41.

6. *Majjh.*, 121.

that consists of gazing at a luminous point reflected by a curved mirror: others will be acquainted with the practice of "divination," based on fixing the sight on a mirror or water or on the fire. We can see from this that the technique of the *kasina*, in itself, is neutral, and may produce one or another result, without in itself determining which. Thus, except for cases of privileged and exceptional predispositions, anyone with sufficient power of concentration will find that the effect of staring at the colored discs or at the discs of light will be merely hypnotic, that is to say, that he will descend to a semisomnambulistic state of reduced consciousness like that of people who are hypnotized. In others, "complexes" of all descriptions may emerge and be projected, resulting in inconclusive visions that may even be dangerous, because not only do they not lead beyond individuality, but they may even disclose and bring up a psychic "subsoil" and so open the way to the manifestation of obscure influences.[7] Yet, others, once they have mastered the exercise, or if they have special natural gifts, may utilize the state of trance into which they pass for the purpose of divining or magic. Lastly, the best that can happen is that apparitions of "divine forms" may occur, of forms belonging to the *rūpa-loka* that, however, as we have already said, is itself left behind by the path of awakening of the Ariya.

For the effective use of the technique in question, the first condition is that consciousness should be already concentrated and detached and capable of maintaining itself by its own efforts: only then, when the peripheral sensitivity has been neutralized, can one keep one's feet, can one go up rather than down, can one set out to attain a purified superconsciousness instead of sinking into the morass of the visionary or low-grade medium. In the second place one needs, as we said, adequate spiritual tension, pervaded by the idea of awakening, almost like the state of a compressed spring on the point of release. In this connection a text states that, as a man with a robust digestion swallows and consumes a spoonful of rice without difficulty, so one who aspires to transcendental wisdom goes beyond the initial act of concentration on the image, absorbs it and transcends it, and achieves the state at which he aims.[8] No one, then, should nourish any illusions about the techniques we have discussed by thinking that they are capable of producing, in the way of genuine spiritual realization, anything more than he has already. They can only create, quickly and conveniently, conditions that favor a particular action that, in itself, presupposes a high development of ascetic, "holy," or initiatic consciousness. The same is also true, although in a lesser degree, of the other, less mechanical forms of approach of which we have spoken: when we are dealing with the path of awakening of the

---

7. It is what, in other ways, nearly always happens in the "mediumistic" states cultivated by modern spiritualism and metapsychics. Cf. our critical studies in *Maschera e volto dello spiritualismo contemporaneo*, 2nd edn. (Bari, 1949).

8. *Dhamma-saṅgani*, trans. C. A. F. Rhys Davids (London, 1900), note on p. 59.

Ariya, a "nobility" and a special internal initiative are always presupposed. Even the continued contemplation of light can lead to little more than hallucinations, instead of to the opening of the "eye of wisdom," if we do not have a living and, in a manner of speaking, intellectualized sensation of this light (intellectual light). There is confirmation of this in the fact that the same practice is sometimes advised for wholly contingent purposes, for example, as an antidote to sleep and torpor.[9]

As the starting point for the five *jhāna* free from form we have, on the one hand, objective detachment from the perceptions of the six senses and, on the other, "pure, clear, ductile, flexible, resplendent indifference" in which the series of *jhāna* we have already considered as well as the series of irradiant contemplations, both culminate. Having made this clear, this is how the texts refer to the contemplative states.

First phase: "Completely transcending perceptions of form, making the reflex images vanish, reducing every perception of multiplicity, the ascetic thinks: 'infinite ether' and reaches the plane of infinite ether."

Second phase: "After completely transcending the plane of infinite ether, in the thought: 'infinity of consciousness the ascetic reaches the plane of infinity of consciousness."

Third phase: "After completely transcending the plane of infinity of consciousness, in the thought: 'non-existence' the ascetic reaches the plane of non-existence."

Fourth phase: "After completely transcending the plane of non-existence, the ascetic reaches the plane beyond consciousness and non-consciousness."

Fifth phase: "After completely transcending the plane beyond consciousness and non-consciousness, the ascetic reaches the cessation of the determined."[10] At this point, it is said, the "mania" of the illuminated ascetic is destroyed, the *āsava* are dissolved, there subsists no longer any "gross or subtle bond"; there is, on the contrary, a flash of absolute liberating knowledge. For this interior vision, which destroys at the root any possibility of conditioned existence, the canonical formula is this: "'This is agitation' *(dukkha),* so comprehends the ascetic, knowing the truth; 'This is the genesis of agitation'; 'This is the destruction of agitation'; 'This is the path which leads to the destruction of agitation.' 'This is mania' *(āsava),* so comprehends the ascetic, conforming to truth, 'This is the genesis of mania'; 'This is the destruction of mania'; 'This is the path which leads to the destruction of mania' so he sees, conforming to the truth. Thus knowing, thus seeing, his spirit becomes freed from the mania of desire *[kāmāsava],* from the mania of existence *[bhavā-sava],* from the mania of ignorance *[avijjāsava].* 'In the liberated one is liberation,' this knowledge arises. 'Exhausted is life, the divine path realised, that which had to be done has been done, this world no longer exists' does he

9. *Angutt.,* 7.58.
10. E.g., *Majjh.,* 13; 66.

then comprehend."[11] The culmination is reached, reintegration has been carried out, life and death are overcome, every thirst is ended, the primordial anguish—the trembling and the burning—is destroyed.

A few words of explanation on these transcendental phases of the ascesis: in the formula of the first *arūpa-jhāna* the perceptions of form that are to be overcome are indicated by the term *paṭighasaññā*, which contains the idea of something that resists. This relates in some degree to experience governed by the law of opposition of object to subject, feeling oneself "I" by contraposition to a non-I, to an *ob-jectum*, to a *Gegen-stand* (something that stands against me, that opposes me). This confirms the idea that, in order to enter into the world that is free from form, one must be capable of really abandoning this consciousness of self as an individual "I," conditioned by a particular "name-and-form," which endures just because of this law. And since all that is individual in an immediate and effective sense is supposed already to have been overcome by means of the preceding catharsis, there remains to be eliminated only the subtle residue of "I" that persists, as one text says, in the same way as the scent remains even when the flower that has produced it is no longer there.[12] As for the "reflex images" that have also to be eliminated in this phase, these refer to the secondary reflected images, void of form, subtle and wholly intellectual, that are obtained by the color and light *kasina*. When this reflex image is also suppressed, in the state of "voidness" that comes to be present, the thought "infinite ether" leads to the apprehension of the plane of infinite ether.

Ākāsa (Skt.: *ākāśa*) is frequently translated as "space" instead of as "ether." This can only cause a misunderstanding. In the Indo-Aryan tradition, *ākāśa* means essentially what "Quintessence," the "Fifth Element," the "Ether-Light," the *aor* and so on meant in the ancient Western traditions. It is not three-dimensional physical and mathematical space, but something that stands in relation to it as does spirit to body. Even etymologically the word *ākāśa* evokes the idea of "light." In a Upaniṣad, the *brahman* is understood as being identical with the "ether" both outside and inside the man.[13] The ether is, rather, called the internal, essential side *(ātma)*, while light is called the external side.[14] In the *jhāna* in question the idea "infinity of space" can only serve as a basis for the evocation of space in its aspect of *ākāśa*, live and luminous infinite ether, and as a preliminary to the transformation of consciousness into ether, which is the first broadening out of pure "being," beyond the sphere of Brahmā.

Having thus considered the object of the first *āyatana*, the passage to the second, whose object is "infinity of consciousness," is quite natural. It is, in fact, a question of

11. E.g., ibid., 27.
12. *Saṁyutt.*, 22.89.
13. *Chāndogya Upaniṣad*, 3.12.7–8.
14. Ibid., 3.14.2.

overcoming the residue of outsideness and of "cosmicity" present in the experience of *ākāśa*. The term used is *viññāṇāñcāyatana* and it is related to the second *nidāna* of the descending series, in the sense of being a "purification" of it. We have conceived the *nidāna* "consciousness" in terms of a determined manifestation. To cut off the bond that it represents, we must pass over to the third *āyatana* or *arūpa-jhāna,* whose object is experience of the sphere of "nonexistence." This sphere must be understood as the negative counterpart of "consciousness," that is, the power of nonmanifestation correlative to that of manifestation, whose principle is "consciousness." The experience of the *āyatana* can also be denoted by the formula "nothing exists," since to penetrate the power of nonmanifestation means to apprehend in everything the possibility of its nonexistence, the lack of its own reality, even in the case of him "in virtue of who everything that exists is." For this reason, some have conceived the experience in question as a liberation from *Etwas-heit,* from objectivity in general, extended even to the supercelestial spheres. The state of the fourth *āyatana* is *nevasaññā-nāsaññā* or that which is neither consciousness (second *āyatana*) nor nonconsciousness or nonbeing (third *āyatana*), that is to say, the element that is anterior to and higher than the two spheres previously realised. It is the "purification" of that which in the descending series corresponds to the *"sankhāra" nidāna,* that is to say, to the impulse that leads to "conception" in general, to the differentiation of possibility, insofar as it is a passive impulse.

The last *āyatana* leads to the ultimate point of the $\overset{"}{\alpha}\pi\lambda\omega\sigma\iota\varsigma$, of the transcendental simplification or purification. Its state is denoted by the term *saññā-vedayita-nirodha,* which refers to "cessation" not only of the element "consciousness," but also of that which, on the plane of psychology, would correspond to perception, to perceptibility or elementary determinableness. It is a matter of going beyond the double category of being (manifestation, consciousness) and of nonbeing (nonmanifestation) in order to attain every conceivable potentiality, conceivable, that is to say, beyond this double sphere of manifestation and nonmanifestation. One achieves, then, the state of consciousness (to continue to use this term, although it has become quite inappropriate at this point) that is absolutely unchained, simple, and intact, the state that in the chain of *nidāna* precedes the primordial form of any determinableness whatsoever: we have quite clearly, therefore, the immediate antecedent of the complete destruction of the *āsava* and of "ignorance," and therefore the herald of the realization of extinction.

It is hardly necessary to say that, although each realization may be conceived on various planes and in varying degrees, here, even more than in the case of the four *jhāna* of the world of forms, any "psychologistic" interpretation must be resolutely rejected. We can hardly take seriously the suggestion that we are dealing here with delvings into the semiconscious or into the "subliminal," until we reach an "oscillation about a zero-point in consciousness" (C. A. F. Rhys Davids).[15] Reference even to the Leibnizian *petites perceptions* is entirely inadequate since the fact is that we are dealing with a "voyage" in superindividual and, in some ways, presaṁsāric states (anterior to association with a particular saṁsāric heredity), in which the transcendental causes of every conditioned existence are rooted. For this reason the Buddhist teaching has "places" *(loka)* or "worlds" or "earths" *(bhūmikā)* that correspond to the five *āyatana*, and it is held that one will rearise in this or that one of them at the level at which ascetic achievement has been arrested, instead of progressing to extinction and absolute illumination.[16]

With regard to the canonical formula for liberation, the term "Exhausted is life" implies the impossibility of any further form of conditioned existence, and not merely of "rebirth" in the grossly reincarnational sense. Similar also is the significance of the formula *itthattāyāti pajānāti* that, following Neumann and de Lorenzo, we have rendered as "He apprehends 'this world no longer exists'"—the world here being understood as the sum total of manifested forms, and therefore also as all that is implied in the Indo-Aryan doctrine by the "threefold world." As for the term *bhavāsava*, that is to say, *āsava* or "mania" of existence, this almost brings us to the same point, if by *bhava* we understand the "becoming" inherent in a "birth," and in the assuming of a conditioned form. But, in a broader and deeper sense, we may see in the destruction of this *āsava* the equivalent of what Germanic mysticism called *Entwerdung*, the overcoming of "becoming" in general. The realization of the Ariya leads beyond both "being" and "becoming." Together with "ignorance" and "craving"—the other two *āsava*—the bond of "becoming" is destroyed at the roots by the clear vision that arrives as a sudden flash of knowledge in face of *dukkha*, the primordial agitation and contingency, and which gives realization of the "incomparable safety," of the state wherein there is no more "becoming," which is the "end of the world," the end of "going," the end of birth and of death. Finally, the formula *kataṁ karaṇīyaṁ*, "that which had to be done has been done," is the extreme expression of the Ariyan nobility. The whole work has been done because it *had* to be done. There are no reasons. There are no rewards. It is *natural* for the man whose spirit is Ariyan to feel these values, to desire this undertaking. The *right* state, in the highest sense, is that of a being who no longer thirsts, who has extinguished craving, who has made his own the Olympian and sidereal nature, as in the origins.

In point of practice, what we have said of the character of "totality" of the *kasina* is valid also for the *āyatana*. The mind, entirely recollected and unattached, receives the basic idea of each *āyatana*—infinite ether, infinity of consciousness, etc.—and

---

15. Page 75 in the English translation of the *Dhamma-saṅgani*.
16. *Majjh.*, 75.

realizes its content in an experience that brings about the corresponding transformation. To use a Buddhist simile, the spirit has become like a jar full to the brim with water, so that it only has to be tipped in one direction or another for the water immediately to overflow in that direction. Here, in the complete concentration of the inner being that is detached from the senses and from the bond of the saṁsāric "I," the images have the power of transformation: to think "infinite ether," "infinity of consciousness," "nonexistence," and so on, means to evoke the corresponding state, to transform the mind into that state, so that it undergoes the corresponding "infinitization" and liberation. We can, furthermore, say of the *āyatana* what we said of the *jhāna*, with reference both to actions that must have an almost spontaneous character, to the neutralization of any tendency toward identification, and finally to the burning process that in every state—even at these heights—discloses something that is conditioned and that may be overcome, thus urging one ever forward.[17]

This is about all that can be said of the five states of ascetic realization in the planes free from form. The indications concerning them in the texts are extremely schematic. Here begins that silence, which will later be absolute—at least in original Buddhism—about the essence of the state of extinction, about *nibbāna* (Skt.: *nirvāṇa*), and about the destiny of the Awakened One after death.

We now have shortly to discuss the other path to extinction, the path considered by another series of texts and that is no longer given as a journey across the world beyond form, but rather in terms of special visions and corresponding "births."

For our point of departure we must refer back to the state of consciousness corresponding to the fourth *jhāna* or to the fourth irradiant contemplation, that is to say, to an extreme, purified equanimity. To the state of mind that the ascetic must assume in order to operate are attributed qualities similar to those of the "pure, clear, ductile, flexible, resplendent indifference." The fixed canonical formula is: "with firm, purified, tense, sincere, unblemished, malleable, ductile, compact, incorruptible mind." With such a mind one strives first of all for achievement of what is known as *ñāṇa-dassana*, the vision that comes from knowledge, having as its object one's own person, in its totality. It is, as it were, the uncoupling of oneself or, better still, a liberating of oneself by self-division, carried out by contemplation of oneself—both in one's own somatic reality and in one's subtle reality—as if one were another person or thing. In fact, it is said that after the fourth *jhāna* one must "hold fast, one must consider in one's mind and penetrate with one's vision the object of self-contemplation—*paccavekkhana-nimitta*—just as one man might look at another, the one standing look

17. Cf. *Majjh.*, 44; 64; 106; *Angutt.*, 10.29; 9.31; 10.72. The passage from one *arūpa* to another occurs at the moment of feeling, firstly, form and the reflex images as a "disturbance" and impurity; then the *ākāśa* or ether element is so felt; then infinity of consciousness; then nonexistence; then the element beyond perception and nonperception; then determination.

ing at him who sits, the one sitting looking at him who stands."[18] It is, then, an extreme intensification of the process that began with the various contemplations on the body and on the mind during the consolidation phase; a process that now passes on to an objective stage that is designed to eliminate completely the bond of "I" and that is distinguished by this characteristic: that which now does the contemplating is the almost ultrahuman mind of one who has reached the fourth *jhāna* or who has followed the path that leads to the possibility of a state of union with Brahmā. The formula of the disidentification or "projection" is: "This is my body, provided with form, made up of the four elements, generated by a father and by a mother, maintained in life by these foods. It is impermanent, subject to change and decay, break-up and dissolution. And this also is my *viññāna* from which it proceeds and to which it is bound." A simile is given: as though on a cloth there lay a gem, a very pure, resplendent, clear, transparent, perfectly cut and faceted jewel, wholly excellent; there might be tied to it a thread, blue or yellow, red or white, and as though a man with good sight, taking it in his hand, were to consider it and see clearly how the one thing was joined to the other. This simile, taken from Sāmkhya, shows that it is a question of "exteriorizing" one's own person in its entirety: the term *viññāna* here refers to the subtle principle that organizes and gives life to bodily form.

But this "knowing," at present, only serves as a preparatory phase. This same "firm, purified, tense, sincere, unblemished, malleable, ductile, compact, incorruptible" mind is directed toward a further "knowing," toward the vision of "previous forms of existence." There arises the memory-vision of "many previous forms of existence, of one life, of two lives, of three lives" and so back through whole series of lives in the periods both of the coming-to-be and of the dissolution of worlds. "There was I, I had such a name, I belonged to such a people, such was my state, such my office; this good and this evil I experienced, thus was the end of my life. Having passed on from there, I entered again into existence." In such a manner, the ascetic recalls multiple forms of existence, each with its own characteristics, each with its own special relationships. A simile is given: as if a man were to go from one village to another and from there to another and finally were to return home and, in recollecting, should think thus: "I, then, went from one village to another, where I stood thus, I sat thus, I spoke thus, I kept silent thus; from that village I went to another, where I did thus and thus, and finally *I returned to my village* ('the country of the ancestors')." This is the first "knowing"—the precise term is *pubbe-nivāsañāna*—a revealing vision having as counterpart an interior liberation, a definite self-elevation beyond the saṃsāric group to which a given particular individual existence belongs, and which now appears as a mere episode.

---

18. *Angutt.*, 5.28.

The next experience concerns a "celestial, clarified, superhuman eye," it is called *dibba-cakkhu-ñāṇa*, which develops the vision, no longer of one's "own" existences, but of other saṃsāric groups, of the appearance and disappearance of beings in the sequence that is determined by the law of action, of *kamma*. "With this celestial, clarified, superhuman eye the ascetic sees beings disappear and appear, beings that are common and noble, ugly and beautiful, happy and unhappy, and he apprehends that beings always appear in life according to their actions." Here, too, we have a simile: as if there were two buildings with doors, and a man with good sight, standing between them, were to see people leaving one house and entering the other, going and coming.

This power of vision, by means of which the contingency of the various forms of existence is directly *contemplated* from a universal, "celestial" standpoint, provides the final catharsis, leads to *paññā* or *bodhi*, to liberation, illumination, and extinction, to the same culmination that crowned and resolved the series of the five *āyatana*, of the five reintegrations in the sphere beyond form. We have, then, as the third and last "knowing," the vision of the "conditioned genesis" that determines the "round of rebirth" of beings, the vision of that which lies at the root of the genesis, of that which is its end and of the states that lead to this end. At this point the *āsava* disappear; there occurs the "redemption of the mind without manias," and again we have the formula: "Exhausted is life, the divine path achieved, that which had to be done has been done, this world no longer exists." There is a final simile, dealing with the crystallinity, the absolute transparency and clarity of this vision that brings to an end the entire catharsis: as if a man with good sight were to stand on the banks of an alpine valley lake and, completely aware, were to consider the shells and the snails, the gravel and the sand and the schools of fish, how they dart about or lie still.[19]

Apart from the initial "projection" of oneself, this second path has thus three stages. It is important to emphasize that in some canonical texts they are related, respectively, to the three watches *(yāmā)* of the night. Thus, the Buddha says: "This knowing [that is, the first, the vision of one's own multiple, previous states of existence] I first apprehended in the first watch of the night, I dispersed ignorance, I apprehended wisdom, I dispersed obscurity, I apprehended light, whilst I dwelt striving ardently, watchful and strenuous." The same formula is repeated for the other two "knowings." The disappearance and reappearance of beings is the second "knowing" to be apprehended, in the middle watch of the night, and the final, liberating vision is the third to be achieved, in the last watch of the night.[20] In one text, it is said: "When the dawn is about to break, at the moment in which sleep is so profound and

19. On all this see *Dighā*, 2.93–98; cf. *Majjh.*, 77.
20. *Angutt.*, 8.11; *Majjh.*, 4. In particular, on the experience, in the watches of the night, of the conditioned genesis and of the conditioned removal of its effects, cf. *Mahāvagga* (*Vin.*), 1.1.2.

to wake so difficult." Another point: the three "knowings" have also been related to so many immaterial births *(opapātika)*. There is the simile of the hen that has completely incubated her eggs and is waiting for them to hatch and for the new being to arise from them, safe and sound. The warmth that nourishes this symbolical birth is that of ascesis, *tapas*. At the moment in which the "knowing" of the various previous tales of existence is apprehended, the ascetic—it is said—"is for the first time disclosed, like the chick come out of the shell." This first birth—beyond physical, saṁsāric birth—is the growth beyond one's own individuality; a growth that is bound up with the ability to gaze beyond the temporal limits of an individual existence, to see the whole group to which it belongs. A second opening is achieved with the "knowing" of the passing and uprising of beings and, finally, a third when the sudden flash of knowledge destroys the *āsavā* and determines the state of *nibbāna*.[21] Each of the three "transcendental knowings" is, then, an awakening, an "opening," a change of state, the passage from one mode of being to another, from one "world" to another. Thus we find in Buddhism a traditional symbolism that is used in many forms of initiation, probably in connection with similar experiences. Besides these three births, which are of a real nature, there is a birth that is symbolical and, above all, moral, the "rebirth with the birth of the Ariya" or the "blessed birth," referred to the man who makes the break, who achieves "departure," and who devotes himself to the path of awakening.[22]

We must give an explanation of this new group of transcendental experiences also. It is essential here to distinguish between the deepest content of the doctrine and that which refers to the popular exposition and that cannot be taken in an absolute sense *(paramatthavasena)*.

To begin with, at this point we must forestall the idea that not only is the theory of reincarnation assumed by the Buddhist teaching, but that it is, in fact, demonstrated by a direct form of transcendental knowledge in the shape of an actual memory. It might seem, that is to say, that the situation were thus: that one single being having lived several lives or, at least, several forms of existence, could, at a particular moment, see retrospectively. Such an interpretation, in spite of all appearances, would be mistaken.

In order to understand the true sense of these experiences, we must always remember their point of departure, that is, *ñāna-dassana*, the vision or "projection" of one's own person that allows of its consideration as a thing or as the person of another. In this there occurs, in a manner of speaking, the fulfillment of all the labor of severance from one's own "I," from one's own individuality, which has been

---

21. *Angutt.*, 8.11; *Majjh.*, 53; *Saṁyutt.*, 22.101.
22. *Majjh.*, 86. We also find the image of the snake that sloughs its old skin—cf. *Suttanipāta*, 1.1.1 ff.

carried out in the preceding ascesis. This means that one has become integrated in a new dimension or at a new level, an integration that is inevitably accompanied by a "loosening." Consciousness is no longer tied to a particular "name-and-form," it can move, it can take on the person of other people, both in space and in time. This is the foundation of the first two "transcendental knowings," the vision of many preceding forms of existence (superindividuality in time) and the vision of the disappearance and reappearance of other beings (superindividuality in space, that is to say, with regard to various individual lives copresent in space).

With reference to the first experience, we could speak, in a certain sense, of "memory," but not as though it were one particular "I" that remembered having lived other lives or, more generally having passed through other forms of existence. We can see that this would be absurd for the simple reason that the condition for achieving such a "memory" is no longer to be an "I," to be free from "I" or from the consciousness connected with a particular "name-and-form" and with a particular life. We are no longer dealing with the memory of an "I" but with the emergence, in the individual consciousness, of saṁsāric consciousness, with the "memory" associated with the groups of craving, or daemon, or *antarabhāva* with which one was identified: for—as we saw—one does not adopt a "name-and-form," a physiopsychical organism drawn from nowhere, but a more or less preformed saṁsāric force carrying with it a heredity, a complex of tendencies, which continue from the dead lives in which this force was previously active. The continuity and therefore also the basis of "memory" is contained in this force: it is not contained in an identical and permanent "I" to which Buddhism rightly denies an existence on the saṁsāric plane. At the moment when consciousness becomes disindividualized, breaks the bond of the saṁsāric "I" and becomes universal, this same saṁsāric memory is spread out clearly before it. The very moment of one's dissociation from the "daemon," or "double," is the moment in which one comes to know it. This is the deeper meaning of the first "knowing," of the "memory of preceding forms of existence."

In the second "knowing" there is an increase in the power of the disindividualized consciousness, a consciousness that now extends not only along time and along the group of that particular entity of craving with which it was identified, but also in space, since it becomes capable of identifying itself also with other beings and of examining the saṁsāric heredity that determines them, the will of craving in which they live and where are determined the causes, when the material of one life is consumed, for the same flame to flare up elsewhere in strict accordance with its antecedents.

Thus it is that, in these experiences, we can see the counterpart of liberations that are exactly similar to those of the ascetic who advances through the five planes free from form. In fact, it is not by chance that we have spoken not of "multiple lives," but rather of "multiple states of existence." The assumption of the person of other people, which we have mentioned, is by no means restricted to human lives in space and time, but includes also extraterrestrial lines of existence and of heredity. Now, all this is possible only if one reaches a dimension to be compared to the depths of the ocean, where all the insular and continental parts emerging from the water as separate things are unified in a single mass. We are thus brought back to images of immensity, vastness, immeasurableness, indiscernibility. About such images we shall have more to say later. And it is natural that the texts refuse to apply to the Accomplished One, who has followed this path to the end, any category whatsoever that, in common speech, takes its meaning from the existence or nonexistence, from the life or death of an individual being.

Thus the theory of reincarnation is rejected from two points of view: firstly from the point of view of ordinary, saṁsāric beings, since it is not the same being that has already lived nor that will live again, but rather the groups of craving working in him. On this plane a real substantial "I" does not exist. Secondly, from the point of view of transcendental illumination, since from this point of view the "many existences" can only represent a mirage. The one who contemplates them can no longer be considered as an "I," and he is now also about to break the law that from one saṁsāric group there must spring a new existence. As we shall see, the Buddhist teaching also considers intermediate cases, that is to say, cases of incomplete extinction: but for further states of existence or for new "lives," in the degree in which extinction is not complete, what we have said about the ordinary man is to a large extent still valid: there is no proper continuity, there are only transformations that affect also the "substratum." Buddhism maintains this view in connection with the "mental body" and with the body "free from form," which various texts attribute to the Accomplished One, the term "body" here being used in a general sense, implying other states and modes of being relative to the "worlds," beyond the physical one, that are reached by the *jhāna*. The question was asked if such "bodies" exist simultaneously. The answer is negative. But the doctrine goes still further: the passage from one to another of these states does not present a true continuity. The transformations are absolute, as in the aforesaid simile of the milk that becomes curd and curd that becomes cheese. It is absurd still to call curd milk or cheese curd: in changing the state, it is well also to change the name.[23] With still more reason, the idea of an absolute identity of the "I" in the states to which a partial liberation may lead is to be rejected.

On the subject of "reincarnations" and of "many lives," we must remember that, in spite of the opinions held in some circles, such ideas find no place in serious traditional teachings, Eastern or Western, nor therefore in Buddhism. Those passages in

---

23. *Dīgha*, 9.39; 47–53.

Buddhism and in the Indo-Aryan traditions in general that would seem to indicate the contrary, do so either because of a too literal reading of the texts or because they are popular forms of exposition that only have a symbolical value, rather like the crude images of the Christian purgatory or hell that are common among simple folk. To accept unquestioningly all that can be found in the Buddhist texts on the subject of preceding existences not only opens the way to all sorts of contradictions and incoherences on the doctrinal level, but also breeds doubts as to the efficacy of the historical Buddha's real supernormal vision. The stories in the canon, and particularly in the *Jātaka,* of the presumed previous existences of Prince Siddhattha, notably in the form of animals, are all evidently of a fabulous nature and, even when their origin is not wholly spurious, it is easy to see that they have been invented or introduced into Buddhism from already existing popular traditions for pedagogic use to illustrate and enliven discourses. We do not find, in the texts, a single serious reference to anything like a "memory," like an actual fact of the past seen by supernormal means and then communicated. Here, also, the Awakened One maintains his silence. In any case, the classical and dryly glittering spirit of original Buddhism, so free of sentimentalism, is rarely found in the later texts, beginning with the *Jātaka,* where not only is there a tropical overgrowth of phantasmagorical and fabulous elements, but also not a few distortions of the original doctrine of the Ariya, particularly on the moral plane. It will be enough to remember—one case will serve for a whole series of others—the story dealing with the preceding life of Prince Siddhattha wherein he is supposed to have been an animal that, upon seeing a hungry tiger, allowed itself to be torn to pieces through "compassion," thus acquiring the "merit" that, through the series of other lives, was little by little to lead him to the grade of Awakened One. Whenever higher wisdom is not enclosed in the form of rigorous esotericism—true esotericism, not that of contemporary "occultists"—such alterations are almost inevitable and it is for intelligent people to discriminate accurately, to pick out the essentials, or to clarify what has become obscure: which can be done only by the guidance of sound principles of a traditional and metaphysical kind.

We must mention another point. We have seen that the three supernormal "knowings" have been related by the texts to the first, second, and third watches of the night, respectively. This is an important fact once we remember the Indo-Aryan teachings on the "four states": the state of individual wakeful consciousness, the state of dreaming, the state of sleep, and finally, the so-called fourth state *(caturtha* or *turīya).* In the same "space" in which, when individual wakeful consciousness disappears, the ordinary man starts to dream, passes into the unconsciousness of dreamless sleep, and finally into a state like apparent death, it is possible to achieve, instead, a series of "liberations," of degrees of superconsciousness. In this connection, the state of dreaming (that is to say, what would correspond to dreaming in the ordinary man) is called by the texts *tejo*, from *tejas*, which means "radiant light" and which is related to what we have said about *ākāśa*, "ether"; the state of deep, dreamless sleep "where there is no knowledge, but the subject of knowledge continues to know," is related to the condition of *prajñā* (Pāli: *paññā*) or of "illumination": here "the being reunites with himself in a unity of pure knowledge and beatitude"; here there is "the perfect serenity which, rising up from the body and arriving at the supreme light, appears in its true aspect"; here we are on the point of crossing that dyke, "beyond which he who was blind is no longer blind, he who was wounded is no longer wounded, he who was ill is no longer ill," where "even night becomes day." The fourth condition corresponds to the unconditioned state, absolutely above all duality, all particular forms of manifestation, beyond both interior consciousness and exterior consciousness, and above both together.[24]

When we spoke of the *jhāna*, we considered the possibility of references to transformations of this sort, and a more exact correspondence can be seen with regard to the developments in the world free from form, to the *āyatana*. Thus, we are not unjustified in matching the Indo-Aryan traditional doctrine we have just discussed with the realizations that take place in the three watches of the night: we have a consciousness that ,"like a fire that advances destroying every bond," carries one beyond the state of wakefulness, leaves this state behind, advances to the state that in others would be sleep or profound sleep, and establishes itself there, "dissipating ignorance, achieving wisdom, dissipating the shadows, achieving the light"— just as says the Buddhist formula that refers to the "supernormal knowing" acquired during the first, second, and third watches of the night. Beyond the "luminous" or "radiant" state of *taijasa*, beyond the state of pure illumination (*prajñā*, which, in Buddhism, would correspond to the opening of the "celestial, unclouded, superterrestrial eye") there is the unconditioned state. *Turīya*, the unconditioned state of the *ātmā* in the general Indo-Aryan tradition, would then correspond to the state of *nirvāṇa* in the Buddhist terminology.[25]

In such terms, the "vigil" of the Ariya appears in the grandeur of a change in which the night is transformed into day, unconsciousness into superconsciousness; the vision of an indefinite number of existences dispersed in time spreads out like a memory, and is left behind. During the last hours of the night, where for the others "sleep is deepest," at the dawning of the physical light, there dawns also that

---

24. Cf. *Maitrāyaṇī Upaniṣad*, 6.19; 7.11; *Māṇḍūkya Upaniṣad*, 4–7; *Chāndogya Upaniṣad*, 8.11.1; 12.3; 6.3–5; 4.1–3, etc.

25. There are also specific references with regard to the experiences that take place in the Awakened One in the state corresponding to that of sleep. Cf. *Sumangala-vilāsinī* (commentary to the *Dīgha-nikāya*), 1.47 (W. 94–95), where it is said that in the second watch of the night he sleeps and simultaneously enters into contact with some divinities. In the third watch, arising, with his superterrestrial eye he perceives those who have decided to tread the path of awakening.

wisdom, that awakening, in which every mania is destroyed and which towers over all worlds with their ranks of angels, evil and good spirits, gods and men, ascetics and priests. Thus the Accomplished One, when the final watch of the night changes into light, returns to the world of men at the moment in which the day once again shines on him, and awakening corresponds to awakening, the physical and the metaphysical elements meet, and truly may we use for him a similitude of the texts: that of the sun, "when, in the last month of the rainy season, after it has dissipated and put to flight the rain-swollen clouds, it rises in the sky and disperses with its rays the mist in the air, and flashes and shines." This is the mighty appearance of the Awakened One among men. "Light of the world," the Buddha has been called—"the light of wisdom becomes light of the world";[26] "the sage, who appears in the world of men and of gods, proceeding alone, in the midst [of the people], dispersing every shadow."[27]

---

26. *Therīgāthā*, 148 (quoted by de Lorenzo in his translation of *Majjh.*, vol. 2, p. 65); cf. *Mahāparin.*, 52–56.
27. *Suttanipāta*, 4.16.2.

14

Discrimination
Between the "Powers"

The Buddhist teaching admits the possibility of acquiring extranormal and supernormal powers *(iddhi)* along the path of awakening: this is one of the signs that the Buddhist ascesis does not move toward a state of nothingness, toward a crepuscular frontier between consciousness and unconsciousness, there to wait for a final "annihilation," but that it is accompanied by ever greater degrees of consciousness, completeness, elevation, and power.

We have no need to consider the "difficulties of belief" that, with regard to the *iddhi,* may arise in the minds of modern "critical" commentators. It is, of course, well known how often these individuals, after denouncing as fabulous all that touches the supernormal in the history of great figures of the past, are capable of falling into ecstasy before some petty "mediumistic" phenomenon that, in the ancient world, would not have merited the attention of any person of consequence.

The problem of the extranormal and supernormal powers is connected with the view of the world. When nature is not conceived as an independent reality, but rather as the outward form in which immaterial forces manifest themselves; when, furthermore, one admits the possibility of removing, under certain conditions, the purely individual, sensory-cerebral consciousness of a man so as to allow of positive contacts with those immaterial forces—then, assuming these premises, which are those of every normal and traditional concept of the world, the general possibility of extranormal powers follows as a natural consequence.

The true problem does not, then, consist in the reality or otherwise of certain phenomena—admittedly not capable of being explained by the physical or psychical laws known today—that in the past boasted a science *sui generis,* of which many, although fragmentary, traces still remain: the true problem is, rather, the significance and the value to be attached to such phenomena.

We have already discussed the difference between "prodigies" of the noble,

Ariyan type and those not noble, non-Ariyan—*anariya-iddhi*. We must add that, by Buddhism as by any traditional doctrine, both the quest after the "powers" in themselves, and worse, the quest after them for temporal and individual ends, more or less in the spirit with which technology and the power associated therewith have been developed today, were considered not only as having nothing to do with ascetic and spiritual development, but even as being positively harmful to this development. The practice of the "powers" was held to be dangerous.[1] "My instruction," says the Buddha, "is not this: Come, O ascetics, and acquire powers which surpass those of ordinary men."[2] The life that is led in the order of the Accomplished One is not directed to the acquisition of powers that produce clairvoyance or clairaudience but has a higher aim, namely, liberation.[3] This, however, does not prevent the transcendental forms of experience and detachment that we have considered from being capable of giving rise to extranormal modes of action and of vision. And when there is adequate cause, an Awakened One may use such faculties, much as an ordinary man uses his speech or his arms.

The *iddhi* are divided, in the Buddhist teaching, into three sections: "magical" powers, powers that reveal what for the ordinary man remains hidden (powers of "manifestation"), and finally, powers that work in the miracle of the doctrine and of right discernment. The last are considered as the most noble and august of them all. They are the ones to which we referred when we spoke earlier of the "miracle" whereby there may arise in the saṁsāric consciousness an extrasaṁsāric force and vocation, a will that is no longer the normal will, a will that overcomes the normal will and arrests the "flux," a vision that can now discern what is noble and what is common, the rational and the irrational, the unconditioned and the conditioned. Together with the power of achieving this "miracle," the Awakened Ones—it is said—also comprehend and acquire those of the first two sections, which we shall shortly discuss;[4] but they fully realize that, in themselves, they have very little value. If anyone should be tempted to show them off or brag about them, he should remember that it is possible to arrive at analogous results by means of certain forms of sorcery.[5] Thus the *iddhi*, the extranormal powers, are never used, in the tradition of the Ariya, even to astonish and convert men of low intellectual capacity; the miraculous phenomenology that occurs in some later Buddhist texts is clearly of a fabulous, allegorical, or symbolical type, just like the stories of the multiple existences. The attitude of the pure doctrine of the Ariya is almost exactly that which the last exponents of the Aryan and aristocratic Roman tradition assumed, in the person of Celsus, in opposition to certain forms of

1. *Dīgha*, 11.5–7.
2. Ibid., 11.1.
3. Ibid., 6.1–13.
4. *Dīgha*, 11.3; *Angutt.*, 3.60.
5. *Dīgha*, 11.5–7.

Christianism. Celsus, in fact, asked what the Christians were trying to prove with all their excitement about this "miracle" or that, since it was well known that anyone with a taste for such things and wishing to produce similar phenomena had only to go to Egypt and learn about them from the specialists.

With this in mind, let us see how we are to understand these powers that are mentioned in the texts of the oldest canon. As the starting point for the *iddhi* of "manifestation" the texts postulate the purified, ductile, malleable, compact, unblemished mind, isolated from peripheral sensitivity, which is also presupposed for the achievement of the "three knowings" in the threefold watch. Free from the bond of the senses and of saṁsāric individuality, neutral, extremely balanced, this consciousness, aroused in one or other of the *jhāna,* can directly realize the object whose image is evoked, by producing either telepathic knowledge, or objective penetration of the mind of others, or, finally, vision of distant things.[6] In this connection we can recall a simile already quoted: just as it is enough to tip a vessel that is brimful, in a particular direction, for the water to overflow in that direction, "so also if he has devoted himself to, developed, often practised, established and brought to its just fulfilment the right, fivefold contemplation of the Ariya [here is meant the four *jhāna* after being integrated by the vision-projection of one's self—cf. p. 174–75], then if he directs his mind to any element whatsoever that is susceptible of being the object of a higher knowledge [the ascetic] can apprehend this element in wisdom, provided he has developed the faculty, and provided the right conditions are present."[7]

When it is applied to the persons, the minds, and the hearts of other people that the Awakened One is able to observe with the same clarity and with no greater effort than every one of us can observe his own features in a mirror,[8] such power may be regarded as an elementary grade of the first and the second "knowing," which embrace multiple "lives" and multiple saṁsāric groups. In some texts, indeed, this twofold "knowing" is listed among the *abhiññā* or supernormal faculties, some of which are also called *iddhi.*[9] In this case, however, we must distinguish between ascetic experiences proper, in which those "knowings" are the concomitants of liberation, and these powers of vision in themselves, when they are used for a particular purpose. We must not, in any case, forget that it is the "celestial, supermundane eye" *(dibba-cakkhu)* with which the Awakened One perceives the whereabouts of others of whom he is thinking, sees into the heart and mind of his interlocutors as well as of people at a distance, and perceives that a particular being, to whom he has directed his thought, is dead, and so on.[10]

6. Ibid., 2.91–2.
7. *Angutt.,* 5.28.
8. *Dīgha,* 2.92.
9. Ibid., 2.93–96.
10. *Majjh.,* 4; 6; 26; 27; 36; 76; 85; 109, etc.

The counterpart of this latter *iddhi* is the faculty of supernormal hearing *(dibba-sota)*. The Awakened One is able to perceive two kinds of sound, "the divine and the human, the far and the near."[11] To understand the "divine" or "immaterial" sounds, we must refer back to the traditional teachings that had already served as the basis for the Vedic doctrine of ritual and that, occurring as wisdom in the mantras, were particularly developed in some forms of yoga, and then, in the tantras. We have already discussed this elsewhere. To hear the "immaterial sounds" is not to perceive an indeterminate and almost mystico-aesthetic "harmony of the spheres," but rather to arrive at a special form of perception of the formative forces of things and of elements, a perception that, in its working, is distantly analogous to what the common man experiences as sound. The man who is really capable of perceiving and grasping the "divine sounds" is then also capable of pronouncing the word that is power, the mantra, a thing that, among others, lies at the root of every liturgical practise that has not been reduced to a mere recitation.[12]

Other *iddhi* considered by the texts consist of appearing and disappearing, of walking on water without sinking, of moving great distances in a moment, of "wielding power over one's body right up to the world of Brahmā."[13] In order to understand that such phenomena are possible we must start from the production of the body "made of mind" *(manomaya)* that we have already mentioned. In the text to which we are principally referring this state occurs immediately after the contemplation-projection of one's own person (cf. p. 174–75) and is given in the following terms: "With this firm, purified, tense, sincere, unblemished, malleable, ductile, compact, incorruptible mind, he [the ascetic] turns toward the production of a body made of mind. From his body he extracts another body having all its organs and all its faculties, furnished with form, but supersensible, made of mind." To illustrate this there are similes of a man drawing a sword from its scabbard, removing the pith from a rush, or a snake from a basket.[14] An important detail that warns us not to confuse this experience with a simple act of magic is that we are here—it is said—in the realm of transcendental knowledge, *paññā*.[15] Besides we have seen that the practise in question comes immediately after the apprehension of one's own person as that of another by means of the eye that has opened in the *jhāna*. We have mentioned the transformation of the sensation that one normally has of the body: it is a matter of taking this process further by achieving an ever more detached and disindividualized consciousness, on the one hand, and on the other, by penetrating down into the deep, "vital"—in a superbiological sense—forces that rule the organism and that make up

12. Cf. our *The Yoga of Power*, and J. Woodroffe, *The Garland of Letters* (Madras, 1922).
13. *Dīgha*, 2.87.
14. Ibid., 2.86; *Majjh.*, 77.
15. Cf., e.g., *Dīgha*, 2.20–26.

the "double," or "daemon," and the saṁsāric being in us. Here the transcendental knowledge cannot do other than produce a special transformation, if only by degrees. The transfigured mind, in this profundity, works almost, one might say, as a catalyst; it transmits its own nature to the group of forces with which it comes in contact, so that eventually the half vital and half opaque sensation that one has of one's bodiliness clarifies into the sensation of a transparent and luminous "form." It is luminous or radiant since, actually, these experiences happen in a condition corresponding to *taijasa*, that is, in the condition of luminosity or radiance that, for the Awakened One, takes the place of the state of dreaming. This is the true sense of the "extraction of the body made of mind," which is not "another" body, but a particular experience of the power of which the body is the sensible manifestation.

We have yet to see how far this power has been "purified," to what extent the disindividualized sidereal principle has divested itself of its saṁsāric nature and directly controls this force. Bodily manifestation *depends* on this power: depends, in the same sense that speech depends on the faculty of speaking, the faculty by which it has been forged, that directs it, and that can either change it or reabsorb it into itself. If the catharsis has been taken as far as it will go, this force, which here appears as "supersensible body made of mind," plays the same part in relation to the manifested bodily form. It follows from this that anyone who realizes and controls his body as a "supersensible body," has, virtually, also this twofold power: of extracting or projecting from the same trunk another bodily image, either the same as or different from his own; or else of reabsorbing the whole manifested form into the energy from which it came, in order to reproject it completely elsewhere. The first of these powers is that of ubiquity, and it may be developed up to the capacity, recorded in the texts, for "appearing as many, being one sole person, and of returning to be one sole person, having been many." Here, the real, physical person of the agent is always supposed to persist in a particular place, while the other forms are only projected images, extracted from the agent's own subtle form which we can call the matrix of corporeality. The second implies the faculty of appearance or disappearance, of passing through "solid barriers, walls and mountains without hindrance, as if they were air," of walking on water or of passing through the air. The simile commonly used by the texts for this extranormal and, in an Awakened One, supernormal phenomenology is: as a strong man stretches his bent arm or bends his stretched arm, so the ascetic disappears from one place and reappears in another: and this other may well signify a condition of existence differing from the terrestrial.

We must forestall the mistake that would be made by anyone who, in attempting to explain such phenomena, were to entertain the idea of "dematerialization." This would presuppose the existence of a "material" that, in the current modern sense, is quite unknown to the traditional teachings. Material existence is only manifested existence, a form of manifested existence. It is not, then, a question of "dematerialization" but rather of reabsorbing a manifested form into its unmanifested principle in order to reproject it elsewhere; one should not, therefore, even think of it as a kind of voyage *through* matter, from one place to another, but as a *withdrawal* of the manifested form, that is, of the bodily figure, at a particular place, to make it reemerge, newly visible, elsewhere. This occurs by "passing underneath," that is by the means of a principle that, since it is outside and above manifestation, is free of the condition of space and that may therefore be said to be everywhere and, at the same time, nowhere. As the mind is now the center of the body, the image of a place, adequately fixed in the mind under the right conditions, determines *eo ipso* the phenomenon, quite irrespective of distance, so that it is said that projection in a nearby place needs the same "time" as projection in a very distant place, since the mental act of evoking either has the same duration.[16]

All this may possibly help to clarify the internal logic of the phenomena that are recorded in the Buddhist texts; phenomena which, although extremely rare in the modern world on account of the ever more intense "physicalization" and "saṁsārization" of the human being, are, nonetheless, quite real. We have, here, referred to phenomena that are "real" in a specific sense, distinguishing them from phenomena, which can be produced quite cheaply by means of collective or individual suggestive devices. Finally, we must consider the possibility that these same phenomena, rather than originating in the metaphysical and ascetic way we have discussed, are achieved along more or less shadowy paths through certain contacts with elemental forces. The Buddha touches on this point when he says, for example, that the forms of supernormal vision that he and many Awakened Ones also have, are created by mental concentration and are not those that are related to inferior practices or contacts with spirits or angels.[17]

In order that the *iddhi* we have considered may be perfect, it is naturally essential that "ignorance" should have been destroyed without leaving any residue and that there should have been an equally complete resolution of the saṁsāric being:[18] only then is the power over the root from which the body is manifested complete, and only then can all the elements on which the manifestation of the bodily form is based be mastered. In this extreme case, rather than of a "body made of mind, furnished with form" we should speak of the "body made of spirit" and of pure consciousness, free from form *(arūpa atta paṭilābha)*, which is related to the "blessed body" *(tusita kāya)* in which one who is on the path of awakening will rearise after death,[19] and to

16. *Milindapañha*, 82 (W. 306).
17. *Angutt.*, 3.60.
18. Using the Taoistic terminology, this would be called the complete distillation of the *yin* to pure *yang*.
19. Cf. *Majjh.*, 123; 143.

the "body of transfiguration" that occurs in some Gnostic schools. It is to this that we must clearly turn when the texts deal with the *iddhi* connected with having one's body in one's own power as far as the world of Brahmā, that is, up to the condition of pure being. Particularly in Mahāyāna developments of the Buddhist teaching we find extensions of these views, through which we can arrive at the deepest meaning that was, perhaps, hidden in Christian docetism. According to these Mahāyāna conceptions, the Accomplished Ones, the *Tathāgata,* do not actually have a body. In reality, it is not a question of not having a body, but, rather, of completely possessing, on the summit of an absolutely liberated consciousness, all the principles on which its sensible manifestation is based. And here, if it were the place to do so, we could devise interesting interpretations of the true sense of the various traditions that relate to beings who never "died," but who were "carried away," who disappeared from the physical world without leaving a body behind them.[20] In any case, the most ancient Buddhist conception of the twofold "body" beyond the physical one, as well as the Mahāyāna conception of the *trikāya,* the threefold body of the Buddha, refers to three degrees of the same realization, and is related both to the general Indo-Aryan doctrine of the "three worlds," and to the views (particularly those of Sāṃkhya) on the three bodies, material, subtle (or vital), and causative (*sthūla*—or *kariya*—*liṅga* [or *sūkshma*] and *kāraṇa-śarīra*). To experience the body as a pure, dominated, free, plastic, intangible instrument of manifestation—this is the extreme limit.

We must briefly discuss one last point on the subject of "miracles." Buddhism states that, if they are not sought for their own sake but occur as natural possibilities in particular stages of awakening, the "powers" may be used where necessary with a pure mind, with the same indifference as the ordinary man uses his senses and his limbs. There are, however, particular cases in which the "prodigy," the extranormal fact, is invested with a "sacred" and "noble"—Ariyan—character: such cases occur when the "marvel" has an illuminating power on account of the phenomenon being a symbol and a manifestation of a transcendental significance, since, in this manner, it produces striking evidence of the dependence of "nature" on a higher order.[21] One can find, also in Buddhism, a few references to these true, sacred marvels. For example, walking on water: when the ascetic, in profound meditation, achieves the state of one who has escaped from the "current," from the "waters"; of one who, like the lotus in a simile we have quoted, arises above the water, untouched by it—then

---

20. Cf. on this our work *The Hermetic Tradition.* There also occurs in Buddhism the *"nibbāna* of fire which leaves no residue," cf. *Udāna* (8.10): Dabba rises in the air and plunges himself into contemplation of the fiery element, then passes over into *nibbāna.* "Neither grease nor ashes remained of his burned body." This concentration on fire also takes us back to the tantras. Cf. de la Vallée-Poussin, in the translation of the *Abhidharmakośa,* 4, p. 229.

21. Cf. our *Maschera e volto dello spiritualismo contemporaneo.*

in particular circumstances he may reveal a cosmic sign of this achievement, the actual power of walking on water without sinking. One text relates that a marvel of this kind began to be neutralized at the moment when the mind of the ascetic relaxed its spiritual concentration.[22] Again, it is well known that the symbol of one who has passed over the current and who, when on the other shore, helps the noble sons to cross, is applied to the Buddha.[23] Now, it can occur that at the very moment of the spiritual realization of this a fresh cosmic evidence in the form of a "marvel" is produced: the Buddha and his disciples in the act of crossing a river, find themselves magically carried to the other bank.[24] Another example. When the Buddha meets the feared bandit Angulimāla he prevents the bandit, who is running toward him, from catching up with the Accomplished One, who is standing still. He who stands still walks, he who walks stands still.[25] A transcendental significance is once more manifested in this marvel: locomotion, which does not take one forward, by which "one does not reach the end of the world," is opposed to being still, in a supernatural stability that, to beings that are carried along by the saṃsāric current, must appear as a vertiginous, fearful going.

Whether or not such irruptions, so full of meaning, of a higher order into the natural order, ever historically took place, they serve, in the texts, to illustrate the significance of a particular category of "sacred" and "noble" marvels. As for the other extranormal or supernormal phenomena, from what we have just said it is clear that, in Buddhism, they do not have the character of "miracles," of incomprehensible and irrational happenings, as they do in many popular, and even in some not so popular, forms of religion. They have, instead, their own logic, they are connected with a particular view of the world, and the path of awakening, in its various phases, affords the explanation of the fact that they can really take place.

22. *Jātaka*, 190. In ibid., 263, it ceases as he becomes contaminated with a woman.
23. *Suttanipāta*, 3.6.36.
24. *Dīgha*, 16.1.33–34.
25. *Majjh.*, 86.

15

⚜

Phenomenology of the Great Liberation

The pure, original doctrine of the Ariya is explicitly anti-evolutionist. "Becoming" has no significance. The "cycle" of rebirths does not lead to the death-less.[1] There is neither beginning, nor progress, nor end in the succession of the states conditioned by "ignorance" and by "agitation." It is said that, even as there is no lofty and massive mountain that one day will not crumble, no ocean that one day will not dry up, similarly, there is no end to the changing undergone by ordinary beings who, through their saṁsāric self-identification, pass from one state of existence to another, like a dog that goes round and round, firmly tied to a post or to a column.[2] Returning to the symbolism of the two shores, it is said that while few enter the water, fewer still reach the other side, while the great mass of living beings runs up and down on this bank.[3] Rare is the appearance in the world of a Perfectly Awakened One.[4] Such an appearance is like the miraculous blossoming of a flower close to a pile of dung that represents, in fact, the worthless mass of ordinary beings.[5]

That Buddhism sees an essential difference between the "sons of the world" (*puthujjana*) and the "sons of the Sākya's son" we know already, as we also know that by "world" Buddhism does not only mean terrestrial existence, but any conditioned form of existence whatsoever, be it higher or lower than the human state. The Ariyan path of awakening is, then, of an absolutely "vertical" nature, it does not conceive of "progressivity"; between the state of *nibbāna* and any other state, demonic, titanic, human, or celestial, it sees a gap. The state of *nibbāna* cannot be found by "going"; it cannot be found in the horizontal direction of time, nor in the

---

1. *Saṁyutt.*, 2.179.
2. Ibid., 22.99.
3. *Angutt.*, 10.117; *Dhammapada*, 85.
4. *Dīgha*, 16.5.5.
5. *Dhammapada*, 58–59.

perpetuity, longevity, or indefinite existence that are ascribed to the various angelic and celestial beings and to the theistic god himself, Brahmā. Bodhi, absolute illumination, the "wisdom" that liberates, is sometimes therefore likened to lightning,[6] a description that clearly shows its extratemporal character. Everything, therefore, that is connected with extrasaṁsāric development is to be considered from a quite special point of view. The oldest texts themselves remark on the relativity of the time needed to achieve fulfillment: seven years, seven months, seven days, the very day of hearing the doctrine.[7] In Mahāyāna and in Zen Buddhism this idea is very much accentuated. In a Mahāyāna text it is said that one should not feel fear or anguish at the thought that "one will awaken late to the incomparable, perfect knowledge" since this awakening is the work of a single moment, and is "the extreme [frontier] limit with something that has no past, and which therefore is a non-limit." One must not even formulate the depressing idea: "Great and long is this limit that has no past," since "this limit without a past, and which is therefore not a limit, is connected with a unique spiritual moment."[8] By this it means that what, from the point of view of saṁsāric consciousness, might seem to be a distant final aim, in reality stands outside any sequence, so that to apprehend it means to apprehend it also as something that has not had a past, that has no antecedents, that is without time; whence it may be said that all that has led up to it is *eo ipso* destroyed. The path, the effort, the gradualness, the "made" *(sankṛta)* all this vanishes, disperses like mist. The Sāṁkhya theory relating to the *puruṣa,* and the Upaniṣads and then the Vedānta theory relating to the *ātmā,* have the same sense: the *ātmā,* have the same sense: the *ātmā* or *puruṣa,* is eternally present. It is not this that "revolves," that "acts," that strives, that advances. Illumination is the flash in which, beyond all time, this presence without a past is apprehended.

Recognition of this discontinuity of the state of absolute illumination does not, however, prevent us from considering a series of cases corresponding to various approximations of the point from which the jump in the transcendental direction may

---

6. *Angutt.,* 3.25. In this text the spirit of the man who, still alive, has destroyed mania and has achieved liberation is also likened to a diamond. The Sanskrit term *vajra* (Tibetan: *dorje*) includes both these meanings—lightning or diamond—and has been particularly used in Tibetan Buddhism to designate the essence of illumination and the nature of one who is made of illumination. At the same time, it also designates the scepter of the supreme representatives of Lamaist spiritual authority. This symbolism would take us much further in terms of comparative mythology—as far as the lightning-force symbolized by prehistoric hyperborean axes and the symbolism of the lightning that always accompanied divine "Olympian" figures of the Aryan civilizations. The "path of the *vajra,*" or the "path of the diamond and of lightning *(vajra-yāna),* is the designation of Tantric and magic Buddhism, on which cf. *The Yoga of Power.*

7. Cf. *Majjh.,* 10; 85. On this subject we can recall the words attributed to the Buddha by the *Vajrasamādhi-sūtra,* when he said that the passage of fifty years did not represent a period of time, but only the awakening of a thought *(apud* Suzuki).

8. *Prajñāpāramitā,* texts in M. Walleser (Göttingen, 1914), 19, p. 120.

be achieved, provided the necessary energy has been acquired. Even the ancient Buddhist texts discuss, in this connection, various possibilities that should not be interpreted without reference to the general Indo-Aryan views on the hereafter and on the various forms of liberation.

The highest degree is that where, while yet a living man, one has completely achieved extinction through having destroyed—without leaving residue or possibility for fresh germination—*avijjā*, the primordial ignorance, *taṇhā*, thirst, the *āsava*, the transcendental intoxications. A relapse, a passing to any conditioned form of existence whatsoever, is as impossible for him as it is for the Ganges to flow toward the west.[9] Even the "mania," through which he might have rearisen as a god, is "extinct, cut down to the roots, made like the stump of a palm tree which cannot sprout again, can no more reproduce itself."[10] He is called the noncombatant, one who has no further need of fighting in the threefold realm of right living, of contemplation, of transcendental knowledge, besides that of the powers.[11] That "he should let attachment be joined again to his body or that his heart should beat again: this cannot be."[12] Powerful and impalpable being, there is nothing that can reach him, alter him, or threaten him. With regard to all that he can still "do," we may quote the simile of the uninjured hand: "he whose hand is without wound may touch poison: poison cannot enter where there is no wound."[13] Whether "he walks or is still or sleeps or wakes," in him the perfect clarity of knowledge conforming to reality, that "mania is exhausted in me," is always present, just as in a man whose feet and hands had been cut off there would always be present the knowledge: "My feet and hands have been cut off."[14] The term *nirupadhi* is also used here; it means destruction of the "substratum" *(upadhi)*. This substratum (which in its turn is related to the *sankhāra* and to *kamma,* Skt.: *karma*) corresponds, in general, to the "entity of craving" that every life that is not liberated strengthens and nourishes so that it creates the possibility of a new arising, of a fresh bursting into flame after the material offered by that life is exhausted. In the "perfectly Awakened One" this substratum no longer exists: being an obscure and oblique form born of ignorance and of "sleep," it is destroyed and dissolved by the steady naked light that he has kindled within himself.

Jarā, therefore, the exhaustion of the possibilities of life, the "fulfillment of time" and the dissociation of the aggregates that make up the individual being, for the Awakened One means final dissolution. He can say: "The outward form of one who

---

9. *Saṁyutt.*, 35.203.
10. *Angutt.*, 4.36.
11. Ibid., 11.11. Cf. *Jātaka*, 70: "Not a good victory is that, after which you may still be beaten. A good victory is that through which you become invincible."
12. *Majjh.*, 105.
13. *Dhammapada*, 124.
14. *Majjh.*, 76.

has achieved truth stands before you, but that which binds him to existence has been cut off . . . at the dissolution of the body neither gods nor men will again see him."[15] With physical death, there collapses something that had only an automatic existence, conditioned in a positive sense—conditioned, that is to say, by the pure will, devoid of craving, of the Fulfilled One: that is what is known as *khandha-parinibbāna* which, in any case, is a wholly contingent occurrence, without consequences for a state that, by definition, has "neither increase, nor diminution, nor composition." The term *parinibbuta,* "completely extinct," is applied, in various texts, to the living Buddha. Material, physical death only dissolves the last material elements, without leaving any remnants, of a being who is already dead to the world.[16]

Besides, since we have seen that the Buddhist ascesis is not limited to detachment, but goes on to penetrate and control the deepest energies of the bodily manifestation, the death of an Awakened One is always of a voluntary nature, at least in the sense of assent, of nonintervention. It has rightly been said that "in order to die, a Buddha must wish to die, otherwise no infirmity can kill him." The true death of Prince Siddhattha took place when, some time before his actual decease, he consciously decided not to live any longer. "From that moment he knows and repeatedly predicts the hour and the minute, the place and the couch in which his breath will cease for ever. The death of the body becomes so much a secondary fact, a thing of no account, that it matters very little what may cause it."[17]

Buddhism, like Stoicism, does *not* condemn suicide. "Taking arms"—that is, killing oneself—is not proscribed by the doctrine of the Ariya, always provided that the person in question has actually achieved extinction. In vain, Māra, the demon not only of this world, but equally of the world of Brahmā, seeks the spirit of the ascetic Channa who had "used the knife."[18] In this case, it is not a question, in fact, of seeking death as a result of any weakness in face of life, of any form of despair, attachment, or pain. We already know that the premise of extinction is to have conquered desire even for extinction itself, to have achieved the state of one who is free and who has no desire either for existence or for leaving existence.[19] The taking of one's own life, here, is no more than a wholly irrelevant act, rather like that of someone who, sitting in one position, decides at a certain moment to change it, or who finally

---

15. *Dīgha,* 13.73.

16. *Saṁyutt.,* 3.119.

17. C. Formichi, *Apologia del buddhismo* (Rome, 1925), p. 29. The Buddha had declared that, had he so wished, he could even have lived for aeons (cf. *Dīgha,* 16.3.3). On the power of the Buddhas and of certain Ariya of prolonging life or of dissolving the vital energies, cf. *Abhidharmakośa,* 2.10; 7.41.

18. *Saṁyutt.,* 35.87, *Majjh.,* 144.

19. *Suttanipāta,* 4.10.9. Cf. *Udāna* (3.10): "Those who believe that they can go out of existence by means of nonexistence will not free themselves from existence." Buddhism condemns both thirst for existence and thirst for nonexistence *(bhava-vibhava-tanhā).*

chases away an insect that had been buzzing ceaselessly around him and that he had suffered with calm. This, like any other act of an Awakened One, does not create *sankhāra;* in no way does it alter the realization he has achieved, nor does it give rise to causes for future effects.

We must remember, however, that the spiritual stature of an Awakened One is such that the moment he may choose for leaving his human form of appearance cannot be arbitrary nor can it depend on accidental considerations. There is a text that, in declaring against voluntary death, sets forth not only all the positive elements of an Awakened One's life, but also everything that, by continuing to live, he can give to beings in need of guidance.[20] An Awakened One will always have, to some extent—an extent that Mahāyāna considerably exaggerates—the sense of a mission on which will depend the course and the moment of the end of his life. Prince Siddhattha declared the he would not finally enter *nibbāna,* disappear from the physical world, or agree to die before the doctrine, by means of the existence of a group of worthy and illuminated disciples who had apprehended it, had been established and well-proclaimed in the world of men and of celestial beings.[21] At this point, the Accomplished One, with perfect consciousness and clarity, "laid aside his will to live" and, "concentrated and inwardly joyful," destroyed his personality "as one shatters a cuirass."[22] To this decease, legend has added cosmic signs and portents not unlike those connected with the death of the Christ.[23] Some texts speak of the movements of the mind of an Accomplished One at the moment of death: it passes upward through the four *jhāna* and, beyond these, enters the planes of the first four realizations free from form, that is to say, it passes up to the state beyond consciousness and nonconsciousness. From this height the spirit then descends by degrees to the first *jhāna,* and then passes up to the fourth *jhāna* that, as we have seen, corresponds to the limit of individuated consciousness as "name-and-form"; and from there, under the impulse of this power come from the world beyond form, it detaches itself, it passes beyond, it "departs no more to return."[24]

All this, then, concerns the highest form of liberation, the liberation achieved in life while still a man: it corresponds exactly with what, in the general Indo-Aryan tradition, is called *jīvan-mukti,* which means, in fact, "liberated while alive." As well as the case of *jīvan-mukti,* the same tradition also contemplates what is known as *videha-mukti,* where liberation is achieved at the moment of physical death. Death, in this case, unlike the first, affords an opportunity for full realization of liberation and

20. *Milindapañha,* 195, 1 ff. (W. 436).
21. *Angutt.,* 8.70.
22. Ibid.
23. *Dīgha,* 16.6.10.
24. Ibid., 16.6.8–9; *Saṁyutt.,* 6.5.

illumination already virtually gained during life. This possibility also is considered by Buddhism: the mental faculties, it is said, can become completely clear, and the eye of supreme knowledge open at the moment of death. The end of physical life then coincides with the end of mania, with the final destruction of the *āsava*. Such a case is known as *samasīsī*. This supreme transformation is supposed to be facilitated if either an Awakened One or a disciple of the Awakened One is present to recall the doctrine to the one who is dying, unless one has the strength to recall it oneself at this moment.[25] We have already said that awareness of breathing constantly practised and properly understood, is considered to be one of the best means of maintaining a clear awareness up to the last moments of earthly existence. For our part, we may add that the condition of modern Western man is such that, in the vast majority of cases, the possibility of liberation can only be conceived in this form; it can only take place, that is to say, in the state produced by that act of disruption that is the dissolution of the aggregates of the personality: this, of course, assumes that one's entire existence has been devoted to the focusing of every energy of one's own being, including those that lie deepest and that are hardly perceptible, in the direction of transcendency.

We shall now go on to discuss the possibilities that are considered by the Buddhist texts for those who tread the path of the Ariya and who do not reach liberation while alive, nor at the moment of death.

The class of beings that we are now discussing comes under the heading of *sotāpanna*, that is to say: "one who has entered into the current." They are the "noble sons" who have so acted that the fundamental force of their life is pervaded by what is beyond life, and they have therefore quite eliminated the danger of taking a "descending path." More specifically, to "enter the current" is to nourish an unshakable faith in the doctrine, to have an eye trained to recognize each phenomenon according to its conditioned genesis, and to maintain five of the fundamental precepts of "right conduct": abstention from killing, from taking what is not given, from lust, from lying, from the use of intoxicants.[26] Other texts have a slightly different view: those who have entered the current are principally those who have overcome three of the five bonds, namely, mania of the "I," doubt, and the blind practice of rites and precepts for the sake of a divine hereafter. Two other bonds, however—desire and aversion—although weakened, continue to persist, and for this reason those in the category in question do not achieve extinction either during earthly life or at its end. Such a being may, however, be sure that his destiny is already decided. The enemy forces will not prevail. He is already established in the right law, he is not exposed to permanent lapses, he has a higher knowledge. He has escaped perdition, he possesses sureness, he may be certain that he will put an end to the state of *dukkha* and

25. *Angutt.*, 10.92.
26. Ibid.

that he will achieve illumination and perfect awakening.[27] The simile provided here is that of the firstborn son of a warrior king legitimately crowned, who is certain of one day ascending the throne: the same feeling is possessed by an ascetic who is a "blessed warrior," who has trodden the path of the Ariya, and who, inwardly unshakable, waits for the supreme liberation.[28]

The future course of one who, in the deepest nucleus of his own being, no longer belongs to the world of becoming, depends on the strength of the *sankhāra* that correspond to the two bonds that have not yet been dissolved. Some texts, which deal with what we may call the pessimistic solution, envisage one who expects a single rebirth in the sense-world *(ekabījin)*; one who expects repeated rebirths *(kolankola)* reappearing, in due course, two or three times in noble families; or, finally one who expects to reappear, at the most seven times, in states that are not all necessarily human *(sattakkhattu-parama)*. After this, the condition of *dukkha* will have been destroyed once and for all.[29] These references in the texts are very schematic, and one cannot therefore be quite sure of the true sense of the doctrine. Since such possibilities are distinguished from others, shortly to be discussed, which refer unquestionably to extinction achieved in one of the worlds of "pure form" or "free from form," it would seem that we are here dealing with reappearances in the *kāma-loka*, that is, in the subcelestial sphere to which the human condition essentially belongs. Are we again faced with an idea of "reincarnation"? Perhaps one who "has entered the current" will appear again as a man? We must here refer to a viewpoint that is rather different from the simple idea of the multiple earthly lives of an "I" that is supposed to pass from one to another; a view, to which the term "shoot forth again," or "germinate," of the text offers a way of approach. One who "has entered the current" has transformed the root from which he sprang into life: in the "current" of which he is made, we now find the element *bodhi*, something that is extrasaṁsāric, which is destined to determine a new line of heredity—if thus we may call it—and, above all, a certain kind of continuity that—as we have already seen—is not possible in one who belongs to the world of becoming and of ignorance. We can thus think of a superindividual matrix or root, no longer exclusively saṁsāric, of existences that tend toward liberation, as it were in a series of attacks (corresponding to each life) and that are destined finally, in one of the existences, the last of the series, to triumph. If one of these does not produce success, there appears another, taking over the attributes of the first, in order to carry it further; the duration of this process is determined by certain cyclical laws and is bound up with the number seven, whose importance in the field of all that concerns development is known even in profane science. We no longer have the absurd idea of a single "I" that

27. Cf. Ibid.; 6.97; *Majjh.*, 68.
28. *Angutt.*, 4.87.
29. Ibid., 3.86.

returns or that travels from existence to existence but, rather, of various manifestations of one same principle that is already superindividual, but not yet fully conscious: manifestations that are ruled by the extrasaṁsāric force that has already been awakened and that is destined, sooner or later, to produce the perfectly illuminated being with which it will "pass beyond," by completely releasing itself. From two books by Meyrink, which are more than just novels—*Der Engel vom westlichen Fenster* and *Der weisse Domenikaner*—the reader may, perhaps, get a more intuitive idea of this kind of process.

For successive manifestations, Buddhism has laws that are not unlike those discovered by Mendel for physical heredity. We know that, according to Mendelian laws, some elements of a heredity may, through a series of generations, have a "recessive" character while others are "dominant": they seem to disappear although they are only latent and ready to reemerge and to reestablish themselves once the power that predominated before has been weakened or, as in the present case, once the material needed for renewed burning is present. This, according to Buddhism, is true both for the positive and for the negative elements that, at the end of a life, will represent an *upadhi,* a substratum of existence. Illusory forms of liberation are therefore possible; illusory because they are paramount only until the negative residues, which had apparently disappeared, reestablish themselves and lead to conditional forms of existence. The opposite may well happen: a principle of liberation and illumination may be well established, but it can only blossom and act fully after the total exhaustion of the power of unresolved negative and saṁsāric elements. These elements sometimes seem to predominate when, in fact, their roots have already been cut off.[30] This should be borne in mind when we consider the case of discontinuous reappearances in a series of births (the isolated emergence of superior, extrasaṁsāric types, with intervals of qui-

---

30. Cf. *Angutt.,* 10.206; 3.98. With regard to the *sankhāra* and to the *upādhi,* that is, to the potentialities of a possible fresh combustion, normal psychological consciousness must not be taken as the final criterion. It may be that with ageing and decay of the organs, a tendency or craving that was alive and unmastered before, may no longer make itself felt. But as a *sankhāra,* it has not therefore vanished: it has only returned to its latent state, and is waiting for a fresh occasion. The Buddhist doctrine of the "possessions" *(prāpti)* refers to this. When, for example, a desire has been satisfied and seems to be exhausted, it has not therefore been eliminated—on the contrary, it remains united to the "I" and to the stem to which it belongs. Nonexistent in act, it subsists in potentiality. And the "possession" *(prāpti)* will lead, sooner or later, to remanifestation *(sammukhībhāva),* (cf. de la Vallée-Poussin, *Nirvāna,* p. 164). We must also, eventually, take into account forces that are not fully manifested or "spent" and that, in certain cases, we must lead to consummation, even at the cost of causing ourselves as individuals and other men to suffer their natural effects. Something of the sort was intuited by the Carpocratian Gnostics. Cf. also the image given in *Golem* by G. Meyrink, chap. 18: "Man is like a tube of glass in which many-colored balls are running. In the life of most men, there is only one ball. If it is red we say that the man is 'bad.' If it is yellow we say he is 'good.' If there are two balls—one red and one yellow—he has an 'unstable character.' We, who have been 'bitten by the serpent,' live in our life that which normally happens to the whole race in an entire age: the many-colored balls cross the tube of glass in a mad rush, one behind another, and, finite as they are—*we have become prophets*—images of the divinity."

escence) and also as what may appear as a "spontaneous initiation." But the same idea also applies in the cases we have yet to consider and, as we said, this will refer to liberations that are to be later but inevitably achieved in posthumous "celestial" states.

Even for these cases we can find an equivalent in the general Indo-Aryan tradition, where it takes into account so-called "deferred liberation" or "liberation by degrees" *(Krama-mukti)*.[31] In order thus to attain the state of *nirvāṇa* in modes of being that cannot be called human, it is necessary to have also virtually cut off the two bonds of craving and aversion, which constitute the elementary differentiations of the primordial mania. And if this mastery is not to be of an entirely psychological character, and therefore ephemeral, the ascetic must, in his earthly existence, have developed to a high degree both the contemplations that produce a superior calm *(samatha)* and the "wisdom" that is closely connected with the will for the unconditioned, which leads to change of heart and detachment, and that brings realization of the nonsubstantiality of all that is saṃsāric *(vipassanā)*.[32] When these conditions have been fulfilled, one possesses the principle of a supreme "neutrality" beyond any craving desire, beyond any aversion, and the "divine" world itself may be overcome; the bond of the "I," which has already been cut off as regards the human state of existence by the one who "enters the current," is now also cut off as regards any individuated and conditioned form of existence whatsoever, not excluding the highest and most resplendent. In the "current," then, a force operates that will prevent any lingering on the "celestial voyage"— spoken of, with varying symbolism, in all traditions including the Dantesque—from being taken as the final destination; this force guarantees that, by definitively bringing to an end every attachment, one will gain, in superhuman states of existence, the opportunity for extinction that could not be achieved in the human condition, not even at the moment of death. The ascetic has here created the conditions for a real survival of death, for a survival that various religions, notably the Christian, imagine is achieved by all beings; whereas it is only logically thinkable for those few who, as men, have been able to conceive of themselves as more than men and who have taken part, in full awareness—even if only through some flash of insight—in states that are free of the condition of the individual.

We are now in a position to give the various possible cases of liberation beyond death that are considered by Buddhist teaching:

(1) he who frees himself and "disappears" halfway in his development
(*antarāparinibbāyin*);

(2) he who succeeds in this after the halfway point in his development
(*upahacca-parinibbāyin*);

---

31. Cf. R. Guénon, *L'Homme et son devenir selon le Vêdânta* (Paris, 1925), p. 181ff.
32. Cf. *Angutt.*, 4.124.

(3) he who achieves liberation without an action *(asankhāra-parinibbāyin);*

(4) he who achieves liberation with an action *(sasankhāra-parinibbāyin);*

(5) he who proceeds against the current toward the highest gods
   (uddhamsota akaniṭṭha-gāma).

All these liberations take place in one of the spheres of "pure forms" *(rūpa-loka)* or in one of the spheres free from form *(arūpa-loka)* making up, together, the "pure abodes" or "pure fields" *(suddhāvāsā)* whose equivalent, in the ancient Western Aryan traditions, were the "Elysian Fields" or "Seat of the Heroes."[33] The order in which we have just given these cases is one that descends from the highest forms to the lowest. They are all, however, qualified by the term *anāgāmin,* "a nonreturner," one who does not pass again to another form of conditioned and manifested existence, since he has entirely conquered any force that could lead to this against his will. The term is the same as that used in the Upaniṣads for one who, after death, does not tread the lunar and ancestral path *(pitṛ-yāna)* but who treads, instead, the "divine path" *(deva-yāna).*

It may be easier to understand the sense of these various possibilities by referring to a simile given by a text that makes use of the example of lighted chips flung into the air.[34] One such chip may get cold even before it touches the earth—and this would be the case with one who liberates or "extinguishes" himself before or after the halfway point of his path (cases 1 and 2); or it may fall to the ground and immediately find a patch of dry grass that goes up in flames, and the chip may only get cold after this fire has died out—the case of liberating oneself without an action; or, again, it may land in a large pile of wood or hay, set it alight, and get cold only when this much larger fire has ceased—the case of liberating oneself by means of an action; or, finally, the chip may fall directly into a forest, and the fire continues until the other side of the forest itself is reached, where there is running water or a field of green grass or rocks—the case of going against the current toward the highest gods.

By way of clarifying this phenomenology of the various posthumous developments possible for ascetic consciousness, the following remarks will suffice. The heat of the lighted chip, that is capable of starting a fresh fire, clearly represents the residual thirst for, and pleasure in, satisfaction still existing in the new current. Already extinguished as regards the forms of earthly existence, this residual potential heat can be finally eliminated while going along the path, before the end of a particular development, "before falling to earth," that is to say, before the complete

---

33. *Angutt.,* 7.16–17; 9.12; 10.63; 3.85–86; *Puggala-Paññatti,* 40–46; *Visuddhi-magga,* 23 (W. 391).
34. *Angutt.,* 7.52.

transformation of state that follows death, and could result in the adoption of a new residence. This then, corresponds to cases 1 and 2. In case 3 this potential heat comes again into contact with combustible material and produces a fresh flame: consciousness rearises in a celestial state of existence, where rapture and "supersensible joy" may promote new forms of identification, of greater or less duration. The extrasaṁsāric and sidereal force that has already been awakened will, however, sooner or later, lead onwards—whereas a "son of the world" is always liable to degenerate again, to pass, even, into a state lower than that from which he started, although he has experienced for a time these supersensible states.[35] In case 3 craving is exhausted by a natural process; in case 4, however, a certain active intervention must be made, which is spoken of in the texts sometimes as "effort," sometimes as "deepening of knowledge." The most unfavorable case is the fifth, which in the simile corresponds to a fire that, little by little, spreads to an entire forest and does not stop until it has reached the natural limit of the forest itself. The potentiality of heat and of attachment, here, is such that it resumes, one after another, in ascending order (against the current), the various possibilities of superhuman life. This case could be compared to "deferred liberation," the fundamental idea of which, as Guénon has rightly pointed out,[36] is to be found in the Judeo-Christian and Islamic symbolism of the "Universal Judgment." The final experience takes place at the moment in which an end is made, in obedience to the cyclical laws, to the celestial forms of existence themselves, and there occurs, in order of precedence, the dissolution of each manifested form into its respective unmanifested principle. It is on such an occasion—almost a reproduction, *mutatis mutandis,* of the possibility offered by physical death (cf. p. 46)—that final extinction may be achieved at the exhaustion of a cosmic cycle of manifestation.

On the subject of symbolism, we may see, in the greater or less quantity of fire that burns again in the posthumous states and that must be allowed to die out before an advance can be made, the deeper significance of what Christian mythology calls "purgatory." We must remember, however, in making this comparison, that this experience is by no means common to all, but only to those who, through a virtual mastery of the human condition and of the saṁsāric bonds, have indeed gained the chance of consciously surviving physical death and of taking themselves further, into superterrestrial states of existence.

Finally, the mention of liberation with or without action gives us the opportunity of remembering that, not only at the point of death, but also in the successive changes of state and in the various phases of the "celestial voyage," much may depend, according to the traditional teaching, on a spiritual initiative that is naturally connected

---

35. Ibid., 3.114.
36. *L'Homme et son devenir,* p. 187.

with the accumulation of knowledge achieved and realized on earth as a man. We can only talk of quasi-automatic and predestined posthumous developments in the case of the ordinary man; but, as we have said, to speak of his "survival" is merely to be euphemistic. On the matter of this transcendental initiative, we refer the reader to the *Bardo Thödol,* the *Tibetan Book of the Dead,* which we have quoted earlier, and to what, on the basis of this book, we have discussed at greater length in the second edition of our book, *The Yoga of Power* (appendix 1).

16

Signs of the Nonpareil

There is, in original Buddhism, a well-known negative expression for the highest point of the Ariyan ascesis, *nibbāna* (Skt.: *nirvāṇa*). Its etymology is rather intricate. The Pāli term is related to the root *vān* and includes the idea of a "vanishing." The Sanskrit term seems to have a different root, *vā*, to blow, with the negative prefix *nir*, and is best translated, in fact, by "extinction," but also with reference to "vanishing." Extinction of what? It has been rightly pointed out[1] that the same root *vā* appears in the terms *vana*, *vani*, which mean, "to wish," "to crave," "to desire," "to rave," "to dote." Nibbāna expresses the cessation of the state described by these terms: a fact that is confirmed by the whole Ariyan ascesis, in its comprehensive significance, particularly as *nibbāna* is attained at the moment in which the *āsavā* and *taṇhā*, that is to say, the intoxicating manias and craving, are completely neutralized. We do not, therefore, propose to put forward a learned argument designed to confute the ideas of those who hold the *nibbāna* is "nothingness." It could only occur to a chronic drunkard that the ending of intoxication was also the end of existence; so, only someone who knew nothing but the state of thirst and of mania could think that the cessation of this state meant the end of all life, "nothingness." Besides, if "ignorance" and "mania" are a negation—and normal beings can hardly think otherwise—then *nibbāna* can only be described, after the manner of Hegel, as a "negation of the negation," and therefore as a restoration, as something that, taken in conjunction with a negative designation, indicates an entirely positive reality. The fact of the matter is that modern man has moved so far from the world of spirituality and of metaphysical reality that, when faced with this kind of experienced achievement, he finds himself totally unprovided with points of reference and with organs of comprehension.

---

1. De Lorenzo, in his edition of *Majjh.*, vol. 1, p. 7.

"Awakening" is the keystone and the symbol of the whole Buddhist ascesis: to think that "awakening" and "nothingness" can be equivalent is an extravagance that should be obvious to everyone. Nor should the notion of "vanishing," applied in a well-known simile of *nibbāna* to the fire that disappears when the flame is extinguished, be a source of misconception. It has been said with justice[2] that, in similes of this sort, one must always have in mind the general Indo-Aryan concept that indicates that the extinguishing of the fire is not its annihilation, but its return to the invisible, pure, supersensible state in which it was before it manifested itself through a combustible in a given place and in given circumstances.

The point is that Buddhism has very largely adopted the method of "negative theology," which seeks to give the sense of the absolute by means of an indication, not as to what it is—a task that is considered to be absurd—but as to what it is *not*. We may say, rather, that Buddhism has gone further still: it has refused to use the category of nonbeing and has understood that even to define the unconditioned by negation would, in fact, make it conditioned. This has been rightly noted by Oldenberg:[3] when the contrast between the contingent world and the eternal world is pushed to the extreme limit of Buddhism, it is no longer possible to imagine any logical relation whatsoever between the two terms. All we can do is to use as a symbol, as an allusive sign, a word, that is to say, *nibbāna*. Zen Buddhism would say: reality is to the word and to the doctrine as the moon is to the hand of the man who shows its direction.

One thing, in any event, is quite sure: the theory that claims that one who has destroyed the manias has also "broken himself and will perish, not surviving the death of the body" is regarded by Buddhism as a heresy, born of ignorance.[4] But the demon of dialectics must not, in this way, be resurrected. When it is asked if the Awakened One exists after death, the answer is: No. Does not he, then, exist after death? The same answer. Does he both exist and not exist after death? Again, no. Does he neither exist nor not exist after death? Once more, the reply is no. And should the questioner ask what, after all, does this mean, then the answer is that such things were not revealed by Prince Siddhattha, that they cannot be discussed since they are transcendent—*abhikkanta*—since nothing intelligent can be said about a state in which everything that might have been included in any concept or in any category whatsoever has been destroyed.[5] *Nibbāna*, indeed, "has nothing that is like it."[6]

---

2. A. B. Keith, *Buddhist Philosophy* (London, 1923), pp. 65–66; de la Vallée-Poussin, *Nirvāna*, pp. 145–46.
3. *Buddha*, p. 269.
4. *Saṁyutt.*, 22.85.
5. Ibid., 44.1.11.
6. *Milindapañha*, 315 ff.

"This has not been revealed," "this cannot be discussed," "this is nonpareil." But where concept and word fail us, the evocative power of the simile may take their place. The simile is one of vastness, depth, immeasurableness, ocean-size. The king who asked the questions in the first place, is now questioned: "Have you an accountant or reckoner who is able to number all the grains of sand in the Ganges?" The reply is naturally negative. He is then told that it would be a similar undertaking to try to define the Accomplished One. "He is deep, unbounded, immeasurable, inscrutable, just like the mighty ocean. Thus it may not be said that he exists, nor that he does not exist, nor that he exists and does not exist, nor that he neither exists nor does not exist after death."[7] From each of the five components that make up common personality an Accomplished One is free: from material form, from feeling, from perception, from the formations and from finite consciousness—all this that was in him has been made like "a palm tree, that is cut off at the root so that it can germinate no longer, no more redevelop." It is quite useless for those who, in trying to understand, refer to one or other of these components, to set themselves the problem of what an Accomplished One is or of where he is going.[8] Since that of which we might say "is" or "is not" is absent, there is no definition or discussion possible.[9] The fundamental point is that the Awakened One, while still alive, is not to be considered as material form, feeling, perception, formations, or consciousness, nor as living in these groups of the person, nor as distinct from them, nor as one deprived of them. If, then, while he is still in this life, the Accomplished One cannot be considered as really "existing," there is no logical category that can enable us to understand the state of pure *nibbāna*, of total extinction.[10] "For one who has disappeared from here, there is no more form: that of which we say 'it exists' is no longer his; when all the *dhammā* are cut away, then all the elements on which discursive thought is based also vanish."[11] We may then justly say: "it is as difficult to follow the path of those whose dwelling is void and whose liberation is without sign, as it is to follow that of the birds through the air."[12] The Accomplished Ones, those who have "entered the current," the *anāgāmin* in general, are also likened to powerful animals of the deep water of the sea.[13] "Deep"—says a Mahāyāna text[14]—"is the denomination of the 'void'; of the 'signless,' of the 'without tendency,' of the not-come, of the not-gone-out, of the

7. *Saṁyutt.*, 44.1.
8. *Majjh.*, 72.
9. *Suttanipāta*, 5.7.6–8.
10. *Saṁyutt.*, 22.85, 86; 44.2.
11. *Suttanipāta*, 5.7.8.
12. *Dhammapada*, 92.
13. *Angutt.*, 8.19. In *Milindapañha*, 320, there is this simile: "As the sea is the abode of great portentous beings, so also *nibbāna* is the abode of great and portentous beings, such as the *arahant*, those who have achieved extinction."
14. *Prajñāpāramitā*, 8.106.

not-issued, of the not-being, of the passionless, of the destruction, of the extinction, of the coming-out, the denomination thereof is profundity."

Besides all this, two reasons of a historical nature have, in Buddhism, imposed silence on all superontological and supertheistic references to the state where thirst no longer exists. Here we must turn back to the considerations that we discussed in the first part of this study. It will be remembered, in the first place, that the doctrine of Prince Siddhattha arose, in contrast to every form of abstract speculation, as an essentially practical and spiritually progressive guidance; in the second, that it had in mind a type of human being for whom the *ātmā*, the "unconditioned" of the preceding Indo-Aryan metaphysics, had already ceased to correspond to any real experience. This absolute, which could no longer stand for anything according to the only criterion that was decisive for the Indo-Aryan tradition—*yathā-bhūtam,* the "vision conforming to reality"—and which could therefore also be denied or profaned by the skeptical or philosophizing manner of thought that had already pervaded a large variety of disputing sects and schools—this absolute becomes, in Buddhism, the object of a single demonstrative organ: action itself, ascesis, *bhāvanā.* As a result of this, silence about the problem of the nature of the state of *nibbāna* and of the destiny of an Awakened One after death was imposed for a practical reason also. Any ideas on the subject could only be "opinion" $(\delta \acute{o} \xi \alpha)$ and, as such, useless and vain, if not positively harmful. Whence the justification for the absence of any reply from the Buddha: "This has not been declared by the Sublime One, because it does not belong to the fundamental principles of a divine life, because it does not lead to renunciation, to detachment, to cessation, to calm, to transcendent knowledge, to illumination, to extinction."[15] In this connection, too, one must cut back the agitation and the imagining of an inconsistent mind: "I am," "I am this," "I shall be," "I shall not be," "I shall be with body," "I shall be without body," "I shall have consciousness," "I shall not have consciousness," and so on—all this, it is said, is a wavering, a sore, a vain imagining. It is the effect of craving, it is a tumor, it is the point of the arrow. "Therefore," says the Buddha, "you must cherish this purpose: 'I wish to dwell with a mind that does not waver, that is not obsessed, with a mind that has destroyed these vain imaginings.' Thus, O disciples, must you train yourselves."[16]

There are those who have held that one reason for not admitting that the state of *nibbāna* might correspond to the unconditioned *ātmā* of the preceding Upaniṣadic tradition lies in the fact that, in the latter, there was always an inseperable connection between this same *ātmā* and the *brahman,* the universal subject, the root of cosmic life.[17]

15. *Saṁyutt.,* 16.12; *Majjh.,* 62.
16. *Saṁyutt.,* 35.207.
17. M. Walleser, *Prajñāpāramitā,* p. 9.

Buddhism, on the other hand, as a doctrine of purification and restoration that is principally Aryan in spirit, is especially characterized by its overcoming of this relationship. With regard to the supreme term of the ascesis, we certainly find in the Buddhist texts a number of passages that can be referred back to the doctrine of the *ātmā* but not one that can be reconciled with the theory of the *brahman;* and this is because Buddhism was resolutely opposed to any pantheistic deviation and cosmic identifications, and because its ideal was an absolutely complete detachment from any form of "nature," either material or divine; it therefore carried the purifying, implacable fire of disidentifying ascesis to almost inconceivable heights. And it is on this account that every bridge falls down and every word, every conception, seems vain and impotent. Less than in any other doctrine, is it possible to establish, at this point, any relationship at all between *saṁsāra*—or contingent existence, which for Buddhism embraces every manifested state of being—and that for which *nibbāna* is only a negative designation.

Having dealt with this point, it only remains for us to consider a few elements that are simply of value as indicating marks.

First of all, we can see without difficulty from the texts that the Buddhist ascesis sets itself a precise task: to overcome and destroy death, to achieve *amata* (Skt.: *amṛta*), that is, the "deathless." We have already said that Māra, the eternal antagonist of the Ariyan ascetic, is one of the forms under which Mṛtyu, the demon of death, appears.[18] Throughout the *Dhammapada* there are references to the struggle to be fought against the demon of death, against the "finisher" *(antaka).* "Let Māra not break you again and again, as the torrent breaks the reeds."[19] "Victor of death," is the Awakened One called,[20] " giver of immortality."[21] Texts speak of a battle against the great army of death,[22] of a conquering or crossing of the torrent or kingdom of death that is achieved by few,[23] of a contemplation on the deathless element.[24] It is toward this element that the eightfold path of the Ariya leads.[25] One who is born subject to death, goes on to achieve "the death-less, the incomparable sureness, extinction."[26] Nibbāna is called the "incomparable island, in which every thing vanishes and all attachment ceases, where there is destruction of decay and of death"; it is an island for those who "find themselves in the midst of the waters, in the fearful torrent that has formed and whereby they become subject to decay

18. Explicit identification of Māra with the demon of death occurs in *Mahāvagga (Vin.),* 1.1; 2.2.
19. *Dhammapada,* 337; cf. 37, 40, 46.
20. *Majjh.,* 92.
21. Ibid., 18.
22. Ibid., 131.
23. *Angutt.,* 10.117; *Majjh.,* 34; *Dhammapada,* 85.
24. *Majjh.,* 64.
25. Ibid., 26, 75.
26. Ibid., 52.

and to death."[27] "As medicine opposes death, so *nibbāna* opposes death."[28] The Buddha's announcement is: "The immortal has been found." "Let the gate of the death-less open: he who has ears to hear, let him come and hear."[29] "Yes, I have achieved the death-less," declares Sāriputta.[30] "Clarion of immortality, supreme triumph in the battle" is the doctrine of the Ariya called.[31] Allusions to revealing and beneficial contemplations or images, "having as base and as aim the death-less," are very frequent.[32] But that is not all: we must remember that the term *amata*, "nondeath," "deathless," which is etymologically the same as the Greek word αμβροσία, has in the Indo-Aryan tradition a different meaning to the weakened form current in the West. In the West we normally find that immortality is interchangeable with that very different thing, survival. At best, it may refer to the continuation of individual existence, though still conditioned, in "celestial" or "angelic" states that, according to the Aryo-Oriental view, though they may be of indefinite duration, occupying may aeons, yet have nothing of the really eternal, of the "deathless" in an absolute sense. That is why in Buddhism, one speaks of cutting back the roots not only of death, but of life itself, of a path of health that leads beyond the dominion of death and of life:[33] by "life," here, we have to understand any possibility whatsoever of rearising in any conditioned form, even in those that are called, in the West, "immortal" or "paradisal." This may possibly confuse the ideas of those who have not grasped the limitations inherent in the more recent of Western religious conceptions; but, in any case, this should do away with the absurd supposition that an ascesis thus attuned to the "deathless" can possibly end in "nothingness."

Stability is one of the properties of *nibbāna*. As a great river inclines toward the sea, descends to the sea, flows out into the sea, and, having arrived at the sea, *stays still;* so does the life of those who proceed toward extinction unroll.[34] As the high mountain, on which no grass grows, is still and unshakable, so, likewise, *nibbāna*, in which no passions or mania are born, is still and unshakable.[35] As men's houses, with the passage of time, become ruins, but the ground whereon they rested remains, so the mind of an Awakened One remains and knows no alteration.[36] We remember the

---

27. *Suttanipāta*, 5.11.1–4. Cf. *Uttarajjhāvana-sutta*, 13.81: "It is a nearby place, but arduous to reach, where decay, death and disease do not exist."

28. *Milindapañha*, 319.

29. *Majjh.*, 26; *Mahāvagga (Vin.)*, 1.1.5, 7; *Saṁyutt.*, 12.33.

30. *Mahāvagga (Vin.)*, 7.23.6.

31. *Majjh.*, 115.

32. Cf., e.g., *Angutt.*, 5.61; 8.74; 9.36; 10.56; 7.45; *Dhammapada*, 374.

33. *Dīgha*, 16, 2.2–3; 4.2.

34. Cf. *Majjh.*, 73.

35. *Milindapañha*, 323.

36. *Mahāparinirv.*, 4.6. Cf. *Majjh.*, 12.

recurring theme that urges the ascetic continually onward, even beyond the most abstract form of contemplation because "that is compounded, that is generated, that is conditioned."[37] The result of this is to endow *nibbāna*—the state beyond which one cannot go—with the character of unconditioned and ungenerated simplicity:[38] the term *asankhata,* "not made, not performed, not produced," is continually applied to *nibbāna,* and so is *svayambhū,* which indicates the quality of that which rests on itself or—in Mahāyāna terms—of that which rests on the not-resting. A limiting function is ascribed to the three *āsava*—they make beings "finite," it is said.[39] For this very reason, the state that no longer knows the *āsava* must be the unconditioned and infinite state; since *dukkha* has been overcome, it can only be the state of a supreme supernatural calm, and of "incomparable sureness" *(anuttaraṁ yoga-khemaṁ).* The "trembling" is ended, the irrational "recirculation" is ended. Terms such as: "become cold,"[40] should no more be a source of misunderstanding than "extinct": the burning, which no longer exists, is to be understood as that of one who is fevered, of one who is burning with thirst, of one who is weakened by saṁsāric fire. It is the absence of heat in the pure Uranian flame—*flamma non urens*—of sidereal natures: of the Olympian principle of pure light.

"Only that which has no birth does not perish"—it is said in one text[41]—"Mount Meru will crumble, the gods will decline in heaven. How great, how wonderful, then, is the eternal essence that is not subject to birth and to death!" Still with reference to *nibbāna:* "To go out from this state [means to find another] state that is calm, beyond thought, stable, not born, not formed, detached from pain, detached from passion, a joy that puts an end to all contingency and that destroys for ever every mania."[42] And again: "There is, O disciples, an abode where there exists neither earth nor water nor light nor air nor infinity of ether nor infinity of consciousness nor any essence at all nor that which lies beyond representation and beyond nonrepresentation nor this world nor another nor Moon nor Sun. This do I call, O disciples, neither coming nor going nor staying nor birth nor death; it is without base, without change, without pause; it is the end of agitation."[43]

We have already had occasion to mention some of the traits attributed by the texts to those who, while still in this life, have achieved the perfect awakening, the supreme liberation—beginning with the son of the Śākya. With the end of identification they are free. Having destroyed the roots of the mania of the "I," for them the net of illusion

---

37. Cf. *Majjh.,* 52.
38. Cf. *Dhammapada,* 383.
39. *Saṁyutt.,* 41.7; *Jātaka,* 203.
40. Cf. *Angutt.,* 3.34.
41. *Dīgha,* 16.3.48.
42. *Itiyuttaka,* 43.
43. *Udāna,* 8.1.

has been burned, their hearts are transparent with light, they are divine beings, immune from intoxication, untouched by the world. As the "lion's roar" their word sounds: "Supreme are those who are awakened!"[44] "Invincible and intact" beings, they appear as "sublime supermen";[45] lions who have left behind fear and terror,[46] they see the past, they see heavens and hells,[47] they know this world and that world, the kingdom of death and the kingdom free from death, time, and eternity.[48] They are "like tigers, like bulls, like lions in a mountain cavern," and are yet "beings without vanity, appearing in the world for the good of the many, for the health of the many, through compassion for the world, for the benefit, the good and the well-being of gods and of men."[49] "I have overcome the bramble of opinions, I have gained mastery over myself, I have followed the path, I possess the knowledge and I have no one else as my guide"—thus says the Awakened One of himself.[50] The Awakened One is he who is detached from life and death and who knows the way up and the way down,[51] he is "bold, not knowing hesitation, a sure leader, pure of passion, resplendent as the light of the sun, resplendent without arrogance, heroic"; he is the Knower "whom no mania dazzles, no trouble conquers, no victory tempts, no spot stains"; he is one "who asks no more, and who, as a man, has mastered the ascetic art"; he is the "great being, who lives strenuously, free from every bond, no longer slave to any servitude"; he is "the Valiant One, who watches over himself, constant in his step, ready to the call, who guards himself within and without, to nothing inclined, from nothing disinclined, the Sublime One whose spirit is powerful and impassible"; he is the "Awakened One whom no thirst burns, no smoke veils, no mist clouds; a spirit who honors sacrifice and who, like no other, towers in majesty."[52] Unconquered, supreme, he has laid down his burden, he has no "home" and he has no desires. Passion, pride, and falsity have fallen from him like a mustard seed from the point of a needle. Beyond good, beyond evil, he is loosed from both these bonds and, detached from pain, detached from pleasure, he is purified. Since he knows, he no longer asks "how?" He has touched the depths of the element free from death. He has abandoned the human bond and has overcome the divine bond and he is freed from all bonds. The path of him, who can be conquered by none in the world and whose dominion is the infinite, is not known to the gods, nor to the angels, nor to men.[53]

44. *Saṁyutt.*, 22.76.
45. *Majjh.*, 116.
46. *Suttanipāta*, 3.6.37.
47. *Saṁyutt.*, 3.58–59; *Dhammapada*, 422–23.
48. *Majjh.*, 34.
49. Ibid., 4.
50. *Suttanipāta*, 1.3.21.
51. *Majjh.*, 91.
52. Ibid., 56.
53. *Dhammapada*, 402–20, passim, 179; *Majjh.*, 98.

In these terms with timeless grandeur, the supreme ideal of the purest Aryan spirit is continually reaffirmed. The contacts are reestablished, there is indeed an awakening, a return to the primordial state whose echo we find in the cosmicity of the Vedic hymns and in the supernatural framing of the deeds of the first Indo-Aryan epics. Nibbāna is, in fact, announced as a state of which nothing had been heard for a very long time.[54] Beyond both the labyrinths of speculation and the poverty of all human sentiment, beyond the saṁsāric world that "burns," and beyond every phantasmagoria of demoniac, titanic, or celestial existences, there is affirmed the knowledge of a nature that, for its purity and power, could be called Olympian and regal, were it not that, at the same time, it indicates absolute transcendency, it is inherently ungraspable, not to be qualified by "this," nor by "here," nor by "there."

Such is the goal of the "noble path" or "path of the Ariya" *(ariyamagga)* that some have chosen to regard as "quietism" induced by an "enervating tropical climate" and leading, as though through an ultimate collapse of the vital force, toward "nothingness."

---

54. *Mahāvagga (Vin.)*, 1. The period, actually given here, "for myriad *kalpa*," is typical of the tendency toward fabulous exaggeration.

17

The Void: "If the Mind Does Not Break"

We have already quoted a text that sees in the "void," in the "signless," and in the "without tendency" the characteristics of the "contacts" of those who emerge from the contemplations free from form. And we have also shown that the *Dhammapada,* in its reference to those "whose path is as difficult to follow as that of the birds through the air," associates "void" and "signless" with *viveka,* aloofness or detachment. These are not the only places where the concept of "void" *(suñña* or *suññatā)* appears in the texts of early Buddhism. One who is detached from pleasure and from desire, from predilection and from thirst, from fever and from craving is called "void."[1] Elsewhere the texts speak of a "superior man" dwelling principally in the state of "real, inviolable, pure voidness"[2]—it is in this state that Prince Siddhattha receives and speaks to kings.[3] He has said that the perceptions no longer cling to those who know, who are troubled by nothing in the world, who ask no more questions, who have rooted out every loathing, and who crave neither existence nor nonexistence.[4] As one who is detached he experiences every kind of perception or sensation or feeling.[5] With particular reference to the triad "void," "signless," "without tendency," all this is associated with the form of experience—either internal and psychological or of the outside world—of one who continues to live with the center of his own being in the state of *nibbāna* or in one or other of the higher contemplations; and the Buddha said of himself that he could dwell without effort or difficulty in one of the four *jhāna* or in one of the irradiant contemplations, walking or standing, sitting or lying.[6] It is thus considered that the realiza-

1. *Saṁyutt.,* 22.3.
2. *Majjh.,* 151.
3. Ibid., 122.
4. Ibid., 18.
5. Ibid., 140.
6. *Angutt.,* 3.63.

tions of the Ariya are not only superhuman forms of consciousness but are also kinds of profundity wherein we can comprehend the multiple variety of the *dhammā*, that is to say, the various elements of internal and external experience.

This experience is itself liberated thereby, and the threefold category defined by the expressions "void" *(suññatā),* "signless" *(animitta),* "without inclination or tendency" *(appaṇihita)* refers to the very essence of this liberation or transfiguration. The category marks the "perfection of knowledge" or of illumination, the knowledge "that has gone beyond," the *prajñāpāramitā,* a term that also designates a series of later Buddhist texts of distinctly Mahāyāna character. Those three terms must then be understood essentially *sub specie interioritatis,* beyond any speculative construction.

The "void" defines the mood of an experience free from the "I," and therefore disindividualized, whose substratum may, analogically, be compared to infinite space, to the ether—*ākāśa.* Its fulfillment is, among other things, given by formulae such as this: liberation from the "I" *(ajjhattaṁ vimokkha)* the destruction of all attachments produces a mental clarity that paralyzes every *āsava* and removes belief in the personality.[7] And again: "Since the world is without 'I' and without things having the nature of 'I,' therefore the world has been called void."[8] "'This is the calm, this is the supreme point, the end of all formations, the freeing from all substrate of existence, the overcoming of thirst, the final change, the ultimate solution, extinction.' In this manner the ascetic may achieve a state such that when confronted with earth he is without perception of earth, so with water, fire, wind, infinity of space, infinity of consciousness, non-existence, the region beyond perception and non-perception, and such that when confronted with this world he is without perception of the world; confronted with the other world, with what he has seen, heard, felt, cognised, attained and sought in the mind, even when confronted with this he is without perception, yet possesses perception."[9] Thus, a cycle is completed. The beginning corresponds to the end. The void, the "I"-lessness, which we had found to be the final truth of saṁsāric existence, where all individuality or substantiality is ephemeral and pure flux, and where thirst for eternal rebirth is the final instance, this "void" also marks the limit of ascetic experience where, however, it reverses its significance: here it expresses the absolute, the superessential, the supercosmic consciousness, freed without residue and become illumination, where no forms nor perceptions nor feelings nor any other *dhammā* can take root any more, or gain a foothold. That which is identical, then, is simultaneously the absolute opposite. To the "I"-lessness of saṁsāric consciousness we may contrast the "I"-lessness of the state of *nibbāna* and of perfect illumination: *suññatā.*

7. *Saṁyutt.,* 12.32.
8. Ibid., 25.85.
9. *Angutt.,* 11.8; cf. 11.10; *Saṁyutt.,* 22.89.

The second category, the "signless" *(animitta)* expresses what, in fact, was known in Vedāntic speculation as the "supreme identity." It is the nondifferentiation of characteristics *(nimitta)* on account of which normal consciousness cannot help distinguishing among beings, states, and things. Not that things lose all their characteristics: it is simply that, in a manner of speaking, their varying weights, their varying distances in relation to liberated consciousness, come to disappear. Each becomes the extreme case of itself. Thus, *in their very diversity* they appear identical, as distinct places in space become identical if they are not referred to particular coordinates, but are considered from the point of view of space itself, of something simple, limitless, and homogeneous. Beings, states, or things are "signless," then, if they are lived as a function of "void"; and this now takes us on to the deeper significance of the third category, *appaṇihita*. We have translated this term as "without tendency." While the bond of an "I" still existed, all things "spoke" to this "I": all things participated in subjectivity and nourished the illusion of "tendency," of "intention." Man projects his soul on the world and makes it personal, he endows the world with feelings, desires, and aims; he projects onto it a pathos, he gives it values and distinctions, all of which, in one way or another, inevitably lead back to the force that supports his life, to appetite, aversion, and ignorance. Man does not know the bare world, undisguised nature, precisely because his perception is itself a "burning," a self-identification, a continual self-binding, which takes place in a simultaneous process of consuming and being consumed. But such a state has been surmounted. Thirst is exhausted, the mist of impurity is dispersed. All nature, every perception, every phenomenon, the entirety of the *dhammā* that make up "internal experience," the "content of the psyche," are freed from "subjectivity," separated from what is "human," and appear pure, without words, without affects, without intentions, in a freshness, an orginality and an innocence that a Western man might call the innocence of the first day of creation. This, then, is the meaning of *appaṇihita*, "without tendency," as a form of the experience of those who are liberated, as the third allusive element beyond the "void" and the "signless."

But with this we have already passed from the tradition of original Buddhism to the fundamental views of the texts of the *Prajñāpāramitā* and of the school of the "Greater Vehicle" itself, the Mahāyāna: our transition must, under the circumstances, be considered quite natural, and we shall therefore say a few words about the doctrine in question.

The theme of a double truth *(satya-dvaya)* spoken of by the Buddha, is here particularly stressed: the school of the Mādhyamika, especially, placed in contrast to the truth that corresponds to normal consciousness *(vyavahāra-satya),* a higher, metaphysical truth *(paramārtha-satya),* about which, however, many misunderstandings arose. Often, in fact, a speculative system was made to correspond to it, a system where the true point of reference should have been an experience or a state. After the early period of Buddhism, there occurred in the two principal schools to which it gave place (Hīnayāna and Mahāyāna) a definite twofold process of regression and of degeneration. Although the nucleus of the original doctrine of the Ariya was made up of ascesis and of experience, and therefore had nothing to do either with morality or with speculation, yet these same two elements eventually became paramount in the two schools. In Hīnayāna the ascesis frequently became weakened through the prevalence of the ethical-monastic element that even then evinced a certain similarity to Western monasticism; in addition, a pessimistic interpretation of the world was usual, *dukkha* being commonly understood only as "universal pain" and *nirvāṇa* as a beyond rigidly contrasted with *saṁsāra*. In Mahāyāna, on the other hand, the philosophical element came to prevail, in the sense that—quite apart from the religious aspect, of which we shall speak in a moment—there was a paradoxical attempt to make use of the view of the world attributed to a consciousness that was liberated and become illumination, as the basis for a philosophical system that some have compared to Western "idealistic" philosophy. This comparison is, however, largely invalid. There is a fundamental difference: for Western idealistic philosophies are simply products of the mind and their authors and followers are, and remain, men as saṁsāric and as devoid of all superrational and superindividual illumination as any of their contemporaries ignorant of university philosophy. The "idealism" of the speculative Mahāyāna Buddhism is, on the other hand, an attempt at a rational systematization of superrational experience behind and above it. Without the dominating figure of Prince Siddhattha, not even the speculative idealism of Nāgārjuna could have made its appearance, yet the existence of such figures as Fichte, Hegel, Schelling, and the like is conceivable without any such antecedent; at most, no more is required than the background of a particular historical phase in Western critical and philosophical thought.

We can now go on to discuss the views that in Mahāyāna are more closely connected with our last considerations. Here, a single term marks the ultimate essence of every state, object, or phenomenon of internal or external experience: *tathatā*, a term as difficult to translate as it is to express the state of rarefied illumination from which it takes its sense. The English translators use, for *tathatā*, the term "thatness" or "suchness," the German, *Soheit*. The word denotes the "this," the quality of that which is perceived, insofar as it is directly and evidentially perceived, as a subject of pure experience, of simplicity, of impersonal transparency. This quality, moreover, understood to be its own substratum, devoid of conditions and of generation that is expressed by the term *svayambhū*, frequently associated in the texts with *tathatā*. *Tathatā* appears as a primary element, beyond every qualification of experience as world of "I" or of non-"I."

In these texts, the normal designation used for an Awakened One, or a Buddha, is *tathāgata,* a word that in the ancient books of the canon could be translated as "Accomplished One" but that here assumes a more special sense. The Tathāgata is one who "has thus gone," becoming the "this." The "this" is the equivalent of his actual illumination, conceived as an inexpressible and simple existential state. The Awakened One is not an "I" and he does not "have" illumination: he is the *tathatā,* the very substance of the knowledge "that goes beyond," the *prajñāpāramitā.*

For him, every content of experience, every objectivity *(dharmatā)* becomes resolved into this substance; and therefore, into something existing as pure evidence, that is not susceptible of name, sign, or definition, that is imponderable, that is "like the nonpareil," that is *tathatā.* These expressions are found thus in one text: "All objects and states *(dharmā)* are unthinkable, imponderable, immeasurable, uncountable, like the nonpareil—these are the objects and the states of the Tathāgata [the Awakened One]: unthinkable, because the mind has attained calm [as opposed to *dukkha,* the state of saṁsāric agitation]; imponderable, through surmounting the possibility of being weighed. Unthinkable and imponderable are designations for what consciousness comes to attain. Similarly immeasurable, uncountable, like the nonpareil—these are the properties of the Tathāgata [the Awakened One] because of a counting and measuring by peers, who have attained calm and neutrality."[10] Thus, "perfect illumination *(prajñāpāramitā)* neither takes nor leaves any object,"[11] experience develops, that is to say, as if in an ether-light, that knows no change or motion, like "a flower opening from the abyss." The condition of perfect illumination or of "knowledge that goes beyond" is, in fact, related to *ākāśa,* the ether, of which we have already spoken (cf. p. 171), and the truth announced by the *bodhisattva,* by those who are illumination in substance and who move toward perfect awakening, is that form has the nature of ether, feelings, perceptions, tendencies, consciousness have the nature of ether; such is the nature of every thing or state *(dharma),* they do not come, they do not go, they are like space, like ether, they are resolved in the void, in the signless, in the without tendency: for them, there is no other law.[12] In similar terms the nature itself of an Awakened One is defined: "Why the name of Tathāgata? Because it expresses the true *tathatā;* because it has no origin, because it is the destruction of qualities, because he is one who has no origin, and non-origin is the highest aim."[13]

At this height, every form or state or phenomenon or element, every *dharma*

---

10. *Prajñāpāramitā,* 13.83. Quotations from the texts of the *Prajñāpāramitā* are based on M. Walleser's edition (Göttingen, 1914).

11. Ibid., 8.68.

12. Ibid., 15.90.

13. *Vajracchedikā,* 17 (text of the *Sacred Books of the East,* "Mahāyāna Texts," vol. 49).

appears, through its own nature, as *vivikta* or "detached"—freed from its individuality:[14] both in the world that was once without and also in the interior of the Accomplished One. Disindividualization, resolution in the "void," in the "signless," and in the "without tendency" then reaches the highest regions, dissolves them, removes the final limit, and prepares for a unity that, though entirely transcendent, is at the same time entirely immanent. To resolve all residue of duality, to make of the state of *nirvāṇa* something that devours all, without residue, to make of it the "end of the world," that which in reality "leaves nothing behind" *(anupādhi-śeṣa)*, then *nirvāṇa* itself and, with it, the Awakened One, the Tathāgata, must be freed from individuality, that is, from the signs on account of which it might have an "other" in opposition. The *nirvāṇa*, that early Buddhism wished to protect by wrapping it in silence and a refusal to speak of it, is here the target of a speculation that reaches the height of paradox. This is what we read: "The 'this' *[tathatā]* of the Tathāgata [the Awakened One] is the 'this' of every thing, phenomenon or state *(dharma)*, and the 'this' of every thing, phenomenon or state is the 'this' of the Tathāgata, and the 'this' of every thing, phenomenon or state and the 'this of the Tathāgata, that in fact is in its turn the 'this' of the Tathāgata. . . . The 'this' of the Tathāgata and the 'this' of every thing, phenomenon, or state, that in fact is a single 'this,' without duality, without plurality, is a 'this' devoid of duads."[15] And again: "That which has been announced by the Tathāgata as perfect illumination *(prajñāpāramitā)*, is announced by the Tathāgata as not perfect illumination and for this very reason it is called perfect illumination,"[16]—a theme that is repeated for a whole series of other elements and for the attributes themselves of an Awakened One, of a Buddha: that which has been announced by the Tathāgata as a quality of a Buddha, is announced by him as not a quality of a Buddha and for this very reason it is called a quality of a Buddha.[17] To remain in the "void" is to remain in perfect illumination, in transcendent knowledge. In it dwells the *bodhisattva:* not in the world of the senses, not in a special state of ascetic realization or in its fruits, not even in "Buddha-ness."[18] Nor is this all: "There is no knowledge, there is no ignorance, there is no destruction [of ignorance]; there is no knowledge, there is no attainment of *nirvāṇa*. A man who has [only] approached transcendental knowledge, [still] remains shut in by his mind *(citta)*. But when the

14. *Prajñāpār.*, 22.129.

15. Ibid., 16.98.

16. *Vajracchedikā*, 13.

17. Ibid., 8; cf. 13, 26—in this last short chapter the formula is extended to the thirty-two attributes of a superior man (cf. p. 16); these are said really to be such when they cease to be so, as opposed to others. Cf. 26: "One who wished to see me by seeing my form or hear me by hearing my voice would struggle in vain and would not see me. A Buddha must be seen by seeing the law, because the Lords [the Buddhas] have their body made of the law [*dharmakāya*—on this "body made of law" Mahāyāna has a vast doctrine] and the nature of the law cannot be understood, *nor was it made to be understood.*"

18. *Prajñāpār.*, 1.56.

shell of his mind is destroyed, he becomes free from all fear, he is carried beyond the world of change and attains the ultimate *nirvāṇa*."[19] And if one asks: "Is there anything that has been announced by the Tathāgata?" the answer, definite as it is disconcerting, is: "No, nothing has been announced by the Tathāgata."[20] Again: "If someone were to say that the Tathāgata goes or comes, stands or sits or lies, he would not have understood the meaning of my teaching. Why? Because the word Tathāgata says that he is going nowhere, that he is coming from nowhere—and for this reason is he called the Tathāgata, the blessed and perfect Illuminated One."[21]

It is thus that we arrive at the paradoxical equation of the most extreme Mahāyāna schools: *nirvāṇa* and *saṃsāra*, the unconditioned and the conditioned, the "end of the world" and the "world" are without duality, without plurality, they do not make a duad: they are one and the same thing. "Form is the void and the void is form. The void is not different from form. Form is not different from the void. . . . Thus all beings have the character of the void, they have no beginning, they have no end, they are perfect and they are not perfect."[22] The central theme of the *Lankāvatāra-sūtra* is, in fact, the need of taking oneself beyond notions of being and of nonbeing, of cutting oneself off from all residue of dual thought *(vikalpa)* of overcoming the attitude that seeks *nirvāṇa* outside *saṃsāra* and *saṃsāra* outside *nirvāṇa*. Thus, the attitude of the "negativistic" schools themselves is rejected. "All texts that affirm the unreality of things belong to imperfect doctrine," as is said in the *Mahābheri-hārakaparivarta-sūtra*. Another adds that this same doctrine of unreality is, in the Mahāyāna, something that obstructs, it is like a gate.[23]

Nirvāṇa = saṃsāra. This means that *nirvāṇa* is not an "other"; it is the absolute dimension (superior both to *saṃsāra* and to itself, if it is understood in opposition to *saṃsāra*) through which the "this," the world can be lived and essayed. And it is only thus, as a function of that which, like the ether, is infinite, ungraspable, like the nonpareil, imponderable, not susceptible to contamination by anything that is contaminated, immobile in any movement—it is only thus that the "world" no longer really exists, that in forms, which ensure one who is ruled by "ignorance," it is no more substantial than an apparition, an echo, or a mirage traced in the limpidity of the open sky.[24] In its existence it does not exist, in its nonexistence it exists: this is true both for the world and for one who is liberated, for the Tathāgata. This is the meaning of the recurring formula of the *Vajracchedikā:* "That which has been de-

19. *Prajñāpāramitā-hṛdaya-sūtra*, in *Sacred Books of the East*, part 2, pp. 147–48.
20. *Vajracchedikā*, 13.
21. Ibid., 29.
22. *Prajñāpāramitā-sūtra*, op. cit.
23. Quoted in K. Nukariya, *The Religion of the Samurai* (London, 1913), p. 137.
24. Cf. our *Fenomenologia dell'individuo assoluto* (Turin, 1930), para. 30.

clared as existing, that very thing has been declared as not existing and it is thus that it has been declared to exist." At this point it is said: "If, indeed, by this doctrine, by this exposition, the mind of one who aspires to illumination is not cast down, does not feel the abyss [does not sink], does not feel anguish, if his spirit is not seized, if he is not as though with a broken back, is not alarmed, does not feel terror—then such a one is to be instructed in the fullness of transcendent knowledge."[25] He will become one of those who are said to be "not comparable with men, not like them," "because unthinkable qualities are the gifts of the Tathāgata, of the Venerable Ones *(arhant)*, of the Perfectly Illuminated Ones."[26]

Such is the attitude of the esoteric, "supreme truth" in the teaching *(paramārtha)*. To stand up to it, "one needs a threefold cuirass." The profane, when it faces them, tremble and cry: "Rather *saṁsāra! (varaṁ saṁsāra evāvasthanam)*." [27]

---

25. *Prajñāpār.*, 1.35; cf. 44.
26. Ibid., 22.127.
27. *Bodhicaryāvatāratīkā*, 9.53. In their turn, these Mahāyāna views have constituted one of the premises of Buddhist Tantrism, of the "path of lightning and of the diamond" with its development into a magic outlook on the world; on which, see our work already quoted, *The Yoga of Power*.

18

Up to Zen

Since our aim has been to give the original Doctrine of Awakening as it appears from a study of the Pāli texts, we have no need to deal in detail with the changes and transformations of Buddhism in later epochs: besides, this would be more in the province of history than in that of doctrine. We shall confine ourselves, then, to a few short notes.

We have already said that Buddhism, in its true essence, is of an eminently aristocratic nature. At the beginning, Buddhism was the truth understood by those few, who alone had really achieved illumination and who appeared as *bhikkhu* or wandering ascetics. Then, around these, the *upāsaka,* lay followers, collected and increased and who, according to the canonical formula, had taken refuge in the Buddha, the doctrine, and the order. The order, however, did not resemble a church and the doctrine still less a religion. Women were originally excluded. The unity of the order was essentially due to a strict style of life. It was only later, and with a decadence fully recognized as such by the ancient texts, that precepts and rules multiplied.

The decadence of Buddhism was inevitable once it began to spread: for the Ariya Doctrine of Awakening is closer than any other to a path of initiation that may be understood and trodden only by the few in whom, together with exceptional strength, there is present a lively aspiration for the unconditioned. And even racial and caste influences played their part: not for nothing have we insisted on the "Aryan" quality of the doctrine under discussion. Frontiers to comprehension exist in the normal way, and they are conditioned by the race of spirit and, in part, by the body itself. As soon as Buddhism was adopted by the masses and not only passed to levels where foreign influences survived or were rearoused, but spread even to peoples of notably different stock, changes and alterations became inevitable.

After the original period, the two principal streams of Buddhism have been, as we have said, Hīnayāna and Mahāyāna. There is probably more formal purity in the former than in the latter. Hīnayāna remained the custodian of the canonical Pāli texts, which every Buddhist recognizes as "Scripture," and made them the base of its orthodoxy. But, as we said a few pages back, this stream eventually developed a prevalently ethical-ascetic interpretation of the Doctrine of Awakening on a pessimistic and claustral foundation; an interpretation that represented, in fact, a fall in level. Yet Hīnayāna retained more traces of the clarity, simplicity, and austerity that reflect the original Ariyan style.

Things went differently in Mahāyāna, which developed in Northern India, Tibet, and Nepal, where the presence of Mongolian elements mixed with even more ancient ethnic strains was noteworthy. Mahāyāna presents a particularly complex and composite picture, which it is not always easy to analyze. On the one hand its metaphysical level is undeniably much higher; on the other, cracks and changes in the structure become equally evident.

If we look at the negative elements, we must in the first place note that, in Mahāyāna the Doctrine of Awakening from being the heritage of an elite of true ascetics, degenerated into a "religion" with an extensive mythology. Mahāyāna is aware of the aspects that do not allow the Buddha to be considered simply as a man. Mahāyāna, in fact, emphasized the cosmic and supernatural significance of the Awakened Ones and of the *bodhisattva,* who advance toward awakening. But, on the other hand, it allowed the deification in a religious sense of the Buddha, who here ceases to be one who is liberated and instead becomes a god, the object of a cult and of devout adoration that Brahmanic Hinduism tried to arrogate to itself by making him one of the *avatārā,* the manifestations of Viṣṇu. In these aspects of Mahāyāna, feeling and imagination get the better of the purely intellectual and virile principle. As opposed to the Doric bareness of original Buddhism, we have here what is really a fabulous and kaleidoscopic phantasmagoria of thousands of divinities and *bodhisattva,* of beings who are the mythological personifications of the various states of contemplation, of symbols, worlds, heavens, and marvels. The Buddha becomes a transcendent being in the person of Amitābha, whose name means "infinite splendor," and with whom primordial memory is enigmatically associated. Amitābha reigns in the "blessed land of the West," Sukhāvatī, where neither impurity, nor death, nor destruction exist; this has the same traits as those of similar lands in the ancient Aryan-Western traditions, in ancient Egypt, and the myth of Gilgamesh itself. These are mythical transpositions of the memory of the original western (or northwestern) home of the "divine race."[1] Between Amitābha and the world of men stands Avalokiteśvara, with the traits of a divine mediator, the "Lord who looks down," moved by love and compassion for all creatures.

---

1. Cf. our *Revolt Against the Modern World.* On Sukhāvatī, cf. the two *Sukhāvatī-vyāha* in *Sacred Books of the East,* vol. 49.

While these creatures are, on the one hand, led along the path of *bhakti,* of religious "devotion"—and in some cases Avalokiteśvara even changes sex, and becomes a maternal divinity, the Kuan Yin of Chinese Buddhism—on the other, they are each given the quality of *bodhi,* which is the extrasaṁsāric element capable of producing the miracle of illumination. Not only in each man, but—according to the more popular forms of this faith (since we must now call it a faith)—in every living being generally, a potential Buddha had to be seen. And here, naturally, we find a resurgence of particularly virulent forms of reincarnational fantasies that sometimes assume ridiculous shapes as the counterpart of a doctrine of "merits." From life to life, by accumulating "merits" of all descriptions, living beings gradually become Awakened Ones. They are helped, besides, by the *bodhisattva,* who here become semicelestial beings, losing, at the same time, a large part of their Olympian traits: for, not only are men now no longer left to their own efforts to achieve awakening, as they were in the original austere and virile doctrine, but the *bodhisattva* are concerned with universal salvation. They now go to the aid of men, and make a vow not to enter *nirvāṇa* themselves until, with their help, all living beings have arrived there too. These doctrines are certainly "generous" in the equalitarian and, we were almost going to say, Christian sense, but they have little of the Aryan or the really traditional style about them. We no longer have before us the Ariyan Doctrine of Awakening, but a religion put together for the satisfaction of the faith and sentiments of the masses, to the detriment of the knowledge and clear vision that conforms to reality.

A second aspect of the degeneration of Buddhism is the philosophical one. Already the later part of the Pāli canon, the *Abhidhamma,* often shows the same stereotyped, unalive, and rationalistic profile that belongs chiefly to our own medieval Scholasticism. In Mahāyāna, thought certainly has broader play, but it gives place to the misunderstanding we have already discussed. The great merit of Mahāyāna lies in this: that it has taken as its foundation the point of view, not of a saṁsāric being, but of an Awakened One, not of an ordinary man who strives, but of a Buddha, a Tathāgata, not the *terminus a quo* but the *terminus ad quem.* That which for the former cannot help being something negative and indefinite—*nirvāṇa*—and which Hīnayāna, too, considered essentially as being evanescently distant, in Mahāyāna assumes, instead, undeniably positive features. Here is a question not so much of *nirvāṇa* as of its counterpart, illumination, *prajñā,* or *bodhi.* In its highest aspects, Mahāyāna is certainly a doctrine of illumination; but unfortunately the demon of speculation managed to find a way in. Mahāyāna often transforms that which, in its nature, is something superrational and inexpressible, comprehensible only on the basis of a direct transcendent experience, into a speculative concept, and it becomes the organ of a system of thought. The "void" *(suñña)* and the intangible *tathatā* condense, in spite of themselves, into concepts of spiritual theory of knowledge and of the world. We have, thus, the equivalents—anticipated by many centuries—of Western absolute idealism. Things only exist as creations of the mind. Mind is the original and permanent substance *(bhūtatathatā)* intact and identical with itself in any phenomenon. Earthly or celestial apparitions, *saṁsāra*, men, gods, Buddhas, all originate only in the mind. Mind is like the water of the ocean, phenomena are like the waves that wrinkle its surfaces: mind and phenomena are of the same substance. Outside the mind, nothing has real existence. So we arrive at Nāgārjuna's system.

These ideas, which, as philosophical views, have nothing to do with higher knowledge, contain, nevertheless, a reflection of it, and are thus not without a certain cathartic power. The fall of level that they represent was halted in Mahāyāna by the presence of a genuine esoterism that was capable, in a restricted circle of qualified individuals, of rectifying such theories and restoring them to the higher plane to which they belong, and also of discovering the secret knowledge hidden behind the mythological form of the various beings and divinities in the religious aspect of Mahāyāna. This same "idealistic" or "unrealistic" theory, we must admit, was valued less from a theoretical point of view than from a practical one, as it was used as a kind of medicine for the purpose of purification. The misery of beings derives from their taking as reality things that exist only as creations of their mind; deceived by the false appearances of real beings and qualities, and of different natures and values, action takes them ever further away from true reality, nourishes "ignorance," creates ever stronger bonds and perpetuates the irrational round that the living pursue. One who steeps himself, instead, in the reality of the "void," in the unreality of everything that, in heaven or earth, seems objective, leaves his intoxication little by little behind him, feels a loftier calm, detaches himself from action that is due to craving and abandons vulgar interests, hate, and anger. He has now made his mind ready to receive a higher knowledge. It is in this sense that the idealism or unrealism of Mahāyāna, which possesses not a few points of contact with that of the Vedānta, had, and still has, a cathartic value.

In this connection arises the problem of the extent to which a knowledge that, because it refers to transcendent summits, should be inarticulate, while being able, in general, to provide directional "suggestions" and to encourage moments of illumination.

In this very connection, and to end our exposition, we wish to say something about what is known as Zen Buddhism. Zen is one of the most important streams of esoteric Buddhism transplanted into China and Japan and is still in existence. According to tradition, it is actually based on a secret doctrine transmitted from spirit to spirit by Prince Siddhattha to his disciple Mahākassapa. Preserved through an uninterrupted chain of masters, it was carried, at the beginning of the sixth century A.D., into China by Bodhidharma, third son of a powerful Brāhman king of southwest India. From China, Zen passed to Japan, where it grew powerful roots and had important developments. We are dealing, in substance, with a branch of Mahāyāna esoterism, which found, in certain Taoist views (particularly in Lao-tzu's doctrine of the "void") and in certain tendencies of the Chinese mind (above all, in its feeling for nature), congenial elements with which it combined. As for the term Zen, it is itself the abbreviation of the Sino-Japanese term that corresponds to the Sanskrit *dhyāna* and to the Pāli *jhāna*. But here this term must be understood in a wider sense than we have previously given it. In general, it expresses a form of contemplation developed under the sign of the "void."

Zen is not, as a few have claimed, a "Chinese anomaly" of Buddhism; it is essentially a renewal of the exigency that originally gave life to Buddhism in the face of Brahmanic speculation and ritualism. In fact, at one period there had taken place in Buddhism, but using different terms, the same phenomenon of decay, of scholastic formalization and of traditional and ritualistic survival, as in post-Vedic India. Zen appears to have represented as strong a reaction against all this as, in its own time, original Buddhism did against its own background of circumstances. Zen will have nothing to do with speculations, canonical writings, rites, or religious aberrations. It is even positively iconoclastic. It does not, like Nāgārjuna, discuss transcendental truth, but desires to create, through a direct action of the mind on the mind, the conditions for its actual realization.[2]

"The Scriptures are nothing more than useless paper," says Rin-zai, a Zen master. Another thus reprimands one who was burning Confucian books: "You would have done better to have burned the books in your mind and your heart, rather than these written in black and white." Texts, dogmas, precepts are so many bonds or so many crutches, to be put aside that one may advance on one's own. The Buddhist canonical literature itself is likened to a window, from which one contemplates the great scene of nature: but to live in this scene you must jump outside the window. There is also the simile of the finger and the moon: to indicate the position of the moon, a finger is necessary: but woe to those who mistake the finger for the moon. We must think the same of transcendental knowledge and achievement. As nature hates a vacuum—it is said—so Zen abhors everything that may come between reality and ourselves. Reap, if you can, the allusions contained in the doctrines: but beware of binding yourself to words and concepts. The idea of a special passing-on of the true knowledge independently of the texts is the cornerstone of one of the principal schools of Zen. The state of a Buddha—it is maintained—can only be un-

---

2. The data and the quotations from texts, in what follows, are taken from Kaiten Nukariya, *The Religion of the Sumarai*, and D. T. Suzuki, *Essais sur le bouddhisme Zen* (Paris, 1940).

derstood by one who is himself a Buddha. To describe it in words is a task that would have been beyond the power of the son of the Śākya himself.

To illustrate the teaching of inward independence, an anecdote is told of a Zen master who, to warm himself one icy morning, chopped to pieces a consecrated statue of the Buddha and put it on the fire with the remark: "The Buddha would have offered not the wood of his statue, but even his very life to help another." The Buddha, he who has taught how to cut off every bond and how to subsist without support, must not become a bond and a support. With regard to the boundary that separates vision from mental expression, and to the consequent necessity of an act starting from within, we find in Zen some episodes that are downright drastic. A disciple who finally asked his master to reveal to him the fundamental principle of the Buddhist doctrine, is sent to another master. The question is repeated, and the answer is a slap in the face. Referring the matter to his first master, the disciple is again sent to the second. He asks the same question and the answer is no different: a slap in the face. He is sent a third time. This time the disciple, as soon as he is in the presence of the master, without a word, himself gives the other a blow on the face. The master, smiling, then tells him: "You have understood." Another Zen master told a prince who was debating with him: "We ask nothing of the Buddha, of the Law, or of the Order." The prince then says: "If you ask nothing of the Buddha, of the Law, or of the Order, what, then, is the aim of your cult?" Here, again, the answer is simply a slap in the face.

The Zen texts are rich in anecdotes where the impulse to know intellectually is cut off by an answer that is entirely out of key, or by a brusque action by the master; they are answers or actions, however, that sometimes act in a mature spirit as a catharsis. They may suddenly confront you with an empty chasm into which you must jump, leaving everything behind: your self, your own mind, your theories, even your own preoccupation with liberation. A man, wishing to be initiated into the knowledge, knocks at the door of a Zen monastery. The only answer he gets is that the door is shut so brutally in his face that one of his arms is broken. In that instant, illumination flashes over the man. "What is the sacred temple of the Buddha?" asks another. The Zen master replies: "An innocent girl." "And who is the lord of the temple?" "A child in her womb." "What is the true body of the Vairochana Buddha?" The master replies: "Fetch me a jug of water." The disciple does so. The master says: "Take it back to where it was." And this is all. An assembly was called together to hear a lecture, long anticipated, on the essence of the doctrine. The master finally appears and, without speaking, stretches out his arms.

This leads us on to another Zen theme: "the tongue of the inanimate." These are Seigen-Ishin's words: "Before a man studies Zen, for him mountains are mountains and waters are waters. When, thanks to the teaching of a qualified master, he has attained the inner vision of the truth of Zen, for him mountains are no longer mountains and waters are no longer waters. But after this, when he has really reached the haven of calm, once again mountains are, for him, mountains and waters, waters." The second phase evidently corresponds to *nirvāṇa* when it is faced by *saṁsāra;* the third, to *nirvāṇa* that leaves no residue. The "return" must be interpreted on the lines of the liberated experience, where every dualism is resolved, which we discussed in connection with the Mahāyāna doctrine of the "void" and of the *tathatā.* Zen, however, tends to make nature itself suggest this disindividualized and liberated experience, and to produce moments of illumination such as give a sense of the change of state, in which lies the essence of the path. The mind must come to feel that everything becomes manifest and reveals itself according to an absolute and unparalleled perfection: only then will it have intimations also of that *nirvāṇa* that leaves nothing behind it, and that corresponds to the mountains that are once again mountains and to the waters that are once more waters. One simile, in this connection, is quite expressive: "The shadow follows the body, the echo arises from the voice. He who chases his shadow tires his body, not knowing that it is the body that produces the shadow; and he who raises his voice to drown an echo, does not know that the voice is the cause of the echo." It is also said: "The subject achieves calm when the object vanishes; the object vanishes when the subject achieves calm." Lao-tzu had already taught: "Abandon in order to obtain." It is a question of creating a state of absolute identity with oneself, without signs, without intentions. Thus, Zen, following the steps of Taoism, speaks of an act that is a noneffort or a nonintention *(anabhogā-caryā)* and of a corresponding resolution, like a "vow" *(anabhogā-praṇidhāna).* Another saying: "As two flawless mirrors reflect, one in the other, so the concrete fact and the spirit must face each other without any foreign body being interposed." Once again, it is a matter of catharsis from subjectivity, of destruction of "psychology," which had already been the aim of the *yathābhūtam* of ancient Buddhism, the transparent vision conforming to reality. Then nature, in its liberty and impersonality, in its extraneousness to all that is subjective and affective, is able to intimate the state of illumination. This is why Zen declares that the doctrine is found in simple and natural facts rather than in the texts of the canon, and that the universe is its real Scripture and the body of the Tathāgata. "Trees, grass, mountains, streams, stars, the sea, the moon— with this alphabet the texts of Zen are written." "Can the inanimate preach the doctrine?" Hui-chung replies: "Yes, it preaches with eloquent words and without ceasing." The sun rises. The moon sets. Mountain heights. Ocean depths. Spring flowers. Fresh summer breeze. The large autumnal moon. Winter snowflakes. "These things, perhaps too simple for a common observer to pay them attention, have a deep meaning for Zen." "What is the truth?" asks a disciple. As a reply, the master Yo-shan indicates the sky with his finger and then a pitcher of water and says: "Do you see?"

The other says: "No." Yo-shan replies: "The cloud in the sky and the water in the pitcher": that is all. Tüng-shan says: "How wonderful is the tongue of the inanimate. You cannot hear it with your ears, but you can hear it with your eyes": with the unclosed eye of the mind, not through perception, not with logic, not with metaphysics. Another saying of Zen: "The leaves that fall, like the flowers that open, reveal for us the blessed law of the Buddha." We must, however, be very careful not to confuse all this with aestheticism *sui generis*. The Far Eastern simplified and particularly transparent feeling for nature plays its part, as we have said. But the fundamental point is to go up from nature, which is free from soul and is only itself, free from affects and subjectivity, to the perception where, in fact, "mountains are again mountains and waters, waters." A Zen formula, which in some ways sums up its doctrine, is: "Reflect in yourself and recognize your own face as it was before the world" (Huei-neng).

Together with the message of the inanimate, there is a manner in which signs, gestures, and symbols take the place of words. We have already mentioned the master of Zen who, before the assembly of monks collected to hear his discourse, confined himself to stretching his arms. Another simply raises his finger. Another presents a stick. It is said that Mahākassapa was chosen by the Buddha for the transmission of the esoteric doctrine in similar circumstances: the Buddha, in the midst of his disciples, had raised a bunch of flowers into the air; only Mahākassapa among those present had smiled and inclined his head in assent. Words limit. A sign can, however, at a suitable time, cause moments of illumination.

From these antecedents, it is not difficult to understand that Zen insists above all on a spiritual awakening, or change of inner state, that is sudden and discontinuous. The opening of the third eye, *satori,* illumination, is a condition that happens suddenly, destroying all that has gone before, appearing to be without origin, without "becoming." The theme of the *Vajracchedikā* is echoed in Zen: the Tathāgata is so called because he does not come from anywhere and does not go anywhere. "When he appears, he comes from nowhere, and when he disappears, he goes nowhere—and this is Zen." And again: "Where there really is a coming in or a going out, there great contemplation is not. Zen, [the contemplative state, the state of illumination-awakening] in its essence, is without birth."

At one period, nevertheless, Zen became divided into two different schools: that of the south *(yuga-pad)* which lays greater emphasis on the discontinuity of the awakening; and that of the north *(krama-vrittya)* which, instead, allows of a certain gradualness. But both agree that it is essential, at a particular moment, to know how to "jump out of the 'I'," how to "vomit forth the 'I'." This may be brought about also by violent sensations, even by a physical pain, by something, according to a Chinese saying, that "twists the bowels nine times and more." We have already told of the episode of the broken arm; and there are many like it. It seems that, in some places at the present time, an operation not unlike strangulation is carried out, by means of which the disciple, who is suitably prepared, is forced forward toward a void into which he cannot but jump.

As for preparation, the methods of Zen do not differ essentially from what we have already described as Ariyan ascesis.

First, make oneself master of external objects by substituting a condition of activity for the usual one of passivity. Realize that wherever a desire pushes a man toward a thing, it is not he who has the thing, but the thing that has him. "He who takes a liquor believes that he drinks it; whereas it is the liquor that drinks him." Detach oneself. Discover and love the active principle in oneself.

Second is mastery of the body. Establish one's own authority over the entire organism. "Imagine that your body is separate from you: if it shouts, make it be silent, as a severe father does his child. If it shows temper, hold it in, as one does a curbed horse. If it is ill, administer to it what is necessary, as a doctor to his patient. If it disobeys, chastise it, as the master chastises the turbulent pupil." Temper oneself physically. Establish with oneself a "trial of endurance" by accustoming oneself, for example, to undergoing freezing cold in winter and in summer a torrid heat. And so on.

Third is the control of mental and emotive life in order to promote and consolidate a state of equilibrium. There is the appeal to one's inner nobility: "It is ridiculous"—it is said in Zen—"that a being endowed with the nature of a Buddha, born to be master of every material reality, should be enslaved by little cares or frightened by phantasms that he himself has created, should let his mind be swayed by passions or dissipate his vital energy in irrelevant things." Anxieties, recriminations, or nostalgias for the past, imaginings or anticipations for the future, enmity, shame, and disturbance, all these must be put aside. One may help oneself, eventually, by means of the "idealistic" theory (cf. p. 223)—which may help one to realize the irrationality of so many of the mind's impulses, and to regaining power over one's heart. Furthermore, one must simplify oneself, one must resolutely cut down the parasitical overgrowth of vain and muddled thoughts. To the question: "How shall I learn the law?" a Zen master, Poh Chang, replied: "Eat when you are hungry and sleep when you are tired." Calm and equilibrium—the *samatha* that we have frequently mentioned—must become a habit. Here is an anecdote: When commanding an army in battle, even in his headquarters, O-yō-mei would discuss Zen doctrines. He was informed, on one occasion, that his advanced troops had been defeated; he calmly continued his discourse. Shortly after, he was told that, in the later developments of the battle he had become the victor. The commander remained as calm as before, and did not, even then, change his discourse. This is how one gradually apprehends the existence of a principle that cannot be altered by doubt or fear any more than the light of the sun can be destroyed by fog or clouds.

Fourth: When we come to the aforesaid "throwing out of the mind" or "of the 'I';" we find that we are here faced with some sort of discontinuity, for which there is no means of preparing, because it is an actual change of state. To one who was astonished at the saying, that the world enters into the mind, a Zen master replied saying that the difficulty consists, rather, in making the mind enter into the world. It is a matter of the breaking of the shell constituted by the mind, of which a Mahāyāna text we have already quoted, speaks; only then does one have the intuition that *nirvāṇa*, when understood as one term of an opposition, is itself an illusion, a bond, the object of an imperfect knowledge.

Zen uses a twofold symbolism for the structure of its discipline: that of the "five degrees of merit" and that of the vicissitudes of the man and the bull.

The "first degree of merit" corresponds to the "conversion"—similar to *pabbajjā*, the "departure" of the ancient Buddhist teaching: a man turns from the outer world toward the inner world. The illuminated, extrasaṁsāric "I" is here portrayed as a king to whom one declares allegiance. The second degree of merit is "service"— that is to say, faithfulness and loyalty to this inner sovereign. The third degree is "valor," what one must show when confronting and combating all opposition to the king. Then there is the "merit of him who cooperates," due to one who is not simply good at defense and fighting, but who is admitted to the positive government of the state. The final degree of merit: "beyond merit" or "merit that is not merit" (an expression to be understood in the same sense as "acting without acting") is the degree of the king himself, whose nature one assumes. Here action ceases or, if you prefer, action is manifested in the form of nonaction, of spontaneity. The being and the law are here identical.

And now the second Zen symbolism, made up of ten well-known illustrations corresponding to ten episodes in the adventures of a drover and a bull. The mind—represented in the preceding allegory, by the king—or rather, "illumination," the *bodhi* element, is conceived as a precious stone, always fresh and pure, even when buried in dust. It has to be found as the drover seeks a bull. The first figure is, in fact, uncertain search. The second is hope: the animal has not yet been seen, but its tracks have been sighted. Third: the bull is seen in the distance, and a cautious advance toward it is made. Fourth: the animal is suddenly seized, and it tries in vain to escape. Fifth: the animal is tamed, mastered, and fed, so that finally it follows the drover as if it were his shadow. Sixth: the drover is carried home by this animal that serves him as a mount. Seventh: "the forgetting of the animal and the remembering of the man." Eighth: "the forgetting both of the bull and of the man"—the corresponding figure gives only a large empty circle: we are at the point of overcoming all dualism in the "void," in liberated consciousness. Ninth: return to the origins and to the source—we remember the Zen saying: "rediscover your own face as it was before the world." Last figure: going into the town with the hands open; this phase should be compared with that in which, once again, "mountains are mountains and waters, waters." It is the point at which transcendency becomes the clarity of an immanence that is free from the stain of the "I"; it is the state in which there is nothing that comes or goes, that enters or leaves. As a corollary of this, some Zen masters have declared that self-application and self-concentration and the seeking of solitary and silent places belong to the heterodox teachings. "Do not be attached to anything whatsoever: if you understand this, walking or standing, sitting or lying, you will never cease to be in the state of Zen, in the state of contemplation and of illumination."

The Zen masters teach that the blessed order of the ancient Ariya, seated round Prince Siddhattha, is even now gathered at the Vulture's Peak, that is to say, at the symbolical place where, in the Mahāyāna texts, the Awakened One is supposed most frequently to have spoken and that expresses the traditional idea of the "center," the "center of the world."

19

⌒⁊❋⁊⌒

The Ariya Are Still Gathered
on the Vulture's Peak

In this book we have not set out to make Buddhist propaganda but, rather, as we said, to indicate the fundamental elements of a complete system of ascesis: these elements may be found in other traditions also, but they appear with particular clarity in the Buddhist teaching, which lends itself admirably to our purpose for the various reasons that we discussed at the beginning.

It now remains to suggest the significance that an ascesis of this sort may have at the present day.

We need hardly stress the fact that the modern world stands, more completely so perhaps than in any other civilization, at the opposite pole to that of an ascetic view of life. We are not talking here of the religious problem that, as we have seen, has no direct relationship to higher ascesis. We are speaking of fundamental orientations of the spirit.

It would be hard to deny that "activism," the exaltation and practice of action understood as force, impetus, becoming, struggle, transformation, perennial research, or ceaseless movement, is the watchword of the modern world. The world of the "being" is drawing to its close, and this decline has for long been hailed with joy. Not only do we have today the triumph of activism, but also a philosophy *sui generis* at its service; a philosophy whose systematic criticism and whose speculative apparatus serve to justify it in every way while pouring contempt and heaping discredit on all other points of view. Interest in pure knowledge has become ever more displaced by interest in "living" and in "doing" or, at any rate, by interest in those departments of knowledge that can be employed in terms of action or practical and temporal realization. Today the nature and potentialities of pure knowledge, that is to say, knowledge whose peculiar object—as in the traditional ideal of all periods—is superindividual and superhistorical reality is almost unknown. Our contemporaries grow ever more accustomed to disregard the "being" aspect of things and concentrate, instead, upon their aspect as "becoming," "life," "movement," "development," or "history."

"Historicism" and "the cult of becoming" beat out the rhythm of activism, even on the cultural plane. Pragmatism, voluntarism, irrationalism, varieties of the religion of "life" and "actuality," relativism, evolutionism, progressivism, Faustism, are lines of speculation that, in spite of their different guises, all spring from the same motive. And this, then, is merely the translation into terms of self-consciousness and intellectual justification of the central motive of the precipitate life of these times, with its tumult, its agitation, its fever for speed, its mechanization devoted to the shortening of all intervals of space and time, its congestive and breathless rhythm that is, particularly in the New World, carried to its limit. There the activist theme really reaches paroxysmal and almost pandemic heights and completely absorbs the whole of life, whose horizons, moreover, are thereby restricted to the dark and gloom that are natural to wholly temporal and contingent achievements.

It is too an ominous fact that forces of a collectivist and therefore subpersonal nature must gain more and more power over beings who have no real traditional support and are racked by a fundamental restlessness. The activist world is also essentially a featureless and plebeian world, ruled by the demon of collectivism; it is not only the scene of triumph of what has been called "the ideal animal," but it is also a world that is essentially "telluric," moved by forces that are bound up with the elements of "mass" and "quantity," where action, force, strife, and even heroism and sacrifice are seen to become increasingly irrational, devoid of light, "elemental," and altogether earthly.

That which the ancient Indo-Aryan wisdom had denoted by the symbol of saṁsāric existence, and which corresponding Western traditions had styled "the Age of Iron," can now be said to be at the height of its career; and there is no lack, either in Buddhism or in similar traditions, of texts in which such characteristics of times to come were predicted with astonishing accuracy.[1] We repeat, however, that the main characteristic of our times is not that life tends to exhaust itself almost exclusively on the saṁsāric plane, but that our civilization stimulates and exalts this kind of life, and considers it, not so much as a state of fact, but rather as something of value, as something that should be, as something that is right. It must be unique in all history that saṁsāra should become the object of a species of mystique or religion. The new philosophies of life, of becoming, of the *élan vital*, which flourish on the borders of practical activism, have just this significance and even come to exalt in human existence all that is unconscious spontaneity, pure vitality, prepersonal biological substratum and which is therefore, essentially prehuman and subhuman.

1. Cf. *Revolt Against the Modern World*, appendix.

To think that we can effectively react against such a state of affairs, taken as a whole, would be frivolous, and would mean (unless we are simply dealing with intellectual reactions) ignoring the remote causes that have gradually led up to it;[2] they are causes that cannot be removed in a day. But although success on a large scale, taking into account the general orientation of the modern world, is at present very remote, yet it might be achieved locally within the circle of an elite, of a certain number of qualified individuals. The only possible point of reference, here, is ascetic values, in the fullest, purest, and strictest meaning of the term. The affirmation of an ascetic vision of life is today particularly necessary in view of the unparalleled force of the "telluric" and saṁsāric element in the modern world.

The prejudices that have been created or encouraged by certain quite special, abnormal, and un-Aryan forms of ascesis we have already removed. Let no one, then, declare that ascesis means renunciation, flight from the world, inaction, quietism, or mortification. The affirmation of a background of pure transcendency to balance a world that is ever more and more the captive of immanency, is the first point and the first task. But another point, not less important, concerns that very action that lies so close to the heart of our contemporaries. Indeed, one could justly maintain that those who despise all asceticism know nothing of what action really is, and what they exalt is merely an inferior, emasculated, and passive form of action. The sort of activism that consists in fever, impulsiveness, identification, centerless vertigo, passion, or agitation, far from testifying power, merely demonstrates impotence. Our own classical world knew this well: the central theme of the Ciceronian oration *Pro Marcello* is just this: there is no higher power than that of mastery over oneself. Only those who possess this mastery can know what is the true action, which shows them also to the outside world, not as those who are acted upon, but as those who truly act. We remember the illuminating Buddhist saying: he who goes, stands still—he who stands still, goes. For this very reason, in the traditions springing from the same root all movement, activity, becoming, or change was referred to the passive and female principle, while to the positive, luminous, masculine principle were attributed the particular qualities of immobility, unchangeability, and stability. We can, then, definitely affirm the existence of an ascesis that in no way signifies quietism but that is, rather, the prerequisite for a higher, aristocratic ideal of activity and virility.

This ideal—let it be noted—is in no way a monopoly of the East. The basic idea with which we are dealing is traditionally Aryan, whence we can also find it among ourselves. The same idea was expressed on the metaphysical plane by Plotinus when he spoke of the becoming that is only "the flight of beings that are and that are not," or by Aristotle when he discussed the "still Mover," or, on the ethical plane, by the

---

2. Cf. ibid., part 2, passim.

Roman Stoa with its emphasis on the sidereal and unchangeable element of the mind as the basis of all human effort and dignity. One who is the cause and effective master of motion does not himself move. He inspires motion and directs action, but he himself does not act, in the sense that he is not transported, he is not involved in action, he *is* not action, but is, on the other hand, an impassive, utterly calm and imperative superiority, from whom action proceeds and on whom it depends. As opposed to this idea of true and mastered action, which is only thinkable, however, on the basis of purification from the saṁsāric element, one who acts while identifying himself with his action, impulsively, urged by passion, by desire, by the irrational, by restless need or vulgar interest, such a one does not really act, but is acted upon. However paradoxical it may sound, his is a passive action—he stands under the sign, not of virility, but of femininity. And under the sign of femininity, the whole modern "telluric" and activist world also stands.[3] It is only a lower, anti-aristocratic form of action that predominates here. Otherwise, it actually betrays that half-conscious desire to deafen and distract, that agitation and clamor that reveal dread of the silence, the internal isolation, the absolute being of higher nature, or it becomes a weapon employed in the revolution of man against the eternal that indeed marks the limit of the saṁsāric "ignorance" and intoxication of fallen beings.

All this is generally true of asceticism as a whole. More particularly, it is even possible to demonstrate historically that the ancient Oriental Aryan forms of ascesis are also capable of this application. We should not forget that, if the East, whether Indo-European or Asian, has not until now given to a modern man the impression, from certain aspects, of a civilization that is activistically practical, this is due not to a lack of strength, but to the fact of having absorbed its principal energies in the vertical direction that is beyond becoming and history; few of the well-born in these civilizations had, or have even now, much interest in other forms of achievement. But where these achievements, through external circumstance or through the development of special vocations, have acquired a certain power of attraction over the spirit, the East has shown, on the same plane of action, what energy and will can do when they are shaped essentially by the ascetic view of life. Anyone who objects and points out, for example, the more recent political state of India, forgets that this country, quite apart from its original epics, had its own imperial cycle under Candragupta and under Aśoka, a sovereign who was profoundly Buddhist. Besides, we know of no Western text in which heroism and warlike action have received a transcendental justification so precise and a transfiguration so high, as in the

---

3. In reality, all the ancient forms of "telluric" civilizations developed in close connection with feminine and promiscuous cults and with the naturalistic-vital substratum of existence. Cf. J. J. Bachofen, *Das Mutterrecht*, 2nd edn. (Basel, 1897).

Bhagavadgītā;[4] while on another level it is well known that of all the troops England gathered in her empire, those provided by India were the best qualified, composed as they were, not of "soldiers," but of warriors by race and vocation. And it was from warrior stock—as we have seen—that Prince Siddhattha himself came.

But a better example is offered us by Japan. It has been justly stated[5] that "the Russo-Japanese War, to the great surprise of most of the European world, showed us how the supposed 'emasculated Oriental immobility' could purposively and heroically fight, on land and sea, the so-called virile Western mobility. The heroism of the Japanese, educated for a millennium and a half by Buddhist doctrine, has shown unmistakably that Buddhism is not the opiate that everyone previously imagined." Anyone with the interests of the West at heart should indeed hope that the future will not create a change of mind in the Oriental peoples whereby they are led to apply against the West their enormous spiritual potential; that the power that has been created by a millennial ascetic vision of life, should be directed onto the temporal plane on which most of Europe, having cut itself off from its best traditions, has chosen to concentrate.

It was not entirely unintentional that, at the end of this book, we spoke of Zen Buddhism. This particularly esoteric form of the Buddhist doctrine has been the most congenial to the Japanese warrior nobility, and Zen has even been called "the religion of the Samurai." According to the Japanese point of view, if a man is a man, and not an animal, he can only be a Samurai: courageous, upright, trustworthy, virile, faithful and full of controlled dignity and ready for any active sacrifice. But the precepts of virility, loyalty, courage, control of the mind, instincts, action, and disdain for a soft life and empty luxury—all these are elements of Bushido, the ethics of the Samurai warrior nobility, found in the Zen ascesis, which derived from the Buddhist Doctrine of Awakening their confirmation, integration, and likewise their transcendent basis.[6] It was thus that the Japanese nobleman was capable of a quite special and unconditioned form of heroism: not "tragic" but "Olympian," the heroism of one who can give away his complete life without regrets, with a clear vision of the goal in view and with an entire disregard for his own person, because he *is* not life and *is* not person, but already partakes of the superindividual and supertemporal.

These are only examples; and we do not wish to give the idea that we are making a defense of the East or of the Far East. Let us repeat: we are dealing here with general views of life, a distinction between East and West does not enter the discussion since the opposition is one of supernational and supercontinental nature. Our

---

4. Cf. *Revolt Against the Modern World*, pp. 120–21.
5. G. de Lorenzo, *India e buddhismo antico*, 5th ed. (Bari, 1926), p. 7.
6. Cf. Nukariya, *The Religion of the Samurai*, pp. 36–50.

own Middle Ages also knew a sacred heroism, and its history likewise shows, in majestic strokes, how a heroic cycle—whenever the corresponding vocation is present—can develop under the influence of an ascetic view of life, even when this view presents deviations, shortcomings, and limitations of considerable importance as happens in the case of Christianism. Either as detachment beyond action, or as detachment in action and for action, there exists a common tradition. We have purposely made considerable use of the term "Olympian" in order to remind those who might forget. From the ancient Mediterranean "Olympian" world, where the opposition between region of being and region of becoming, between the cycle of generation and the superworld corresponds exactly to the Indo-Aryan opposition between *saṁsāra* and *nirvāṇa*, we derive our highest heritage, that which the modern world has forgotten but which still persisted in some measure among the Germanic and Roman elements of the best of the Middle Ages. The Olympian view of life, to which every true ascetic value is intimately bound, is the highest, most original, and most Aryan of the West. It holds the symbol of all that, in a higher sense, can be called classical and aristocratic.

A return to ascetic values can, then, be conceived in two forms and in two degrees. A formation of life newly oriented toward the extrasaṁsāric and "sidereal" element can, in the first place, teach what real action and mastery are to all those who know only their most obscure and irrational forms. In the second place, ascesis as affirmation of pure transcendency, as detachment, not only in action, but beyond action, toward awakening, can ensure that the immobile is not overturned by the changeable, that forces of centrality, forces of the world of being are set up against forces of becoming. Nor should we think of this second process as though we had to do with the presence of guests of stone at a banquet of the agitated and fanatical. To inspire and establish, even in scattered and unknown beings, extrasaṁsāric forces, may be an action whose invisible effects, even on the plane of visible and historical reality, are considerably more important than many might imagine. It is Buddhist teaching that the Ariya are able to work from a distance, for the good of many, in the human sphere as well as in the "divine,"[7] and these spheres would be harmed by differences among the Ariya.[8] It is Buddhist doctrine that when the Ariya, in their disindividualized consciousness, suffuse the world with the irradiant contemplations, they can liberate forces that go out into it and act invisibly upon distant lands and destinies. We think it possible that should the course of history, in spite of appearances, not deteriorate further, this may perhaps be due, less to the efforts and direct action of groups of men and leaders of men, than to the influences proceeding, through

7. Cf., e.g., *Majjh.*, 31.
8. Ibid., 104.

the paths of the spirit, from the secret realizations of a few nameless and remote ascetics, in Tibet or on Mount Athos, among the Zen, or in some Trappist or Carthusian cloister of Europe. To an awakened eye, to an eye capable of seeing with the sight of one on the Further Shore, these same realizations would appear as the only steady lights in the darkness, as the only peaks emerging, calm and sovereign, above the seas of mist down in the valleys.[9] Every true ascetic realization becomes inevitably transformed into a support—an invisible one, but for all that nonetheless real and efficacious—for those who, on the visible plane, resist and struggle against the forces of an obscure age.

Lastly, let us say a few words about that special class of reader who is interested in "spiritualism." We have already, in our *Maschera e volto dello spiritualismo contemporaneo,* warned such readers against the errors and confusions that have been set afoot by many modern trends through mistaken aspirations toward the supernatural and supersensible. Should anyone seriously harbor such aspirations, he must take careful stock of such errors and confusions and, above all, not deceive himself that true realization of what lies beyond the human condition is possible without rigorous "ascetic" preparation and consolidation. Given the conditions in which the Westerner now finds himself and which we have frequently mentioned, such preparation is, today more than ever indispensable. We should then be under no illusions about the real nature of knowledge or "occult" discipline, particularly when we are dealing with what our contemporaries put forward. A doctrine, such as the one we have discussed, gives a very good idea of the possibility of an Aryan and aristocratic path beyond saṁsāric existence. This path will have no need of "religious" aids, dogmas, or petty moralities, and it genuinely corresponds to the will for the unconditioned. But, at the same time, this doctrine shows no less clearly the preliminary conditions for ascesis and detachment that are absolutely imperative for any enterprise of a transcendent nature. It also shows that the path of awakening—identical in its spirit with every true "initiation"—is absolutely irreconcilable with all that is implied by confused mysticism, mediumistic cults, the subconscious, visionarism, manias for occult phenomena and powers, and neopsychoanalytical contaminations. It is well known that interested circles—either confessionalists or "illumined" in the profane and "critical" sense—rely on such spiritual deviations in their attempt to heap discredit upon the ideals and kinds of wisdom that, in one form or another, were always recognized as the culminating point of every normal and traditional civilization. To realize that, as we have indicated, there is similar content in the path announced by a figure of the dignity and grandeur of Prince Siddhattha,

9. We may here call to mind the words of the *Atharva Veda* (12.1.1): "The great truth, the powerful order (ṛta), the initiation, the ascesis, the rite and the sacrifice sustain the earth."

the Buddha—and that this path, even if only in distant and varied reflections, is now related to the faith of more than four hundred million followers—such a realization should be enough to forestall any attempt by such shortsighted or malicious individuals to cause error and confusion of thought.

In the opposite field, we must say something in particular about two currents: the one, followed by those who, though themselves Orientals, apply themselves to "adapting" ideas of the ancient traditions in their own way and to popularizing them in the West; and the other, which aims at introducing the concept of a new "modern initiation."

The first case brings to mind the Hindu parable of a man who, when surrounded by water in a drenching rainstorm, made a great effort to draw some up from a muddy well. As far as the Oriental traditions go, or rather, the various Oriental forms of the one tradition, the situation we have to deal with is different from that existing in the West. Even in the case of transcendent wisdom there exist ancient texts, for the most part translated and available to all, where we can find, in a purer and more complete form, all that such people would vulgarize and reduce, at best, to an emasculated reflection of the original. Anyone who can lay his hands on the Buddhist texts or the *Bhagavadgītā* or the yoga and Vedānta texts should be able calmly to close the doors on these modern publishers and commentators and adaptors, leaving himself only the serious task of study and achievement. But, the true reason for the success of such new expositions is to be found where they are the most accommodating, least rigid, least severe, most vague, and ready to come to easy terms with the prejudices and weaknesses of the modern world. Let everyone have the courage to look deeply into himself and to see what it s that he really wants.

The second current differs from the first in that it makes no attempt to adapt or spread a kind of wisdom that is either ancient or Oriental. On the contrary it maintains that such forms of knowledge are unsuitable for the man of today who requires an altogether modern kind of "initiation." This is based upon evolutionism applied to affairs of the spirit. An evolutionary development of the world and of humanity is assumed, and it is thought that even the spirit should conform to this law and follow this development. There is no trace of such an idea in the teachings of any school of wisdom. The world is what it is, *saṁsāra*, said the Indo-Aryans; κύκλος τῆς γενέσεως, an eternal cycle of generation, said the ancient Greeks. And in *saṁsāra* there is no "evolution," there is no beginning and there is no end. By "going" one does not reach the "end of the world." The direction in which we may find awakening and liberation, the direction of initiation, is vertical and has nothing to do with the course of history.

Certainly, the condition of modern man is very different from that of ancient man—and in the course of this study we have repeatedly emphasized this fact. A "fall" or a "descent" has taken place, which is in no way a happening in an evolutional scheme, designed to produce, in a "happy ending," something higher than ever existed before. If this fall has any significance, it is that it shows the terrible power of the liberty of the spirit that can design and bring about even its own negation. Therefore the only thing to do is to admit that the ancient teachings cannot be used today without due consideration, and modern man must apply himself to a thankless task of reintegration: he must take himself back spiritually to the state of mind that has, always and everywhere, been the point of departure of a way that is essentially unique. There is no room for a "modern initiation" in a specific sense; by definition all that is modern is the contradiction of anything to do with initiation.

If, when we speak of "modern initiation" we wish to claim for it the characteristics of a "spiritual science," of a discipline that is as clear and exact as regards the supersensible world and the instruments of inward development as modern science is in regard to its own field and instruments, then we must show where in this respect it does more than simply state the problem.

It is, rather to traditional doctrines such as the one that we have laid before him in the present book, that the reader who is attracted by true spirituality should turn, to understand what a "spiritual science" really is: these doctrines will teach him the clarity of pure knowledge, divorced from all forms of visionary "clairvoyance," joined to a spiritual sovereignty, and to the will to break not only the human bond, but the bond formed by any other "world." Modern man has not only to fight against materialism, but must also defend himself from the snares and allures of false supernaturalism. His defense will be firm and effective only if he is capable of returning to the origins, of assimilating the ancient traditions, and then of relying upon the ascesis to carry out the task of reestablishing his inner condition. For it is through this that these traditions will reveal to him their deepest and perennially real content and show him, step by step, the path. In conclusion, we would like to repeat the ancient Roman augural formula: *quod bonum faustumque sit.* We would, that is to say, count it as most fortunate if this further modest contribution of ours to the understanding of premodern spirituality were to serve someone as something more than a simple reading. Only then could we repeat the formula of the Ariya: *kataṁ karaṇīyaṁ*—"done is what was to be done."

Index

Other Titles in the Spiritual Tradition

Power Places of Kathmandu

Hindu and Buddhist Holy Sites in the Sacred Valley of Nepal
Photography by Kevin Bubriski
Text by Keith Dowman
ISBN 0-89281-540-X. 108 color photographs.
$39.95 cloth

This handsome oversize volume features the work of award-winning photographer Kevin Bubriski. He offers an intimate portrait of the sacred places of Nepal's Kathmandu Valley, while noted scholar and Kathmandu resident Keith Dowman details the history and significance of more than thirty of the most important sites.

Here you will see a vital and vibrant spirituality practiced as it has been for centuries by both Hindus and Buddhists. From quiet devotions in misty morning light to exuberant religious processions that sweep you away in a rush of color, both spiritual seekers and armchair travelers will find treasures seldom seen by Western eyes.

Masters of Enchantment

The Lives and Legends of the Mahasiddhas
By Keith Dowman. Illustrated by Robert Beer
ISBN 0-89281-224-9. 32 full-color illustrations
$19.95 paperback

This beautifully illustrated collection of stories, skillfully retold from the original twelfth century A.D. text, tells the legends of the saints and magicians who founded the lineages of the Tantric Buddhist tradition. Extraordinary men and women from all walks of life, the Mahasiddhas demonstrate that enlightenment may be found in the most unexpected circumstances.

"We are drawn into the Mahasiddhas' magnificent magical vision of the universe, and we can take innocent delight in their often quirky personalities, their tremendous sense of humor, and their penchant for miraculous feats. This volume is an exemplary achievement and should be in the hands of every student of spirituality."

Spectrum Review

The Sacred Mountain of Tibet

On Pilgrimage to Kailas
By Russell Johnson and Kerry Moran
ISBN 0-89281-325-3. More than 100 color plates
$24.95 cloth

Spectacular color photography and vivid narrative lead you through the Himalayas to Kailas, a majestic mountain held sacred by both Hindu and Buddhist for more than 1,000 years. During the few years that Westerners were permitted to visit this area of Tibet, the authors joined a group of pilgrims on the path of devotion around Kailas and were able to record a rare glimpse of a region and a ritual almost unknown in the West.

"Both the vivid description and the awe-inspiring color photographs help to capture the mystical experience of this region and its religious significance."   **Booklist**

The Buddhist Handbook

A Complete Guide to Buddhist Schools, Teaching, Practice, and History
John Snelling
ISBN 0-89281-319-9
$14.95 paperback

This is the first book to provide an overview of Buddhism worldwide—the different schools, concepts, interpretations, teachers, and organizations, from its early history, meditation practices, and festivals through the Westward migration of Buddhist thought. It also includes a Who's Who of Buddhism from a modern Western perspective.

Taming the Tiger

Tibetan Teachings on Right Conduct, Mindfulness, and Universal Compassion
Akong Tulku Rinpoche
ISBN 0-89281-569-8
$12.95 paperback

With wit and wisdom, Akong Tulku Rinpoche teaches how to tame the tiger of the mind—a necessary step on the path to self-mastery. He explores the pitfalls that result from our habits of thought and provides a series of exercises by which to change our patterns of living.

Other works by Julius Evola

The Hermetic Tradition

Symbols and Teachings of the Royal Art

Originally published in Italian in 1931, now available for the first time in English, this important survey of alchemical symbols and doctrines draws from a wide variety of writings in the Western esoteric tradition—works on theurgy, magic, and gnosticism from neoplatonic, Arab, and medieval sources. Evola demonstrates the singularity of subject matter that lies behind the words of all adepts in all ages, showing how alchemy—often misunderstood as primitive chemistry or a mere template for the Jungian process of individuation—is nothing less than a universal secret science of human and natural transformation.

"An erudite, superbly knowledgeable collection of hermetic lore…A vast accessible panorama of occult wisdom written with elegance."   **The Book Reader**

ISBN 0-89281-451-9
$16.95 pb

The Yoga of Power

Tantra, Shakti, and the Secret Way

Evola introduces two Hindu movements—Tantrism and Shaktism—both of which emphasize a path of action as well as mastery over secret energies latent in the body. He draws from original texts to describe methods of self-mastery, including awakening of the serpent power, initiatic sexual magic, and evoking the names of power. While the movements of Tantrism and Shaktism have had a major influence on the Hindu tradition from the fourth century onward, Evola focuses on the appropriateness of their practices (known as the Way of the Left Hand) in our present age of dissolution and decadence.

ISBN 0-89281-368-7
$16.95 pb

Revolt Against the Modern World

In what is considered to be his masterwork, Julius Evola here turns his keen powers of analysis to the modern world as he traces the remote causes and processes that have exercised a corrosive influence on what he considers to be higher values, ideals, beliefs, and codes of conduct. He agrees with Hindu philosophers who argue that history moves in huge cycles, and that we are now in the Kali Yuga, an age of dissolution and decadence. Evola challenges our assumptions about the most fundamental aspects of spiritual and social life, and concludes that revolt is the only logical attitude to be adopted by those who oppose the materialism of everyday life.

ISBN 0-89281-506-X
$29.95 cloth

Eros and the Mysteries of Love
The Metaphysics of Sex

"Evola's study of the spirituality of sex focuses on what both science and popular culture have overlooked, invoking the rich symbolism of religious myths and mysteries throughout history, from the I Ching to the Kabbalah, to illustrate the redemptive power of the sexual act. He treats his subject with respect and circumspection."

The Los Angeles Times

ISBN 0-89281-315-6
$12.95 pb

These and other Inner Traditions titles are available at many fine bookstores or, to order directly from the publisher, send a check or money order for the total amount, payable to Inner Traditions, plus $3.00 shipping and handling for the first book and $1.00 for each additional book to:

Inner Traditions
One Park Street
P.O. Box 388
Rochester, VT 05767